STUDIES ON VOLTAIRE AND
THE EIGHTEENTH CENTURY

255

General editor

PROFESSOR H. T. MASON

Department of French
University of Bristol
Bristol BS8 1TE

B. LYNNE DIXON

Diderot,
philosopher of energy:
the development of his concept
of physical energy
1745 – 1769

THE VOLTAIRE FOUNDATION
AT THE TAYLOR INSTITUTION, OXFORD

1988

© *1988 University of Oxford*

ISSN 0435-2866

ISBN 0 7294 0366 1

British Library cataloguing in publication data

Dixon, B. Lynne
Diderot, philosopher of energy: the development of his
concept of physical energy, 1745-1769.
— (Studies on Voltaire and the eighteenth century,
ISSN 0435-2866; 255)
1. French philosophy. Diderot, Denis; 1713-1789.
– Critical studies
I. Title   II. Series
194
ISBN 0-7294-0366-1

Printed in England at The Alden Press, Oxford

Contents

Contents

Abbreviations

AT   Diderot, *Œuvres complètes*, ed. J. Assézat and M. Tourneux (Paris 1875-1877)

Corr.   Diderot, *Correspondance*, ed. G. Roth and J. Varloot (Paris 1955-1970)

Enc.   *Encyclopédie, ou Dictionnaire raisonné des sciences, des arts et des métiers* (Paris 1751-1780)

Her.   Diderot, *Œuvres complètes*, ed. Wilson, Hanna, Desné and others [Hermann edition] (Paris 1975-)

Lew.   Diderot, *Œuvres complètes*, ed. Lewinter (Paris 1972)

Mln   *Modern language notes*

OPhil.   Diderot, *Œuvres philosophiques*, ed. P. Vernière (Paris 1964)

RhlF   *Revue d'histoire littéraire de la France*

Rsh   *Revue des sciences humaines*

Preface

THE original version of this study of Diderot's philosophy of energy[1] owed its origins to Jacques Chouillet's *La Formation des idées esthétiques de Diderot* (Paris 1973). Chouillet's introductory essay on the concepts of *énergie* and *sensibilité* in Diderot's moral, political and aesthetic thought had opened up a virtually untrodden area of Diderot studies, which it had been my original intention to explore and map. In seeking to establish the origins of these concepts in Diderot's scientific thought, however (an issue which seemed to hold the key to understanding their application in his study of man), I gradually came to realise that this too was something of a wilderness, and one which would have to be cleared before the main expedition could get under way.

I am grateful to Chouillet's work for leading to the discovery of that need, and for suggesting, by precept and example, the most appropriate and efficient methodological tools for the original *tentative de déblayage*.[2]

A decade later, I find myself indebted to Chouillet a second time. His recently published survey of Diderot's philosophy of energy[3] has provided the stimulus for reviving my own study, as a complementary contribution to this still relatively uncharted field.

The title of this work may seem to beg an important question, since it rests on the assumption that Diderot *has* a 'concept of physical energy'. Indeed the aim of my study is, in part, to assemble evidence in support of the *acte de foi* implicit in its title. I am using 'physical energy' in a loose sense, as a convenient term to denote 'what matter can do' as distinct from 'what matter is made of'. Hence it may be taken as broadly synonymous with 'power' or 'force', encompassing both active and potential forms, and thus corresponding to a combination of the fourth and fifth senses identified by the *Oxford English dictionary*:

4. Power actively and efficiently displayed or exerted.
5. Power not necessarily manifested in action; ability or capacity to produce an effect.

Modern subatomic physics, of course, recognises no such distinction between

---

1. Submitted, in a different form, as a dissertation for the degree of Ph.D. in the University of Hull in 1982.
2. See Chouillet, p.4, 5, 7.
3. *Diderot poète de l'énergie* (Paris 1984). Personal circumstances have unfortunately prevented my consultation of M. Delon's recent study of energy in the late Enlightenment, *L'Idée de l'énergie au tournant des Lumières (1770-1820)* (Paris 1987).

'being' and 'doing'; at a fundamental level, matter-as-substance and matter-as-energy are interchangeable (and, as I shall argue towards the end of this study, Diderot himself comes close to a similar position). Nevertheless, the division is both justifiable and useful within the context of eighteenth-century philosophies of nature. For, as many scholars have pointed out,[4] the trend towards reinstating nature as an integrated, *active* phenomenon, in place of the cartesian view of passive *étendue* only incidentally endowed with motion, was crucial to the development of scientific thought in the mid-eighteenth century. Debate and research on such issues as Newtonian attraction, inertia, electricity and magnetism, chemical reactions, not only contributed directly to the advancement of physics and chemistry, but also (like cartesian mechanism) impinged upon the perennial biological questions, themselves being investigated from a new and exciting angle.[5]

As a philosopher rather than a practising scientist, Diderot was ideally placed to draw freely and creatively on all these areas, and his speculations on what we might call 'the nature of nature' are highly characteristic of the new approach. He comes increasingly to discuss and define natural phenomena (organic and inorganic alike) from the point of view of nature's powers – in the spirit of Renaissance naturalism, but from the perspective of up-to-date scientific findings. It is in this sense that I refer to a 'concept of physical energy'.

Given the organic quality of Diderot's thought, it is not surprising to find the idea of energy recurring in other areas of his works. If man is composed of matter – active matter – then all human activity, be it moral, political, aesthetic, becomes capable of interpretation in terms of energy. I share Chouillet's conviction that this is a crucial aspect of Diderot's overall philosophy, which deserves to be more widely recognised and more fully understood.

This work, in its successive forms, has been a long time in the making. I am especially grateful to Dr A. R. Strugnell of Hull University French Department for sensitively adopting a non-interventionist policy in his initial role as research supervisor, and for his recent encouragement. I owe him an equal debt of gratitude for his unstinted advice, constructive criticism and practical assistance throughout.

Thanks are also due to Professor R. Niklaus for many helpful observations.

Invaluable material help towards my studies was provided by the Department of Education and Science, in the form of a three-year State Studentship, and by the staff of the Brynmor Jones Library at Hull University, in particular by its efficient and friendly Inter-Library Loans and photocopying departments.

4. See, amongst many others, J. Varloot (ed.), *Le Rêve de d'Alembert*, p.lxviii-lxix; J. Ehrard, *L'Idée de la nature en France* (Paris 1963), p.150.
5. See, for instance, below, chapter 2, section C.

Special thanks are due to my husband Alan, for his good-humoured adjustment to life with a perpetual student, and to our children, Neville, Elizabeth and Claire, for being a distraction only when I needed one.

My longest-standing debt, however, is to Mr D. E. Curtis, the mentor of my undergraduate days, without whom my interest in the history of ideas might never have been kindled.

Introduction

SUCH had been the upturn in Diderot's fortunes by his 250th anniversary year that one scholar felt obliged to issue a warning against overestimating the philosopher's merits.[1] He took, as an illustration of the need for caution, Diderot's philosophy of energy:

Nul génie n'aurait été plus éclatant que celui de Diderot, s'il avait réussi à dégager une notion cohérente d'énergie à partir des trois sens: religieux, physique, moral inclus en ce mot prestigieux d'énergie. Mais il a eu assez de génie pour pressentir que la science y chercherait la clef de l'univers dont, sous l'apparente diversité des phénomènes, l'unité s'imposait à lui comme un acte de foi.[2]

For over twenty years, no comprehensive study emerged to assess and synthesise the dispersed elements of Diderot's notions of energy. Fabre's first contention was therefore left to pass unchallenged, until the publication of Chouillet's stimulating and fresh account of, precisely, the coherence underlying the various levels at which Diderot considers energy: physical, biological, psychological, moral, linguistic and socio-political. Of the various senses of energy detailed by Fabre and Chouillet, it is the physical/biological which has received the greatest amount of critical attention. Yet even this has never been the subject of a thoroughgoing analytical scrutiny.

This study adopts the aim, therefore, of offering an answer, however imperfect or incomplete, to the question (itself only one of many): how did Diderot's concept of physical energy – and of associated philosophical issues, notably the unity of nature and the character of life – develop, up to the time of its expression in the *Rêve de d'Alembert*?

The selection of the *Rêve de d'Alembert* as a *terminus ad quem* is neither arbitrary nor merely a concession to that persistent critical tradition which sees this work as the first – and last – coherent expression of Diderot's materialism. Nonetheless it is true that the *Rêve de d'Alembert* marks a watershed in Diderot's philosophy of energy, a kind of synthesis, in that it is the first work in which the interrelationships of energy, unity and life are fully explored.

This does not, however, amount to claiming that it constitutes a definitive statement of that philosophy. Four later works in particular (*Principes sur la matière et le mouvement*, *Réfutation d'Helvétius*, *Commentaire de Hemsterhuis* and

---

1. J. Fabre, 'Actualité de Diderot', *Diderot studies* 4 (1963), p.29. Cf. his 'Le chemin de Diderot', *Europe* 405-406 (1963), p.16.
2. 'Actualité de Diderot', p.33.

Eléments de physiologie) contain further variations on the same themes. So rich and complex are these variations, however, that to treat them with the fullness they deserve would require a study of equal length to the one I have undertaken. By the same token, it is impossible to investigate here the religious and moral aspects of Diderot's philosophy of energy, despite the frequently striking correspondences between these and their physical counterpart. Both these tasks, and hence the completion of the programme implicitly sketched by Fabre, must be reserved to another time and, perhaps, another hand.

The proliferation of critical studies devoted (in whole or in part) to Diderot's general philosophy of nature imposes a secondary aim on this study: to establish the relationship between the particular (philosophy of energy) and the general (philosophy of nature). It will be argued that the former becomes co-extensive with the latter; that his attitude towards energy determines his attitude towards physical nature as a whole: that the distinction between particular and general cannot be upheld – or, to borrow one of Diderot's own phrases, that 'il n'y a qu'un seul grand individu; c'est le tout'.[3]

Accordingly, the study will also assume the validity of Jean Varloot's term *energetische Materialismus*[4] as a general characterisation of Diderot's philosophy of nature. Varloot prefers this expression to the (admittedly more elegant) 'dynamic materialism' on the grounds that the modern connotations of 'energy' provide a more accurate reflection of Diderot's concept of active matter.[5] It conveys in particular that quality of Diderot's thought which has led W. Krauss to write of 'eine dialektische Überwindung des mechanischen Materialismus'.[6] Callot's alternative of *naturalisme*[7] is rather too broad for the purpose of this study, and the term 'vitalism' has been avoided since it is subject to divergent interpretations.[8]

To the extent that Diderot reacts against the sterility of mechanism and endeavours to reinstate the distinctness of organic phenomena, his may be called a vitalistic philosophy. In the sense of belief in life as a universal property of matter, however, vitalism characterises only one stage in the development of Diderot's thought, and it is in this context alone that I have found it appropriate to use the label. In its spiritualistic forms, finally (more properly termed animism), vitalism is alien to Diderot's thinking from the start.[9] To claim, as Crocker has

---

3. *Rêve de d'Alembert*, p.44.
4. J. Varloot, 'Diderots Philosophie im *Rêve de d'Alembert*', *Sinn und Form* 14 (1962), p.709-10.
5. Cf. U. Winter, *Der Materialismus bei Diderot* (Genève, Paris 1972), p.234.
6. W. Krauss, 'Diderot in dieser Zeit', *Wissenschaftliche Zeitschrift* 13 (1964), p.115. Cf. Winter, p.70.
7. E. Callot, *La Philosophie de la vie* (Paris 1965), p.246.
8. Cf. below, chapter 5, D.iii.a.
9. Varloot, 'Diderots Philosophie im *Rêve de d'Alembert*', p.717-18.

done, that only a marxist would deny the existence of 'pan-vitalism' in Diderot's philosophy[10] is misleading: Diderot's flirtation with the concept is extremely brief. Callot's references to 'hylozoism' and 'panpsychism'[11] are, as I hope to show, highly questionable.

Adoption of the term 'energetic materialism' is not, however, meant to imply that Diderot has a single philosophy of nature which can be fixed, analysed and definitively labelled. It would be difficult to sustain such a position in view of the extensive evidence to the contrary assembled by U. Winter; she seeks to demonstrate, throughout her study, that Diderot neither sought nor achieved a philosophical 'system' with claims to universal validity, and that it is precisely this quality which sets him apart from his contemporaries.[12] Individual works are, for Winter, simply provisional stopping-places.[13] It is, she argues, this very awareness on Diderot's part of the relative nature of his own theories which stands in the way of assigning to him an appropriate philosophical label.[14]

Whilst Winter's conclusions are not acceptable in their entirety, they do have the merit of demonstrating the characteristic at which Naigeon hinted in his *Mémoires*: 'Tout se passait [...] dans son entendement comme dans la nature, où rien ne se fait par sauts et par bonds, mais par nuances insensibles'[15] and which it used to be fashionable to deny,[16] the organic unity of Diderot's thought. It has now become equally commonplace to refute such views as Janet's '[il] ne se soucie pas beaucoup de conséquence et de cohérence' (p.699), substituting a belief in the internal coherence of Diderot's natural philosophy;[17] the concept

---

10. L. G. Crocker, *Diderot the embattled philosopher* (New York 1966), p.143.

11. Callot, *La Philosophie de la vie*, p.275, 280.

12. 'In dieser Denkhaltung, die durch den Verzicht auf alle dogmatischen metaphysischen Aussagen charakterisiert wird, in seiner Art der Annäherung an die Wahrheit, nicht so sehr in den gewonnenen Denkinhalten sehen wir die entscheidende philosophische Originalität Diderots' (*Der Materialismus bei Diderot*, p.77). Cf. p.84.

13. 'nur provisorische Haltepunkte' (p.76).

14. p.225. Cf. Chouillet, *La Formation des idées esthétiques de Diderot*, p.26.

15. J. A. Naigeon, *Mémoires historiques sur la vie et les ouvrages de D. Diderot* (reprint Genève 1971), p.10.

16. In P. Janet, 'La philosophie de Diderot: le dernier mot d'un matérialiste', *Nineteenth century* 9 (1881), p.695, 699; Callot, *La Philosophie de la vie*, p.255, and *Six philosophes français* (Annecy 1963), p.32, 34; J. Charpentier, 'Diderot et la science de son temps', *Revue du mois* 16 (1913), p.550; and even as recently as 1966 by R. Jasinski in *Histoire de la littérature française* (Paris 1966), ii.120 ('un chaos de contradictions'). Cf. the assessment of this tradition by P. Casini, *Diderot 'philosophe'* (Paris 1962), p.6-7, and H. Dieckmann, 'Zur Interpretation Diderots', *Romanische Forschungen* 53 (1939), especially p.50. As Wade has remarked in his perceptive essay on the subject, 'the problem of Diderot's unity is not new' ('Organic unity in Diderot', *L'Esprit créateur* 8 (1968), p.3).

17. For example Winter, *Der Materialismus bei Diderot*, p.8: 'Von der Untersuchung seiner naturwissenschaftlichen und philosophischen Werke her läßt sich nicht Oberflächlichkeit und Widersprüchlichkeit, sondern Einheit und innere Geschlossenheit in Diderots Denken feststellen.' Cf. A. C. Lerel's 'innere Logik' (*Diderots Naturphilosophie*, Wien 1950, p.8).

of *organic* unity proposed by Chouillet[18] has the advantage of abolishing any apparent tension between the fluidity and unity which both characterise his attitude towards nature. Precisely because this philosophy is organic, it grows and ramifies; parts die and are cast off; others develop, sometimes gradually, sometimes suddenly, as the organism comes to maturity.

Groethuysen's 1913 analysis of the quality of Diderot's thought is unusual for its time in that it acknowledges *and respects* this feature. For Groethuysen it is inseparably linked with the philosophy of flux, life and *devenir* upheld by Diderot: 'Devant nous se déroule le spectacle des idées qui naissent, s'agrandissent, deviennent des visions et ensuite se cristallisent et prennent forme',[19] and again: 'la pensée qui s'éveille et qui passe, qui se forme et se métamorphose' (p.324). Whilst Groethuysen lays rather more stress on the instability of Diderot's thought than is strictly justified, his appreciation seems essentially modern and positive in its overall tenor. Indeed it is taken up, some fifty-one years later, in Niklaus's perceptive comment that Diderot's works must be studied 'comme des reflets d'une pensée en gestation',[20] a sentiment echoed by Chouillet, who declares that the outstanding characteristic of Diderot's ideas 'est d'agir continuellement sur elles-mêmes comme un organisme en évolution' (p.26). Callot has claimed that Diderot's philosophy remains essentially the same from 1753 to 1780, except for fluctuations of detail (*La Philosophie de la vie*, p.278). It would seem more accurate to reverse the proportions and say that, whilst the central inspiration remains constant, the detailed formulations undergo radical transformation over the years. It is that transformation which I propose to trace. Remarking on the conflicting views of Diderot offered by existing criticism, I. O. Wade concludes: 'Their error, if error there is, consists not in misinterpreting Diderot's ideas, but in failing to analyze the structure of his thinking until they attain the form of his thought' ('Organic unity', p.9). This, he suggests, should be sought in Diderot's own definitions of eclectic philosophy. *Eclectisme expérimental* seeks to gather new facts to complement and extend selected facts and ideas from past systems. *Eclectisme systématique*, on the other hand, combines these materials from past and present, juggles and restructures them into a new scientific and philosophical whole. Hence it knows no masters. This version, remarks Diderot, 'est celui des hommes de génie'.[21] I concur with Wade (p.13) that it is also essentially Diderot's.

18. *La Formation des idées esthétiques de Diderot*, p.26.

19. B. Groethuysen, 'La pensée de Diderot', *Grande revue* 22 (25.11.1913), p.334.

20. R. Niklaus, 'Présence de Diderot', *Diderot studies* 6 (1964), p.16. Lerel also proposes to trace Diderot's views through 'ihre Geschichte, ihre innere Entwicklung' (p.6). Unfortunately his generally disappointing study does not live up to this statement of intent.

21. *Encyclopédie*, article 'Eclectisme', quoted in Wade, p.13-14. Her., vii.81.

This assumption about the mode of Diderot's thought is reflected in the method of my own research. For the central concern of this study is the internal evolution of Diderot's thought: the changes within a philosophical organism[22] rather than the environmental pressures, as it were, responsible for catalysing such changes. Or, in terms of eclecticism, the process of restructuring rather than the source of its elements. As Niklaus has observed, 'en définitive, c'est bien l'esprit de Diderot qui fascine'.[23] To catalogue the points of contact between Diderot's ideas and those of his predecessors and contemporaries at each stage of their development would be to destroy the very point of the study, especially since, as Mayer has pointed out, Diderot assimilates his borrowings so completely into his vision of nature that they effectively become his own ideas.[24] Consequently such cross-references have been reduced to a minimum, and interpretation confined, by and large, to Diderot's own writings.

This approach has a respectable pedigree. Winter's ambitious study of Diderot's materialism invokes the names of Belaval and Mortier in support of such a methodology and declares her own intention to present the content and development of Diderot's philosophy of nature purely from the texts.[25] Only by interpreting the individual threads, motifs and images of Diderot's thought in the context of his own overall philosophy, rather than that of their outside sources, she argues, can a proper appreciation of their interrelationships be gained. Chouillet had already reached a similar conclusion, distinguishing between historical determinism and internal self-modification, *les causes formatrices* and *les causes constitutives*, the latter of which reveal Diderot's work to be 'porteur de sa propre histoire, comme se conditionnant lui-même indépendamment des contingences extérieures' (p.26). This is not to deny that often the two levels of causality are inextricably linked. On occasion, Diderot takes another's ideas as the explicit starting-point for his own, as in the dialectical interchange with Maupertuis in the *Pensées sur l'interprétation de la nature*. Equally his history of philosophy articles for the *Encyclopédie* provide a wealth of 'sources' which are internal rather than secondary in the conventional sense.[26]

Furthermore, standard accounts of the eighteenth-century background are plentiful, as indeed are specialised comparative studies relating to Diderot

22. Cf. Chouillet's declaration quoted above, p.4.
23. Introduction to *Lettre sur les aveugles* (Lille, Genève 1951), p.liv.
24. J. Mayer, *Diderot, homme de science* (Rennes 1959), p.444. Cf. Crocker's conclusions in his 'Toland et le matérialisme de Diderot', *RhlF* 53 (1953), p.294: 'Son originalité n'est-elle pas surtout dans l'empreinte que sa personnalité enthousiaste et son esprit synthétique impriment sur tout ce qu'ils empruntent?'
25. 'der Inhalt und die Entwicklung von Diderots materialistischer Naturphilosophie [sollen] allein von den Texten her dargestellt werden' (p.15).
26. Cf. for example chapter 4, A.ii.b.2.

himself. Those of greatest relevance will be indicated by means of footnotes in the appropriate place; there seems to be little profit in attempting to duplicate their rôle. Nor is it my intention to undertake the task of seeking to trace Diderot's influence on his contemporaries or on the future course of science or philosophy. Not only is this more difficult to assess even than the question of sources, it is equally irrelevant to the purposes of this study. An oddly insubstantial and ill-judged study published in 1944 declared that Diderot 'was neither a visionary nor a man of science'.[27] I happen to believe that in his links to past, present and future he was both, but this is not the place to demonstrate it.

In thus restricting my approach, I have deemed it essential to practise a sustained close reading of the texts. An apparently trivial instance of rephrasing from one work to another, the associative implications of a particular choice of vocabulary, often prove crucial to a full understanding of Diderot's thought. If errors of interpretation and dangerous generalities are to be avoided, the texts must be treated with the same meticulous attention as Diderot himself devoted to his analysis of such contemporary thinkers as Helvétius and Hemsterhuis.

In view of the general principles outlined above, and the nature of the subject, the plan of this study requires little comment. A straightforward chronological approach has been adopted overall. Thus the first chapter deals with Diderot's early works up to and including the *Lettre sur les aveugles* (1749); the third with the *Pensées sur l'interprétation de la nature* (1753) and the fifth (and final) with the *Rêve de d'Alembert* (1769). Chapters two and four occupy a logical position within this sequence, dealing with the two periods of transition between major works. Internally, however, they are not organised along exclusively chronological lines. The transitional nature of the periods involved lends itself to a partially thematic approach; in addition, both draw on Diderot's articles for the *Encyclopédie*, precise dating of which is notoriously difficult to achieve.

Throughout, the often irregular development of individual themes in counterpoint to the linear progression through time of the works themselves[28] has been indicated by extensive cross-referencing. In this way, I hope to offer a just impression of both the mode and the content of Diderot's speculations on the energy of nature.

27. A. Gregory, 'Denis Diderot', *Horizon* 9 (1944), p.34. Cf. Crocker: 'Il ne fut ni prophète, ni même philosophe profond et original' ('Toland et le matérialisme de Diderot', p.295). Diderot may not have been a practising scientist, or even a systematic exponent of contemporary scientific knowledge, but his was the kind of inspired investigative scientific thinking which can truly be called 'visionary' in that it allows the wood to emerge, albeit briefly, from the trees. Chouillet calls it 'une anticipation qu'on peut à la fois qualifier de géniale et d'irrationnelle' (*Diderot poète de l'énergie*, p.129). Cf. also below, chapter 5, B.i.b, and Conclusion.
28. Cf. Chouillet, p.10, 25-26.

1. The metaphysical foundations

I MAKE no apologies for opening my study with a survey of Diderot's metaphysical thought up to the *Lettre sur les aveugles*. The underlying philosophical positions of Diderot's earliest works have, it is true, been studied on numerous occasions. My purpose here, however, is to draw together those aspects of his early thought directly relevant to the three themes of this study: physical energy, the nature of life, and the unity of nature. Since these are, at the outset, inextricably interwoven with Diderot's quest for a tenable metaphysics – which proves in the end to be a rejection of metaphysics – repetition of a certain amount of familiar material is unavoidable. The premises of an energetic, unified and autonomous universe, in which the phenomena of life occupy a special place, emerge almost imperceptibly from the interplay within Diderot's mind of the various interpretations of nature offered by differing metaphysical models.

A. *Essai sur le mérite et la vertu* (1745)

Diderot's first original philosophical reflections are to be found in his annotations to the text of the *Essai sur le mérite et la vertu*, which he had translated from Shaftesbury for publication in 1745. Whilst the majority of his remarks relate to the moral and apologetic content of Shaftesbury's essay, others are of more direct relevance to his future philosophy of nature.

The *Essai sur le mérite et la vertu* contains, for instance, the first, crude expression of a principle which is to become an integral part of Diderot's philosophy, the unity of nature: 'Dans l'univers, tout est uni. Cette vérité fut un des premiers pas de la philosophie, et ce fut un pas de géant.'[1] On this occasion, Diderot is not concerned to investigate the implications of this principle, nor is he under any illusions as to its originality. As E. R. Briggs has pointed out, Shaftesbury in turn derived his notion of natural unity from the *anima mundi* of Renaissance platonism.[2] Nevertheless, the importance he evidently attaches

1. Her., i.313. Cf. F. Venturi, *La Jeunesse de Diderot* (Paris 1939), p.66; Casini and Spink, Her., i.278-79; Casini, *Diderot 'philosophe'*, p.101, 104; Fabre, 'Le chemin de Diderot', p.5.
2. Briggs, 'The Enlightenment's reception of the legacy of the Italian Renaissance', *British Society for Eighteenth-Century Studies newsletter* 11 (1977), p.23. Cf. S. C. Landucci, 'Diderot "philosophe"', *Belfagor* 18 (1963), p.325. As Y. Belaval points out, however, Diderot actually refers the reader to Cicero ('Note sur Diderot et Leibniz', *Revue des sciences humaines* 112 (1963), p.440). Landucci also makes the pertinent remark that, even if Diderot did derive his concept of unity from Shaftesbury, the two philosophers are nevertheless separated by the distance between spiritualism and materialism (p.325).

to it is worthy of note: the belief will prove to be a source both of inspired intuition and of frustrating contradiction.[3]

It is also clear from the *Essai sur le mérite et la vertu* that Diderot has undergone the influence of the mechanistic teleology which marks early eighteenth-century deism. This teleological form of deism was already commonplace by the time Diderot encountered it in Shaftesbury's work;[4] his stance towards it, however, is already critical, although his analysis of its defects is based on psychological, rather than philosophical grounds: on the adage that 'familiarity breeds contempt' (Her., i.343):

Si nous arrivions dans ce monde avec cette raison que nous portâmes dans la salle de l'Opéra, la première fois que nous y entrâmes, et si la toile se levait brusquement, frappés de la grandeur, de la magnificence et du jeu des décorations, nous n'aurions pas la force de nous refuser à la connaissance de l'ouvrier éternel qui a préparé le spectacle: mais qui s'avise de s'émerveiller de ce qu'il voit depuis cinquante ans?

It is this awareness that the mechanical model of the universe has lost its force as an apologetic device which will lead him, in the *Pensées philosophiques*, to seek a new, biological foundation for his deism. The deism itself is, as yet, under no threat; in 1745 Diderot is, in Roger's words, *déiste enthousiaste* (p.237). Nevertheless, the present work opens with the confident assertion that piety and the study of nature are not incompatible (Her., i.289); the *Pensées philosophiques* will go further and declare them to be mutually enhancing, a shift which will prove to be the source of Diderot's eventual abandonment of deism.

Niklaus has described the years 1747-1759 as a period of 'intensive research and enquiry'.[5] He thus relegates the *Essai sur le mérite et la vertu* by implication to the earlier phase of 'uncertainty' (although he actually dates this 1732-1743). Nevertheless, from the point of view of Diderot's philosophy of nature the *Essai* cannot be denied the status of preface to the more detailed and explicit declarations of his wholly original works later in the decade.

B. The *Pensées philosophiques* (1746)

In the *Pensées philosophiques*, Diderot's first entirely original philosophical writing, the early metaphysical origins of his philosophy of nature emerge more clearly still. The *Pensées philosophiques*, as numerous critics have indicated, are notable both for the nature of the evidence adduced by Diderot in support of his deism[6]

---

3. Cf. Casini, *Diderot 'philosophe'*, p.102.
4. J. Roger, 'Le déisme du jeune Diderot', *Europäische Aufklärung* (München 1967), p.238.
5. R. Niklaus, 'The mind of Diderot', *Filosofia* 14 (1963), p.927.
6. A. M. Wilson, *Diderot: the testing years* (New York 1957), p.58; A. Vartanian, 'From deist to atheist, *Diderot studies* 1 (1949), p.46-63; Crocker, *Diderot the embattled philosopher*, p.70; R. Niklaus (ed.), *Pensées philosophiques* (Genève 1965), p.xvii.

and for their sympathetic account of atheism.[7] Both aspects have important implications for the future movement of Diderot's thought.

i. *Deism: the rôle of biology in metaphysics*

Previous studies[8] have brought out the significance of the biological aspect of the *Pensées philosophiques*. In his account of deism, Diderot places the burden of proof squarely upon biological fact, which he sees as providing evidence not only of order, but of purposeful order within the universe (Vartanian, p.48, 49). He thus breaks both with the newtonian teleological approach and with such apologists of deism as the abbé Pluche, whose philosophy, although drawing on the phenomena of natural history, tended to view these within the by now familiar mechanistic framework, regarding them as mere adjuncts to the realm of physics (p.50). To argue, then, as Kiernan has done, that Diderot's rejection of the physical in favour of the life sciences dates only from the *Lettre sur les aveugles*[9] is to underestimate his 1746 position. Already Diderot's version of finalism is distinctly more organic in conception (Vartanian, p.49); it gives living matter a new status, making it crucial to the debate and thus transposing onto the metaphysical plane the contemporary scientific trend towards the biological.[10]

The emphasis within his profession of deism is uncompromisingly shifted from the creator to the creation, from God to matter;[11] the matter of the biologist, moreover, rather than that of the physicist. Although the deism itself will prove fleeting, the orientation it entailed will remain constant, lending coherence to Diderot's evolution towards a scientific atheism.

This evolution has been denied by Etiemble, who maintains, in contradiction to received critical opinion, that Diderot had already adopted atheism by the time of the *Pensées philosophiques*. He seeks to refute Vartanian's thesis by arguing that biology could not have effected Diderot's conversion to atheism since the *Pensées philosophiques* clearly state the mutual hostility of biological research and an atheistic metaphysics.[12] The new science of biology, however, was far from possessing the static content Etiemble assumes for it: the corpus of biological fact was constantly changing, and along with it the philosophical implications

7. R. Niklaus, 'Les *Pensées philosophiques* de Diderot', *Bulletin of the John Rylands Library* 26 (1941), p.127, and edition, p.xvii; Crocker, p.69.

8. Notably Vartanian's 'From deist to atheist'.

9. C. Kiernan, 'Additional reflections on Diderot and science', *Diderot studies* 14 (1971), p.114 and *passim*.

10. Vartanian, p.51-52. For the biological content, see below, ii.b.

11. Venturi, *La Jeunesse de Diderot*, p.87, 88.

12. R. Etiemble, 'Structure et sens des *Pensées philosophiques*', *Romanische Forschungen* 74 (1962), p.1-10.

of such research. There is no discrepancy between Diderot's biological deism and his subsequent atheism: both stances are based firmly upon the biological evidence available *at the time*, particularly in the context of research into the phenomenon of spontaneous generation.[13]

It is indeed, as Diderot says, 'la connaissance de la nature'[14] which presents an obstacle to atheism in 1746; his critique of the atheist position is given primarily biological terms of reference which will become the touchstone for future modifications within his thought, both metaphysical and physical.

ii. *Atheism: the rôle of energy in matter*

The atheist of the *Pensées philosophiques* invokes a dual concept to account for the creation and ordering of the universe: inherently mobile matter acting through the mechanism of chance.[15] Diderot's examination of such a position thus brings about his first formal encounter with the issue of energy in matter. It soon becomes clear that for Diderot there are two distinct sides to the issue: the question of whether or not motive force is inherent within matter and, more importantly at this stage, whether the mechanical physicist's motive force is relevant to the processes of the biological world.

a. *Inherence of motion*

Diderot's treatment of the former question is, at first sight, paradoxical. For a deist, he seems remarkably unconcerned about the materialistic implications of accepting the inherence of motion. The opening words of *Pensée* XIX suggest indifference, or at the least, indecision: 'Que le mouvement soit essentiel ou accidentel à la matière'.[16] Pensée XXI, on the other hand, appears to belie this ostensibly non-committal stance: Diderot details the dangers of accepting the atheist's conceptual framework as a gesture of compromise, as other apologists had been prepared to do, arguing that if the inherence of movement is conceded, there can be no logical refutation of atheistic materialism. An ambiguity remains, however. Firstly it is not on account of this concession that he condemns the reasoning of such apologists as Rivard, but because their attempted refutation of probability theory is defective. The argument that the spontaneous arrangement of atoms into the present world order is as unlikely as the spontaneous arrangement of letters of the alphabet into a literary masterpiece cuts no ice with the atheist: 'Je me garderai bien de faire ce raisonnement à un athée: cette

13. See below, b.1. Cf. Winter, p.155-56.
14. Pensée XIX, Her., ii.25.
15. Pensée XXI, Her., ii.29.
16. Pensée XIX, Her., ii.25.

comparaison lui donnerait beau jeu.'[17] Secondly, nowhere does he deny the accuracy of the hypothetically conceded principle of inherence. In the final analysis, Diderot has given no answer.

The issue was not, in any case, clearly polarised. There was considerable debate even among deists over the relationship of motion and matter, and as to whether this constituted an arbitrary or necessary choice on the part of the Creator.[18] The explanation for Diderot's hesitation, however, must be sought in his attitude towards the rôle of motion in such phenomena as spontaneous generation and biological organisation.

b. Motion in living matter

1. Spontaneous generation

The remaining lines of *Pensée* XIX have been the subject of extensive scholarly analysis, notably in an article by L. G. Crocker and ensuing correspondence.[19] Leaving aside the question of inherence, Diderot considers the rôle of motive force in living matter, declaring it inadequate to bring about the spontaneous generation of organisms: '[Que le mouvement soit essentiel ou accidentel à la matière] je suis maintenant convaincu que ses effets se terminent à des développements: toutes les observations concourent à me démontrer que la putréfaction seule ne produit rien d'organisé.'[20]

Much of the debate over these lines has centred on the word *organisé*. For Crocker it implies only a partial rejection of spontaneous generation, in the case of the higher, organised beings (p.434), although he subsequently attempts to show that Diderot envisaged the possibility of exceptions to this rule (p.436). In reaction to this interpretation, Doolittle and Vartanian both seek to re-establish the universality of Diderot's rejection[21] as does Roger, elsewhere.[22] None of these interpreters, however, has noted that Diderot is less concerned with the denial of spontaneous generation than with establishing the inadequacy of motion to account for it. For Diderot is referring only to the classical/cartesian concept of motive force (whether atomic or mechanical) assumed by materialist atheist[23] and physicist alike rather than to a broader concept of energy. When

17. Pensée XXI, Her., ii.28.
18. G. Tonelli, 'La nécessité des lois de la nature au XVIIIe siècle', *Revue d'histoire des sciences* 12 (1959), p.226.
19. Crocker, 'Pensée XIX of Diderot', *Modern language notes* 67 (1952), p.433-39, and consequent 'Correspondence', *Mln* 68 (1953), p.282-88.
20. Pensée XIX, Her., ii.25.
21. Doolittle and Vartanian, 'Correspondence' (*Mln*), p.282, 283.
22. J. Roger, *Les Sciences de la vie dans la pensée française du dix-huitième siècle* (Paris 1963), p.587, n.16.
23. See for instance the account of Pérelle in E. R. Briggs, 'L'incrédulité et la pensée anglaise en France', *RhlF* 34 (1927), p.499-503.

he subsequently comes to accept spontaneous generation, mechanical motion will have already been discredited as an explanatory concept.

Both Vartanian and Crocker go some way towards recognising the significance of this fact. Vartanian links Diderot's perception of this inadequacy in traditional atheist thought with his eventual turning aside from teleological apologetics. If the universe is no longer considered a machine (powered by mechanical motion) neither the atheist's fateful combinations of mobile matter nor the deist's clockmaker God are satisfactory models of explanation.[24] Crocker points out that the deficiency recognised by Diderot is inherent in any purely quantitative model of the universe, and that Diderot is therefore implicitly seeking a qualitative alternative.[25]

Moreover, it is now clear that Diderot's metaphysical stance hinges on the single issue of spontaneous generation. He rejects it only on the grounds of apparently damning experimental proof against it ('toutes les observations') and implies that were it not for this the atheist's thesis would be unanswerable.[26] Numerous critics have stressed Diderot's eagerness to accept later, contrary findings on the subject, seeing this variously as a precipitating factor in, or a consequence of, his adoption of an atheist position.[27]

Pensée XIX, then, points up a serious conceptual weakness in the atheist's position: even if abiogenesis were a reality, he would have no scientifically acceptable model with which to integrate the phenomenon into a materialistic account of the universe. Consequently the initial question, the inherence of motion, becomes irrelevant to Diderot's purpose in the *Pensées philosophiques*: whether inherent or imparted, mechanical motion cannot present a threat to the doctrine of creation, and decision on this apparently crucial issue becomes somewhat less urgent.

Lefèbvre interprets the entire issue in a quite different way. He claims that Diderot now *accepts* spontaneous generation and that his nascent materialism is, consequently, already compromised.[28] Lefèbvre does hit the nail on the head when he points out that the emergence of organised beings from purely mechanical matter reveals both the efficiency and finalism of some form of divine causation (that is, that spontaneous generation tends to support deism) but to attribute this argument to Diderot would appear to be mistaken since he

24. Vartanian, 'From deist to atheist', p.49.
25. Crocker, *Diderot the embattled philosopher*, p.71. Cf. M. W. Wartofsky, 'Diderot and the development of materialist monism', *Diderot studies* 2 (1952), p.279.
26. Cf. Winter, p.155.
27. Crocker, 'Pensée XIX de Diderot', p.437-38; Vartanian, 'Correspondence' (*Mln*), p.283-84; Niklaus (ed.), *Pensées philosophiques*, p.14, n.; Vernière (ed.), *OPhil.*, p.18-19, n.3; Varloot (ed.), *Textes choisis* (Paris 1953), p.47, n.4; Winter, p.156-57. Cf. also below, D.i.b.
28. H. Lefèbvre, *Diderot* (Paris 1949), p.84-85.

accepts neither spontaneous generation nor, unreservedly, the cartesian view of matter at this time.

2. Biological organisation

Despite his misgivings as to the adequacy of motive force in the context of spontaneous generation, Diderot is prepared to give it a limited rôle within living matter. Motion is made responsible for 'des développements', that is the emergence of an organised being from the original (created) *germe*.[29] Pommier's gloss on this point: 'entendez que le mouvement développe l'organisé, mais qu'il ne produit pas l'organisation'[30] overlooks the fact that such development necessarily implies an element of ordering and organisation. It is not organisation which Diderot considers motion incapable of bringing about, but life.

Another controversial section of *Pensée* XIX sheds further light on this issue: 'je puis admettre que le mécanisme de l'insecte le plus vil n'est pas moins merveilleux que celui de l'homme, et je ne crains pas qu'on en infère qu'une agitation intestine des molécules étant capable de donner l'un, il est vraisemblable qu'elle a donné l'autre' (Her., ii.25-26). For Crocker, these lines indicate a belief on Diderot's part that intestinal fermentation *could* give rise to the spontaneous generation of inferior organisms[31] – an interpretation which is at odds with Diderot's affirmation that 'la putréfaction seule ne produit rien d'organisé' (Her., ii.25). Doolittle and Vartanian, on the other hand, consider that Diderot is here acknowledging that if spontaneous generation were a reality there would be no logical obstacle to its universal application.[32] Certainly Diderot's 'je ne crains pas qu'on en infère' is ambiguous: it could mean either that there is no risk of such an implication being drawn, or that (because biogenesis is impossible) such a hypothetical implication would in any case present no threat to the deist, that is, that the inference is unlikely or that it is irrelevant and therefore unalarming.

The crux of the passage, however, lies in Diderot's readiness to attribute biological organisation – in insect or in man – to the workings of 'une agitation intestine des molécules', that is to an exclusively physical property of matter. Although at this stage there is apparent identity between this property and the mechanists' motive force, it is the starting-point for Diderot's conception of a specifically biological energy. For motion, in cartesian mechanism, tended to be considered as an extrinsic, rather than intrinsic force (hence the need for an immaterial Prime Mover). As Szigeti puts it, 'l'unité de la matière et du

29. Roger, *Les Sciences de la vie*, p.587, n.16.
30. J. Pommier, *Diderot avant Vincennes* (Paris 1939), p.37.
31. Crocker, p.436, and 'Correspondence' (*Mln*), p.285.
32. 'Correspondence' (*Mln*), p.282, 284. Cf. Winter, p.156.

mouvement était disloquée'.[33] Consequently Diderot's concept of 'une agitation *intestine*' can be seen as a step towards the reintegration of matter and energy, towards the reactivation of nature.

Roger has pointed out the loss of autonomy for nature entailed by most deistic apologetic systems,[34] in which the order of the universe is dependent on either direct, constant divine intervention (as in Newton's theories or Malebranchian occasionalism) or upon an initial preordination (as in Leibniz's monadology). He sees the *Pensées philosophiques* as a further instance of the same tendency, Diderot's invocation of the discovery of *germes* (Her., ii.25) representing a defence of 'l'ordre de la création contre une activité anarchique de la matière'.[35]

Pensée XIX is rather more than this, however, for it does permit natural forces themselves to be the instruments of organisation, despite their inability to generate life initially. It thus restores a certain degree of autonomy to nature and, in combination with Diderot's use of organic nature as a source of metaphysical argument, results in what Venturi has called: 'Ce renversement sentimental qu'il faisait des apologies de Dieu à travers la nature pour les transformer en apologies de la nature, en elle-même.'[36] Varloot makes a similar point, stressing that the importance which Diderot attached to biological organisation was twofold in its effect: 'conscient qu'il est avant tout de l'"organisation" dans les phénomènes de la nature, il ne se dégagera pas tout de suite de l'interprétation finaliste du monde; mais, justement, c'est en retournant l'explication finaliste qu'il fondera son matérialisme sur une matière qui tend à l'organisation'.[37] Varloot's reading – that by switching from the argument 'nature is organised, therefore it needs an organiser' to the very different argument 'nature is organised therefore it needs an intrinsic principle of organisation' Diderot changes his conclusion rather than his premise – coincides with my own earlier conclusions regarding the continuity of inspiration behind Diderot's successive metaphysical positions.

Diderot's rehabilitation of nature should not, however, be interpreted too ambitiously. Crocker's suggestion, for instance, seconded by Varloot, that

33. J. Szigeti, *Denis Diderot: une grande figure du matérialisme* (Budapest 1962), p.45.

34. Roger, 'Le déisme du jeune Diderot', p.238. Cf. Ehrard's argument that in the early eighteenth century neither the cartesians nor their opponents offered effective opposition to the attempts by alchemical thinkers such as Guyot to reinstate nature as an inner creative principle (*L'Idée de nature*, p.41-49). For the seventeenth-century background to such attempts, see B. Tocanne, *L'Idée de nature* (Paris 1978), p.18 and *passim*.

35. J. Roger, 'Diderot et Buffon en 1749', *Diderot studies* 4 (1963), p.233.

36. *La Jeunesse de Diderot*, p.88. Cf. H. Dieckmann, 'Diderots Naturempfinden und Naturgefühl', p.76-77; Casini, *Diderot 'philosophe'*, p.100 ('La Natura, animata da una energia elementare e universale, si distacca poco a poco dell'involucro delle sottigliezze teologiche que l'occulta').

37. *Textes choisis*, introduction, p.19.

Diderot is already attempting to establish the premises of an evolutionary universe[38] seems to go too far. As Callot has emphasised, all notion of transformism is absent from the *Pensées philosophiques*, the atheist's *jets* being directed towards the integral formation of the present world-order (*La Philosophie de la vie*, p.302).

Moreover, the deistic conclusions of the *Pensées philosophiques* are not conducive to the immediate further investigation of the issue of biological energy. It is metaphysical questions which remain in the forefront of Diderot's mind.

C. *La Promenade du sceptique* (1747)

In the following year, Diderot pursues his examination of the metaphysical issues raised, and left largely unresolved, in the *Pensées philosophiques*. His evident fascination with the plausibility of the atheist's view of the universe is broadened, in the 'Allée des marronniers' section of the *Promenade du sceptique*, into a survey of the philosophical options open to the eighteenth-century philosopher of nature.

Previous commentators have sought to demonstrate either that Diderot commits himself to one or other of the philosophies expounded in the *Promenade*, or that he retreats into indecision or bewilderment before the alternatives. Thus for Luppol, Diderot's sympathies remain with deism, whereas for Vartanian and Niklaus Diderot's final position is that of scepticism, although this is not necessarily identified with the philosophy labelled *sceptique* in the work itself.[39] For others – Pommier, Wilson, Chouillet, Venturi, Casini and Varloot – the dominant figure is that of the spinozist, or pantheist, though none of these critics make clear the extent to which they consider Diderot has given his allegiance to the philosophy this dominance implies.[40] Roger and Crocker go a little further, the former writing not only of a powerful 'tentation panthéiste'[41] but also of 'positions ambigües',[42] whilst the latter remarks that, although the spinozist has the final word, Diderot himself adopts no viewpoint.[43] This conclusion is echoed to some extent by Dieckmann, who puts forward the thesis

38. *Diderot the embattled philosopher*, p.71; Varloot, *Textes choisis*, p.30.
39. I. K. Luppol, *Denis Diderot: ses idées philosophiques* (Paris 1936), p.140; Vartanian, 'From deist to atheist', p.55; Niklaus (ed.), *Lettre sur les aveugles*, p.xvi.
40. Pommier, *Diderot avant Vincennes*, p.47; Wilson, *Diderot: the testing years*, p.63; J. Chouillet, 'Le personnage du sceptique', *Dix-huitième siècle* 1 (1969), p.203; Venturi, *La Jeunesse de Diderot*, p.117-18; Casini, *Diderot 'philosophe'*, p.127; Varloot, *Textes choisis*, p.14.
41. 'Le déisme du jeune Diderot', p.239.
42. 'Diderot et Buffon en 1749', p.221. Cf. Vernière's 'terrain d'entente' and 'position d'attente', *Spinoza et la pensée française* (Paris 1954), p.572, and *Œuvres philosophiques*, p.xii.
43. *Diderot the embattled philosopher*, p.75-76.

that the entire work is an exercise in objectivation and distancing, its satire directed against all the protagonists.[44] Lefèbvre, finally, sees it as a dialogue between Diderot and the contradictory tendencies of his time: 'Et il hésite, et il oscille entre elles' (*Diderot*, p.95), although he does acknowledge that: 'De confrontation en confrontation, la nature perd peu à peu à ses yeux son empreinte divine' (p.95-96).

These interpretations demonstrate a common reluctance to view the *Promenade* as anything other than a product of the transitional confusion separating the *Pensées philosophiques* from the *Lettre sur les aveugles*. It is possible, however, to identify the distinctive characteristics of this stage in Diderot's philosophical evolution in more positive and certain terms. Diderot's conclusion may be largely implicit, but it is nonetheless possible to discern it from a close analysis of the philosophical exchanges in the 'Allée des marronniers'.

i. *Atheism in the 'Allée des maronniers'*

Atheism is represented in the debate by Athéos, who devotes the majority of his speeches to a sarcastic and somewhat negative attack upon the finalistic view of the universe espoused by the deists.[45] In this respect he appears to be evenly matched with his deist opponents, Philoxène and the narrator. In other respects, however, a certain amount of ambiguity is in evidence.

On the one hand, Athéos's philosophy is clearly shown to be deficient in the question of biology. In reply to the deist's arguments from nature he can declare only that the organisation of living forms proves 'que la matière est organisée' (Her., ii.136). The poverty of this remark, together with his evident discomfiture, suggests that Diderot is merely reiterating the conclusions of the *Pensées philosophiques*.[46] Certainly his conviction that atheism is unequal to the task of interpreting so complex and vast a process as the organisation of living matter remains unshaken.

At the same time, however, there is evidence of a rather different attitude. The atheists as a group escape the satirical tone in which Diderot delineates the other philosophical sects in dispute with deism. They alone are introduced in neutral terms. Similarly, the assembled company do not dismiss Athéos's reasoning out of hand. Whilst conceding that plausibility is on the side of the deist narrator, they acknowledge to Athéos 'que peut-être il avait raison' (Her., ii.137).

44. 'Diderot's *Promenade du sceptique*', *Studies on Voltaire* 55 (1967).
45. For example, sections 39, 45. Her., ii.132-33, 135.
46. Cf. Pommier, *Diderot avant Vincennes*, p.47; Vartanian, 'From deist to atheist', p.52; Niklaus (ed.), *Lettre sur les aveugles*, p.xvii.

It would seem, then, that atheism is overshadowed by deism in the initial stages of the debate only on account of its incompleteness, its lack of a biological dimension. At this point, however, the *Promenade* diverges from the *Pensées philosophiques* by the introduction of an alternative challenge to deism: the philosophy of Oribaze.

ii. *Oribaze's 'spinozism'*

Oribaze's intervention in the debate makes explicit the particular limitations of Athéos's tenets. To him falls the rôle of expressing what appears to be Diderot's own judgement: that Athéos is correct in substance, but has failed to exploit his principles fully: 'il n'avait qu'à faire un pas de plus pour balancer au moins la victoire' (Her., ii.137). Oribaze takes this additional step by demonstrating that matter and the intelligent principle responsible for its organisation are co-existent and co-eternal: 'il s'ensuit donc [...] que l'être intelligent et l'être corporel sont éternels, que ces deux substances composent l'univers, et que l'univers est Dieu' (Her., ii.138). This formula appears to offer the dual advantage of rendering the deist's Creator superfluous and avoiding the narrow-ness of Athéos's philosophy. It transfers the responsibility for organisation and life from an extrinsic First Cause to a self-creative, self-sufficient universe, and thus reinforces the trend initiated by the *Pensées philosophiques*. Venturi expresses a similar conclusion about Oribaze: 'Oribaze représente à la fois l'enthousiasme pour la nature du déiste et la critique philosophique de l'athée',[47] though he erroneously labels this synthesis 'spinozism'.

For Oribaze's philosophy is not spinozism, as several scholars, including Pommier, Vartanian and Niklaus, have pointed out.[48] There is no need to seek the source of this version in Shaftesbury, as Casini has done (*Diderot 'philosophe'*, p.130-34); Spink's study of French free thought has shown that Diderot was not alone in using the label 'spinozist' loosely.[49] The interchangeability and vague philosophical content of such terms as *spinoziste, matérialiste, naturaliste* was commonplace at this time. Luppol, writing in 1936 and thus without the benefit of later research, seems unaware of any distortion.[50]

Spinoza's own formulation had been unequivocally monistic; he had referred,

47. *La Jeunesse de Diderot*, p.117.

48. Pommier, *Diderot avant Vincennes*, p.48; Vartanian, 'From deist to atheist', p.55; Niklaus (ed.), *Lettre sur les aveugles*, p.xvii.

49. J. S. Spink, *French free-thought from Gassendi to Voltaire* (London 1960), esp. p.238-79. The same point is made by H. El Nouty, 'Le panthéisme dans les lettres françaises', *Rsh* 100 (1960), p.437, 442. Cf. Winter, p.227, 236. For Spinoza's fortunes in eighteenth-century France, see also P. Vernière, *Spinoza et la pensée française* (Paris 1954) (esp. p.3, 610), and Ehrard, *L'Idée de nature*.

50. *Diderot, ses idées philosophiques*, p.135-36.

like Oribaze, to the impossibility of interaction between *pensée* and *étendue* (Oribaze's *être intelligent* and *être corporel*)[51] but, adding to this the absurdity of invoking an indefinite regression of causes (i.51 (10)), had gone on to establish that only one substance exists, namely God (i.49 (1) and n.9) and that *pensée* and *étendue* are simply attributes of this single substance (i.57 (28)). Momdzjan's analysis captures precisely the monistic – and energetic – potential of genuine spinozism:

Identifiant la nature à Dieu, Spinoza relie en quelque sorte la matière inerte au principe de l'activité, de la création, et fonde en un tout la *Natura naturata* et la *Natura naturans*. Privé de sens mystique, le panthéisme de Spinoza exprime l'idée de la matière spiritualisée, active, agissante d'une manière autonome, ne nécessitant aucune force de l'au-delà pour engendrer la richesse de l'univers.[52]

It is easy to see the contribution such a philosophy *could* have made to a vision of unity and energy. It must be stressed, however, that this is not the position outlined in the *Promenade*, for Oribaze refers to *two* substances, co-existing as distinct entities rather than as alternative modes of a single entity.

Consequently the superiority of Oribaze's philosophy over deism as an explanatory model is limited. The questions raised by Oribaze himself regarding the interaction of a material and a spiritual substance are only spuriously answered, and as a scientific (as opposed to purely metaphysical) concept, Oribaze's picture is as defective as Athéos's. It is not therefore plausible to suggest that either alternative to deism is fully acceptable to Diderot. His conclusions must be sought not at this explicit level but, as the form of the *Promenade* suggests, within the allegory.

iii. *Symbolic elements*

a. *Defeat of pyrrhonism and deism*

The deist's position is weakened in the course of the debate by both Athéos's and Oribaze's arguments. Far more serious than this, however, is the subtle way in which his symbolic defeat is engineered. Symbolic events conclude each of the two main stages of the debate: in the first, the pyrrhonist Zenoclès plunges into the waters of a river, declaring them to be solid, and has to be rescued from the consequences of his philosophy by Oribaze (Her., ii.134). Few critics have remarked upon this: Chouillet refers only in general terms to the ridicule heaped on Zenoclès,[53] and even Dieckmann, who points to the symbolic nature

51. Spinoza, *Œuvres* (Paris 1964), i.53, n.4 (Court traité ii/17/2/4).
52. H. N. Momdzjan, 'La dialectique dans la vision du monde de Diderot', *Au siècle des Lumières* (Paris, Moscou 1970), p.255.
53. 'Le personnage du sceptique', p.204.

18

of the attack on pyrrhonism,[54] does not bring out the particular rôle of Oribaze in this incident. In effect, Zenoclès's allegorical defeat reduces the number of serious contenders in the discussion to three – deist, 'spinozist', and atheist. Moreover, of these three it is Oribaze who has been cast in the rôle of philosophical saviour, and his status during subsequent exchanges with the other two is thereby enhanced.

This stratagem is reinforced and completed by an occurrence of even greater weight: the darkness which closes the debate. Vartanian indicates the significance of this event;[55] Casini, Niklaus and Dieckmann go further, pointing out a parallel with the device of blindness in the *Lettre sur les aveugles*.[56] The deist is prevented from countering Athéos's lengthy arguments (which are thus left to echo in the reader's mind) by the fall of darkness (Her., ii.138); this not only silences him, but effectively removes his strongest argument, the spectacle of nature. The fragility of this argument, at least at the cosmic level, is clearly demonstrated. Deprived of its teleological evidence, deism is rendered impotent, which leaves only the atheist and 'spinozist' positions (with one victory apiece) open by the end of the work.

b. Equalisation of atheism and 'spinozism'

Further symbolic and structural devices point to the futility of attempting to discern a preference in Diderot's mind for either of these two alternatives to deism. In the *Pensées sur l'interprétation de la nature* he will explicitly recommend the testing of any philosophical hypothesis by examination of its most extreme implications;[57] the method is already applied in the *Promenade* as he satirises the logical moral consequences of atheism on the one hand, and the absurdity of a literal interpretation of Oribaze's tenets on the other.

Athéos returns to find his home and family destroyed by an ex-Christian whom he had liberated from the fear of divine sanctions (Her., ii.138-39). Crocker sees this as evidence that Diderot still considers deism a necessary support for morals.[58] Certainly Diderot remains apprehensive about the moral content of atheism; it could be argued, however, that he no longer sees deism as the only alternative in this respect. Oribaze's display of spontaneous altruism in rescuing Zenoclès may be seen as a symbolic representation of his moral integrity. In addition, it is outside the philosophical world of the *Allée des marronniers* that these consequences are felt, a sign that Diderot is prepared to

54. 'Diderot's *Promenade du sceptique*', p.427.
55. 'From deist to atheist', p.54.
56. Casini, *Diderot 'philosophe'*, p.135; Niklaus (ed.), *Lettre sur les aveugles*, p.xviii; Dieckmann, 'Diderot's *Promenade du sceptique*', p.430, n.
57. See below, 3, B.iii.a.1.
58. *Diderot the embattled philosopher*, p.77.

divorce the philosophically and scientifically useful from the morally desirable. The implied condemnation is thus considerably attenuated.

A similar attenuation of satire marks Diderot's attitude to the literal version of 'spinozism'. This is expounded by Alcméon in a wealth of ridiculous detail as he attempts a physical identification of God's eye with the sun, the stars with his crown, and the like (Her., ii.132). The fact that these notions are immediately and convincingly refuted by pyrrhonist, sceptic and deist is not inconsistency in Diderot's treatment of 'spinozism', as Dieckmann has suggested,[59] but a necessary preliminary if Oribaze's more acceptable version is to be given a serious hearing. Ironically it is the accurately spinozist monism of Alcméon's version, omitted by Oribaze, which receives the brunt of the ridicule, on account of his naïve attempts to represent this in concrete, anthropomorphic terms.

Both alternatives to deism are also accorded favourable treatment in places – the atheists, as already noted, when they are introduced, and Oribaze (significantly) when he joins forces with Athéos against the deist position (Her., ii.137-38). By having Oribaze turn to the atheist for conceptual support, Diderot succeeds in stressing the common ground, rather than the considerable differences between the two philosophies. For, despite its dualism, Oribaze's view of the universe is closer, in its implications for an autonomous nature, to an atheistic monism than to a deistic dualism.

iv. *Diderot's conclusion*

Deism and pyrrhonism are thus eliminated; atheism and 'spinozism' are subtly, but deliberately, equalised. In this way Diderot implicitly defines his own position. He is seeking a metaphysical formula which synthesises atheism and pantheism, partaking of each and yet surpassing both. Atheism is attractive in certain respects, but offers no account of cosmic and biological order; 'spinozism' avoids this mechanical sterility but entails either continued dualism or an unacceptable form of pantheism. It is possible that Diderot is not expressing doubt as to whether deism, atheism or spinozism provides the most acceptable model of nature, only to settle this doubt definitively in favour of atheism in the *Lettre sur les aveugles*. His conclusion may well be dictated not by scepticism but by a positive act of judgement. He seems to have found all the options wanting and to be indicating implicitly, beneath the allegorical subtleties, the alternative he would prefer: an atheistic, monistic materialism, which nevertheless sees nature as an organic, non-mechanical whole.

Two years later he is able to make this conclusion explicit, in the *Lettre sur les aveugles*. Saunderson's declaration, from his personal world of darkness, is

59. 'Diderot's *Promenade du sceptique*', p.429-30, n.

Diderot's reply to the questions being asked as symbolic darkness fell upon the 'Allée des marronniers'.

D. *Lettre sur les aveugles* (1749)

i. *Interim developments*

During the brief period which separates the *Promenade du sceptique* from the *Lettre sur les aveugles*, two major developments occur: Diderot's intellectual commitment to atheism grows, and he gains a new conceptual tool by accepting the reality of spontaneous generation. Both have important implications for his nascent philosophy of energy.

a. Atheism

The *Bijoux indiscrets* of 1748 indicate Diderot's growing identification with atheism. In the early pages of the novel, a theological leader, or *bramin*, pronounces a sermon upon the philosophical turmoil provoked by the appearance of *bijoux parlants*. In it he is made to rail against those disbelievers who refuse to see anything more in the new phenomenon than the 'mécanisme aveugle de la nature' (Her., iii.77-78). Although the allegory parodies all parties, the deist *bramin* is the more immediate object of Diderot's satire, suggesting that his sympathies lie rather with those against whom the sermon is directed: the atheists, who prefer to seek a natural explanation.

The actual mechanism behind the *bijoux parlants* was, of course, inaccessible to empirical investigation, as indeed were the ultimate principles of any natural process. Diderot shows a clear preference for the atheist's honest admission of ignorance ('toutes les propriétés de la matière ne nous sont pas connues') over the deist's arrogant and elaborate attempts at total explanation.[60] It is only the former attitude which constitutes a constructive scientific approach to nature; in a reversal of the situation in the *Pensées philosophiques*, it is now atheism which appears to be most closely in harmony with the aims of biological speculation.

b. Spontaneous generation

Closely associated with this shift was Diderot's conversion to the principle of spontaneous generation. Vartanian has studied in depth the crucial rôle played

---

60. Her., iii.78. Cf. Mirabaud's claim in a manuscript of 1751 that, since matter is not yet fully understood, 'les sensations et la pensée' may prove to be as yet unknown properties of matter (quoted in I. O. Wade, *The Clandestine organization and diffusion of philosophic ideas in France*, Princeton 1938, p.215). Similar ideas appeared in the anonymous *L'Ame mortelle* (Wade, p.223-25).

by the vitalist biology of the 1740s in Diderot's transition to materialism.[61] Kiernan attempts to refute Vartanian's thesis, arguing that Diderot uses science only to uphold 'a philosophy derived by other means'.[62] His alternative, however, is unconvincing and often based upon flawed evidence. He asserts, for instance, that at the time Diderot abandoned deism he already believed that life was a property of matter (p.67) – a clear misreading of the *Pensées philosophiques* – and quotes the *Eléments de physiologie* as illustration of a position supposedly reached some decades earlier (p.68). He also ignores the central fact that *both* deism and atheism are, for Diderot, derived from the life sciences. The transition from physics to biology to which Kiernan refers simply does not exist.

Vartanian stresses that the impact of Needham's work on infusoria, which appeared to reinstate biogenesis, was felt in France precisely during the brief interim between the *Promenade du sceptique* and the *Lettre sur les aveugles*.[63] Such 'discoveries' together with Trembley's experiments on the freshwater polyp, led philosophers to view nature increasingly as an active, rather than passive entity.[64] As Casini has remarked, 'La natura creatrice, lungi dall'essere un mero fantasma erudito, era una realtà che gli osservatori empirici penetravano oggi giorno più profondamente.'[65] La Mettrie's *L'Homme machine* (1748), in some respects an extreme expression of this tendency, was almost certainly instrumental in persuading Diderot to accept the implications of Needham's findings.[66] Buffon, too, may have played a rôle in this conclusion.[67] The outcome, as Winter sees it, is that Diderot was enabled to dispense with the concept of an extrinsic Creator, just as the *Pensées philosophiques* had implied (p.157):

Gemäß seiner methodischen Forderung, daß die Theorien nur die Gültigkeit provisorischer Stufen im Fortschreiten der naturwissenschaftlichen Erkentnisse umfassen und dem Experiment als Kriterium unterworfen sind, gibt Diderot auf der Basis von Needhams Forschungsergebnissen die deistische Theorie auf.

Although erroneous, these conclusions helped Diderot to a positive conceptual breakthrough[68] and, in combination with his commitment to atheism, give rise to his first explicit formulation of materialism.

61. 'Trembley's polyp', *Journal of the history of ideas* 11 (1950), p.259-86.
62. *Enlightenment and science*, p.63.
63. Vartanian, Crocker, 'Correspondence' (*Mln*), p.284.
64. Vartanian, 'From deist to atheist', p.56-57.
65. *Diderot 'philosophe'*, p.123-24. Cf. Roger's comment on the effect of Needham's work: 'Bien que guidée par le Créateur, la Nature se trouvait ainsi douée d'une spontanéité qui pouvait paraître dangereuse à bien des esprits' (*Les Sciences de la vie*, p.502).
66. Vartanian, 'From deist to atheist', p.63, n.; 'Trembley's polyp', p.274.
67. Winter, p.157. Cf. Roger, 'Diderot et Buffon en 1749' and *Les Sciences de la vie*, p.597-98.
68. Vartanian, 'The problem of generation and the French Enlightenment', *Diderot studies* 6 (1964), p.346.

Niklaus points out the way in which external and internal developments are mutually reinforcing in this instance: 'l'idée de générations spontanées, combattue dans les *Pensées philosophiques*, est maintenant acceptée, parce qu'elle reçoit les suffrages des savants, et parce qu'elle entraîne des conséquences qui entrent dans ses idées philosophiques'.[69] The result is what Winter has called 'der erste skizzenhafte Entwurf eines neuen Weltbildes' (p.18).

ii. *The letter to Voltaire: monism*

In June 1749 Diderot wrote to Voltaire commenting upon the latter's reactions to the *Lettre sur les aveugles*. Previous commentators have examined this letter in a somewhat negative light: Niklaus, for instance, sees it only as a vague reiteration of the spinozism and deism the *Lettre sur les aveugles* appeared to have left behind,[70] whilst Roger and Villey consider it only insofar as it casts doubt upon Diderot's full commitment to atheism.[71] This aspect is important and will be assessed in the following section. Equally noteworthy, however, is the letter's value as a document of Diderot's thought processes during the transition to a monist view of matter, presented as a *fait accompli* in the *Lettre* itself. Venturi hints that a close comparison of this letter and parallel passages in the *Promenade du sceptique* is essential for an understanding of Diderot's ideas at this time, but fails to elaborate the point.[72]

In his letter, Diderot takes up the arguments attributed to Oribaze in the *Promenade*, but with certain amendments and additions passed over by Venturi, Casini and Vernière.[73] In the first place he stresses the dualistic implications of Oribaze's 'spinozism' by replacing the *Promenade*'s 'êtres intelligents' with the term 'êtres spirituels', which has the effect of underlining the distinction between these and the 'êtres matériels' or 'corporels' which constitute Oribaze's second substance (*Corr.*, i.76). Secondly, he inserts a sentence which rules out even more firmly than before the possibility of any interaction between the two substances. The letter's version of Oribaze's conclusion is extended in such a way as to bring out its internal contradiction: 'il s'ensuit donc [...] que l'être corporel n'est pas moins indépendant de l'être spirituel, que l'être spirituel de l'être corporel, qu'ils composent ensemble l'univers, et que l'univers est Dieu'

---

69. Niklaus (ed.), *Lettre sur les aveugles*, p.xxii, n. Spontaneous generation is discussed again below, iv.a.

70. Edition, *Lettre sur les aveugles*, p.lxviii. Cf. Szigeti, *Denis Diderot: une grande figure*, p.15.

71. Roger, 'Diderot et Buffon en 1749', p.221; P. Villey, 'A propos de la *Lettre sur les aveugles*', *Revue du XVIIIe siècle* (1913), p.429.

72. *La Jeunesse de Diderot*, p.117.

73. Venturi, p.117; Casini, *Diderot 'philosophe'*, p.158; Vernière, *Spinoza et la pensée française*, p.571. G. Roth juxtaposes the two versions, but without comment of any kind (*Corr.*, i.76-77).

(*Corr.*, i.77). The separation of the two substances leads to a dualism, whereas 'l'univers est Dieu' is a potentially monist statement. This ambiguity had been left unresolved in the *Promenade*. Now, however, Diderot demolishes both alternatives, dualism *and* pantheism, by suggesting that intelligence is not the province of an autonomous substance, but contained within the potentialities of matter itself: 'Quelle force n'ajouterait point à ce raisonnement l'opinion qui vous est commune avec Locke, que la pensée pourrait bien être une modification de la matière.'[74]

Certainly spinozism is one of the origins of this transition to monism, as several critics have indicated. Vartanian, for instance, considers that Spinoza's influence 'acted as a valuable precipitant on Diderot's emerging materialism' and that it provides the key to the continuity of Diderot's thought during this early period.[75] Niklaus, too, sees spinozism as 'un pas dans le sens du naturalisme'.[76] This letter indicates the exact point at which he transcends spinozist philosophy by positing not that matter and intelligence are alternative modes of God, but that intelligence is a mode of matter. Diderot's is clearly a materialist, not a pantheist monism. In this it differs also from Leibniz's philosophy of nature which, like Spinoza's, posited a spiritual substance.

Such a monism must, by definition, be atheistic. The letter to Voltaire confirms this paradoxical synthesis of spinozism and atheism by placing Oribaze's arguments in the mouth of the atheist Saunderson. The atheism itself, however, is only fully presented in the *Lettre* itself.

iii. *Diderot and Saunderson*

a. Atheism

There is strong evidence within the *Lettre* to support the assumption that Diderot shares the philosophy expounded by Saunderson. As in the *Promenade*, Diderot's position is indicated largely by symbolic and structural elements.

In the first place, he validates the methodological principle behind Saunderson's metaphysical speculation, namely that of cartesian – or occamite – simplification, by declaring: 'Un moyen presque sûr de se tromper en métaphysique c'est de ne pas simplifier assez les objets dont on s'occupe.'[77] The sentiment is not particularly striking in itself. A few pages later, however, Saunderson invokes the very same principle in support of his atheism. In terms reminiscent of the implicit conclusion of the *Bijoux indiscrets*, he argues that using God as a means

---

74. *Corr.*, i.77. See below, iii.b. for the treatment of this issue in the *Lettre sur les aveugles* itself.
75. 'From deist to atheist', p.55.
76. Niklaus (ed.), *Lettre sur les aveugles*, p.xviii.
77. *Œuvres philosophiques*, p.98. Her., iv.32.

to cut through the Gordian knot of nature is self-defeating, since such a Being is even less accessible to human reason than the phenomenon it is designed to explain in the first place: 'Si la nature nous offre un nœud difficile à délier, laissons-le pour ce qu'il est; et n'employons pas à le couper la main d'un être qui devient ensuite pour nous un nouveau nœud plus indissoluble que le premier' (*OPhil.*, p.119; Her., iv.49). It is difficult to believe that Diderot did not intend these two statements to be taken together, the first guaranteeing the validity of the metaphysical conclusions drawn in the second. Incidentally he will use the same principle to introduce the atheistic monism of the *Rêve de d'Alembert* twenty years later (*OPhil.*, p.257).

This is only one element of a strategic framework clearly discernible within the *Lettre* despite its apparent looseness of construction, a framework of which Niklaus asks: 'Tout n'est-il pas ordonné pour entraîner le lecteur avec lui dans la prodigieuse aventure intellectuelle qu'il annonce?'[78] Several pages before Saunderson's speech, Diderot vouches for the soundness of his ideas: 'L'aveugle-né aperçoit les choses d'une manière beaucoup plus abstraite que nous, et [...] dans les questions de pure spéculation il est peut-être moins sujet à se tromper' (*OPhil.*, p.98; Her., iv.32). Saunderson's strongest argument against the existence of a benevolent, ordering deity is his blindness; this not only prevents him from appreciating the teleology on which deism depends, but also constitutes a serious physical flaw, inconsistent with the beliefs of deist finalism. Diderot makes use of this, after the speech, to alienate sympathy for the deist viewpoint just as surely as that for Saunderson had been aroused before it. His ostensibly orthodox objections to Saunderson's atheism deliberately remind the reader of the argument behind it: 'Quelle honte pour des gens qui n'ont pas de meilleures raisons que lui, *qui voient*, et à qui *le spectacle étonnant de la nature* annonce [...] l'existence et la gloire de son auteur. *Ils ont des yeux, dont Saunderson était privé.*'[79] And again: 'Je demanderais volontiers si le vrai Dieu n'était pas encore mieux voilé pour Socrate par les ténèbres du paganisme, que pour Saunderson par *la privation de la vue et du spectacle de la nature.*'[80] In each case the imperfection is carefully juxtaposed with the *spectacle*; together with Diderot's earlier guarantees, this represents a clear invitation to read between the lines.

Nevertheless, several critics have questioned the strength of Diderot's commitment to atheism at this time, notably Venturi, Niklaus, Vartanian and Villey.[81]

78. Niklaus (ed.), *Lettre sur les aveugles*, p.xxxi. Niklaus does not, however, bring out exactly the same structural points as the present analysis.
79. p.124. Her., iv.52-53. My emphasis.
80. p.124-25. Her., iv.53. My emphasis.
81. Venturi, *La Jeunesse de Diderot*, p.150, 156, 161; Niklaus (ed.), *Lettre sur les aveugles*, p.xlii-xliii; Vartanian, 'From deist to atheist', p.60; Villey, 'A propos de la *Lettre sur les aveugles*', p.429. Villey fails to appreciate the symbolic value of Saunderson's blindness and seeks to deny any

Their reservations are based on Saunderson's dying words: 'O Dieu de Clarke et de Newton, prends pitié de moi!' (*OPhil.*, p.124; Her., iv.52) and on Diderot's disavowal of Saunderson's philosophy in his letter to Voltaire: 'Le sentiment de Saounderson [*sic*] n'est pas plus mon sentiment que le vôtre' (*Corr.*, i.75-76). It is tempting, though doubtless quite unjustified, to dismiss the latter remark as a piece of pure casuistry on Diderot's part. It might, after all, be only the *dying* sentiments of Saunderson which Diderot disowns. There are, however, more soundly based indications that no serious inconsistency is implied by these lines.

It seems unlikely, in the first place, that Saunderson's final invocation would be seconded by Diderot even if he were still inclined to cling to the shreds of his deism. The concept of the Newtonian divinity, guarantor of a passive, mechanical nature, had been rejected as long ago as the *Pensées philosophiques*.[82] Moreover, it is so at variance with the philosophy of active, autonomous nature just elaborated by Saunderson that these words can be ascribed only to the speaker's delirious state – of which Diderot is careful to inform us.

Indeed there is a close parallel between this situation and Diderot's confession to Voltaire that it is only during the hours of darkness that his belief in God wavers (*Corr.*, i.76). In both cases there is a clear distinction between intellectual conclusions and those drawn at a time of emotional vulnerability. Diderot makes it plain in the letter that he is concerned with the emotional dimension of his personal beliefs; the 'raisons métaphysiques' of Saunderson's atheism are not called into question.

In fact he echoes the strategy of the *Lettre* itself, adding to his disclaimer the insidious rider: 'mais ce pourrait bien être parce que je vois' (*Corr.*, i.75-76). If he were blind, in other words (that is, in permanent darkness), he would probably think like Saunderson – and it is the blind who tend to be right about such matters. There is no inconsistency here: Diderot's intellectual commitment to the atheism professed by Saunderson seems complete.

b. Materialism

Having given his general endorsement to the blind man's speculations, Diderot also appears to accept the materialist interpretation of nature which complements Saunderson's atheism. As Diderot implies in his letter to Voltaire, the transfer of intelligence to matter is crucial to such a philosophy. In the *Lettre* he integrates both references to this point into the strategic framework designed to manipulate the reader's sympathies. In the early pages of the work he inserts a deceptively casual remark to the effect that the blind do not share the common preconceptions which would rule out such a tenet: 'comme ils voient la matière d'une

measure of intellectual commitment to atheism on Diderot's part.
82. Cf. above, B.ii.b.1.

manière beaucoup plus abstraite que nous, ils sont moins éloignés de croire qu'elle pense' (*OPhil.*, p.93-94; Her., iv.28). This is followed by Diderot's suggestion that it is to this same quality of abstraction within the blind man's vision that his accurate perception of speculative truths may be attributed.[83] Towards the end of the work, after the reader's intellectual sympathies have been suitably orientated, the point is made again: 'combien nos sens nous suggèrent de choses, et que nous aurions de peine, sans nos yeux, à supposer qu'un bloc de marbre ne pense ni ne sent!' (*OPhil.*, p.144; Her., iv.70). Previous commentators such as Niklaus and Varloot,[84] who have drawn attention only to the first formulation, miss the force of its repetition and the structural subtlety with which Diderot imposes it.[85]

The concept of thought (and sentience) in matter is, as yet, only crudely stated. It will however recur, as will the motif of the marble block, in Diderot's elaboration of a philosophy of natural energy. Already the attribution of sentience and consequent intelligence to matter serve to confirm both Diderot's intuition that the structure and functions of higher biological forms differ only in complexity from those of the lower (*Pensée* XIX) and his definitive abandonment of pantheism.

It is not, therefore, unreasonable to take the materialistic content of Saunderson's speech as fully indicative of Diderot's own philosophy of nature in 1749.

iv. *Saunderson's account of natural energy*

The metaphysical synthesis adumbrated in the *Promenade* is given expression in Saunderson's vision of a universe invested with energy: 'das Bild, einer Welt, die in dauernde Bewegung und Umwandlung begriffen ist' (Winter, p.18). On the one hand, material forces are presented as the first cause of the present world order; on the other they are seen as the source of a continuing, creative dynamism within nature. The first rôle corresponds to that played by mechanical motion in cartesian and classical atheist thought; the second provides a viable alternative to the pantheistic monism offered by Spinoza.

The emergence of living forms is ascribed to spontaneous generation, which is envisaged as a twofold process involving the primary combination of matter, through a process akin to fermentation, and a second combinatory stage attributed simply to motion, in which discrete organisms emerge.

---

83. *OPhil*, p.98, Her., iv.32. Cf. above, a.
84. Niklaus (ed.), p.95 n.12; Varloot, *Textes choisis*, p.34.
85. *OPhil*, p.124-25; Her., iv.53. Cf. above, a.

a. The origin of life

As in the *Pensées philosophiques*, Diderot remains reluctant to accept that motion, as understood by Epicurean philosophers or contemporary physicists, is capable of initiating life. He therefore adopts a term with specifically biological associations, *fermentation*: 'dans le commencement [...] la matière en fermentation faisait éclore l'univers' (*OPhil.*, p.123; Her., iv.51). Contemporary definitions indicate that *fermentation* was applied by chemists in the eighteenth century, as now, to the process whereby organic matter is decomposed or converted into new compounds, accompanied by the production of movement and heat.[86] Although at the time it was considered to be only a specialised form of motion provoked by a suitable agent, the distinction between this view of chemical interaction and that proposed by the mechanist's colliding atoms is substantial. Already the term had evolved from its early seventeenth-century sense of 'a process [...] involving pressure, collision and particles in motion'[87] to something involving spontaneity, creativity: a definitely *organic* dimension.

Crocker also notes the significance of Diderot's choice of terminology, but interprets it rather differently: 'We must avoid the error of always taking the word *"fermentation"* in its chemical sense, which it sometimes has; it is often a metaphoric expression of the turbulence of matter in motion, and is more accurately rendered as "ferment". It is not opposed to mechanism, but rather to creationism.'[88] These readings are not necessarily mutually exclusive.

In any case, Diderot's intuition of a special biological force is as yet very limited. In the first place it is clear that the issue of distinguishing organic from inorganic matter has not yet presented itself to him.[89] Matter is still, for Diderot, a totally homogeneous substance, and he remains oblivious to the vitalistic implications of Saunderson's vision.

The second limitation arises within his concept of secondary combination.

b. Biological organisation

Diderot is apparently content to retain the rôle given to movement in the *Pensées philosophiques*: that of the secondary organisation of organic matter. The *germes*

86. For example, 'un mouvement intestin qui s'excite de lui-même entre les parties insensibles d'un corps, duquel résulte un nouvel arrangement, et une nouvelle combinaison de ces mêmes parties': 1766 translation of David Macbride's definition, itself based on Macquer, quoted in G. Bachelard, *La Formation de l'esprit scientifique* (Paris 1947), p.66., and the anonymous *Encyclopédie* article 'Vin' (*Enc.* xvii.283). Cf. also below, 5, B.i.b.

87. E. I. Mendelsohn, 'Philosophical biology versus experimental biology: spontaneous generation in the 17th century', *Actes*, 12e congrès international d'histoire des sciences, 1b (1971), p.219.

88. *Diderot's chaotic order* (Princeton 1974), p.12-13.

89. Hence my reluctance to use either of the conventional terms biogenesis or abiogenesis of his version of spontaneous generation. It is simply not clear which he has in mind.

arise now, it is true, through spontaneous generation, but their development is ascribed as before to the workings of mechanical motion: 'le mouvement continue et continuera de combiner des amas de matière, jusqu'à ce qu'ils aient obtenu quelque arrangement dans lequel ils puissent persévérer' (*OPhil.*, p.123; Her., iv.51).

This trial-and-error succession of arrangements is nothing more than the multiple *jets* of the *Pensées philosophiques* atheist. As Crocker points out, Diderot has as yet no concept of a creative force leading to qualitative differences at this level.[90] Crocker is, however, a little severe in his judgement that Diderot has no principle of action other than the mechanical forces of nature until *sensibilité* is formulated. The concept of *fermentation* is available; it is simply not applied. The potential for transcending mechanism is there.

Diderot's account of biological organisation also reveals the extent to which he has detached himself from deism. Paradoxically, it guarantees both spontaneous creativity and purpose to nature. Unlike the 'programmed' *germes* of deist biology, the rudimentary forms thrown up by spontaneous generation are unpredictable, even fallible. They are the fruit not of a pre-ordained, regularly unfolding scheme, but of 'agitations irrégulières' (*OPhil.*, p.123; Her., iv.52). Moreover, by dispensing with God, Diderot now assumes the inherence of energy within matter.[91]

At the same time, the rôle played previously by divine design is taken over by a material equivalent: the principle of viability. The process of interaction has as its end product the formation of organisms able to survive and reproduce themselves. This belief in the existence of a state of optimum organisation evidently satisfies Diderot's previous misgivings about the ability of an atheistic philosophy of nature to account adequately for the apparent purpose discernible in the biological world. Harmony and stability can, after all, be shown to emerge from the free interplay of energetic matter. Physical energy thus not only possesses the immanence which both traditional atheism and pantheism claimed for their first cause; it also takes on the creative and directive powers hitherto reserved for a deistic God.

c. Universal dynamism

The stability created by this energy can be nothing more, however, than a temporary equilibrium. New interactions will occur, existing forms decay and new ones be thrown up: 'Qu'est-ce que ce monde [...]? Un composé sujet à des révolutions, qui toutes indiquent une tendance continuelle à la destruction; une succession rapide d'êtres qui s'entresuivent, se poussent et disparaissent;

90. *Diderot the embattled philosopher*, p.122. Cf. following section.
91. Cf. below, 2, B.ii.a.

une symétrie passagère; un ordre momentané' (*OPhil.*, p.123; Her., iv.52). It is a widely held view that Saunderson's vision of a dynamic universe prefigures evolutionary, or at least transformist, theory. This opinion is shared by commentators as diverse as Luppol and Niklaus, Villey and Wilson, and by many more besides.[92] Others are more cautious: Venturi and Crocker are aware that Diderot's theories do not yet amount to evolutionism or transformism,[93] whilst Vernière points to the largely literary inspiration of his speculations on the formation of monsters.[94] Only Callot and Roger, to our knowledge, have attempted to refute the 'transformist' interpretations and show that Saunderson's speech, despite its substitution of the successive rather than simultaneous emergence of life forms, is essentially anti-evolutionary.[95]

For the *Lettre*'s vision is of an ever-changing mosaic; there is no sense of overall progression, such as an evolutionary philosophy implies, nor any suggestion of the transmutation of one organism into another, as in transformism. Any balance achieved is precarious: new forms arise in isolation and at random. Diderot's philosophy is thus already one of universal dynamism and of flux.

Crocker has made a plausible and interesting attempt to integrate the concepts of optimum organisation and flux by speculating that they constitute an early theory of entropy. He thus refers to the *Lettre*'s dynamic view of nature as: 'a constant search for structure, order, stability – and, simultaneously, a constant breakdown and increase in disorder, involving the same energy' (*Diderot's chaotic order*, p.10). Optimum organisation, then, is the expression of matter's struggle to achieve and maintain an organised form, to resist the entropy entailed by 'the inevitable destruction of this precarious stability'. This may be a little ambitious, but it certainly captures the spirit of Diderot's speculations.

In four years, under the catalytic influence of spinozism, Diderot has cast aside his sentimental and somewhat uncritical deism in favour of atheism, and established the principles of a self-sufficient, self-creative nature.[96] During the

92. Luppol, *Diderot: ses idées philosophiques*, p.264; Niklaus (ed.), *Lettre sur les aveugles*, p.xxliii, xliv-xlv, l-li; Villey, 'A propos de la *Lettre sur les aveugles*, p.427-28; Wilson, *Diderot: the testing years*, p.98. Cf. Mayer, *Diderot homme de science*, p.228; Mornet, *Diderot* (Paris 1941), p.47; Varloot, *Textes choisis*, p.31; Vartanian, 'From deist to atheist', p.59-60; Wartofsky, 'Diderot and the development of materialist monism', p.317; Lefèbvre, *Diderot*, p.87, 110-11; Casini, *Diderot 'philosophe'*, *passim*; Ehrard, *L'Idée de nature*, i.233-34.

93. Venturi, *La Jeunesse de Diderot*, p.148; Crocker, *Diderot the embattled philosopher*, p.100-101; cf. O. Schmidt, 'Die Anschauungen der Encyclopädisten über die organische Natur', *Deutsche Rundschau* 7 (1876), p.85.

94. *Œuvres philosophiques*, p.121. Cf. Roger, 'Diderot et Buffon en 1749', p.231, and C. M. Singh, 'La *Lettre sur les aveugles*: its debt to Lucretius', *Studies in 18th-century French literature presented to R. Niklaus*, ed. Fox and others (Exeter 1975), p.233-42.

95. Callot, *La Philosophie de la vie*, p.303-305; Roger, *Les Sciences de la vie*, p.593-94 and n.50.

96. Cf. Winter, p.18, 19.

next four years, he turns aside from religious polemic to consolidate, explore and expand the methodological and conceptual foundations of this philosophy. Towards the end of the *Lettre sur les aveugles*, Diderot reflects on the limitations of human knowledge: 'que savons-nous? ce que c'est que la matière? nullement; ce que c'est que l'esprit et la pensée? encore moins; ce que c'est que le mouvement, l'espace et la durée? point du tout' (*OPhil.*, p.144; Her., iv.72). These lines are no mere profession of scepticism; they sketch out a programme for his future speculations: matter, energy, vital faculties, and their relationship through time and space.

2. Transition: from the *Lettre sur les aveugles* to the *Pensées sur l'interprétation de la nature* (1749-1753)

THE foundations for Diderot's first major work of scientific speculation, the *Pensées sur l'interprétation de la nature*, are laid in the *Apologie de l'abbé de Prades* and his early *Encyclopédie* articles. From 1749 to 1753 he not only reaffirms and develops the materialism of the *Lettre sur les aveugles*, but also declares certain principles of methodology on which this philosophy is henceforth to be based. There is no division between these two aspects of his thought: one serves constantly to illuminate the other. Thus anti-finalism is associated inevitably with atheism and the concomitant replacement of God by natural energy as both an explanatory and a physical concept. Relativism (the epistemological approach and its physical counterpart, the flux within nature) and unity (Diderot's belief that knowledge, like the world, is an organically unified whole) demonstrate a similar parallelism. Both aspects, finally, draw their inspiration primarily from the world of biological rather than mechanical phenomena.

A. Anti-finalism and the autonomy of scientific enquiry

For many commentators it is not until the *Pensées sur l'interprétation de la nature* that Diderot abandons metaphysics in favour of science. Vernière, for instance, remarks of the *Interprétation*: 'Diderot semble abandonner les spéculations métaphysiques et donner pour but à la philosophie de couronner l'édifice des sciences.'[1] The essentials of this process, however, are completed well in advance of 1753. Several earlier writings are concerned to declare theology irrelevant, even detrimental, to the work of the scientific investigator of nature. This concern was provoked by the large number of popular contemporary scientific works, especially those devoted to biological subjects, which were essentially apologetic in aim and manner (a trend reflected in Diderot's own *Pensées philosophiques*). The concern was shared by Buffon, La Mettrie and Maupertuis, among others.

Traces of Diderot's growing impatience with the appeal to final causes to

1. *OPhil.*, p.xiii. Cf. Varloot: 'il ne s'attarde pas à la polémique religieuse banale; il croit mieux faire en faisant progresser le matérialisme' (edition, *Pensées sur l'interprétation de la nature*, p.26).

account for natural phenomena had been in evidence as early as 1748, with the satirical treatment meted out to the 'deists' of the *Bijoux indiscrets*.[2] It is given more extensive expression, with varying degrees of explicitness, in the *Prospectus* to the *Encyclopédie* (1750), the *Apologie de l'abbé de Prades* (1752) and the *Encyclopédie* article 'Chaos' (volume iii, published in 1753).

i. Prospectus

Any overt declaration of anti-finalism would have been out of place in the *Prospectus*, attracting hostile attention from the censors. The careful reader, however, would have noted Diderot's amendment to a key section of Bacon's outline of human knowledge, on which the *Prospectus* was based.

Bacon's definition of the science of matter, which Diderot quotes, had accorded equal status to the study of efficient and final causes: 'Division de la Science spéculative de la Nature en *Physique particulière* et *métaphysique*; la première ayant pour objet la cause efficiente et la matière, et la Métaphysique, la cause finale et la forme' (Her., v.127). Diderot, however, combines the two categories; the artificial, scholastic distinction between matter and its form is eliminated, and his 'metaphysics' clearly involves only a study of the physical properties and energy of matter: 'Nous avons vu par la réflexion que de ces abstraits [abstract notions] les uns convenaient à tous les individus corporels, comme étendue, mouvement, impénétrabilité etc. Nous en avons fait l'objet de la Physique générale, ou métaphysique des corps' (Her., v.112). The scientist is thus freed from any obligation to take final causes into account in his work.

ii. Apologie de l'abbé de Prades

This work proclaims, in turn, the independence of scientific enquiry from scriptural authority. De Prades's thesis on the origins of the world had been condemned on the grounds that it contravened the teachings of Genesis. Diderot's defence of its author is equally a defence of his own *Lettre sur les aveugles*: 'Je suis bien éloigné de croire qu'on ne puisse abandonner la physique de Moïse sans renoncer à sa religion' (Her., iv.337). Speaking in de Prades's name, he declares the total incompatiblity of the two modes of enquiry, the theologian's and the scientist's: 'Demeurons en repos, suivons paisiblement notre objet, et permettons aux physiciens d'atteindre le leur. [...] Notttre devoir est de les éclairer sur l'auteur de la nature; le leur, de nous dévoiler son grand ouvrage' (Her., iv.338). It is the same sentiment which will inspire the better-known declaration of the *Interprétation*: 'Le physicien, dont la profession est

2. See above, i, D.i.a.

d'instruire et non d'édifier, abandonnera donc le *pourquoi* et ne s'occupera que du *comment.*'[3]

The distinction was not new: Descartes had differentiated between the realms of theology (truths of revelation required for salvation) and philosophy (truths of reason required for science and action) in the previous century.[4] Descartes, however, had considered both orders of truth valid and relevant to man. Diderot, on the other hand, seconds Bacon's contention that the traditional confusion of the two 'n'a déjà que trop retardé le progrès des sciences' (Her., iv.338) and states unequivocally that the progress of human civilisation depends on science, not theology: 'Si, à la première découverte qui se fera [...] nous devons renouveler, dans la personne de l'inventeur, l'injure faite autrefois dans la personne de Galilée, allons, brisons les microscopes, foulons aux pieds les téléscopes, et soyons les apôtres de la barbarie' (Her., iv.337-38).

Clearly physics must take precedence over metaphysics. Diderot's ambiguous position in this work as defender of orthodoxy allows him to insinuate the inferiority of theological truth by denying it the status of scientific fact: 'Gardons-nous bien d'attacher la vérité de notre culte, et la divinité de nos écritures, à des faits qui n'y ont aucun rapport, et qui peuvent être démentis par le temps et par les expériences' (Her., iv.338).

For the materialist, of course, the provisional nature of scientific truths does not detract from their validity. Diderot had made use, for instance, of successive, contradictory 'facts' about spontaneous generation without his faith in biological science being shaken. He rejects the static world-view of faith, with its refusal to take account of potentially threatening scientific evidence, in favour of the philosopher's flexible vision, capable of assimilating new elements. The investigation of final causes belongs to the former approach and is therefore declared barren for the scientist: 'Occupons-nous sans cesse de causes finales, mais n'assujettissons point à cette voie stérile l'Académie dans ses recherches' (Her., iv.338).

To replace the conceptual framework of finalism, Diderot – again basing his ideas closely on those of Bacon – advocates a working hypothesis of atheism: 'Le physicien doit faire, dans ses recherches, une entière abstraction de l'existence de Dieu, poursuivre son travail en bon athée.'[5] Although aware, as the *Pensées philosophiques* showed, that real scientific progress had been made under the banner of finalism, Diderot now felt a need to free science from the shackles of such an approach: his own emerging philosophy is dependent on the premise

3. Her., ix.90. As Winter points out, this does not constitute a rejection of research into causal explanations (*das Warum*), simply of teleology (*das Wozu*) (p.96).

4. Cf. A. Vartanian, *Diderot and Descartes* (Princeton 1953), p.203, 291.

5. Her., iv.338-39. Cf. Winter, p.179.

of atheism. He therefore praises the atheists of antiquity, although he no longer wholeheartedly shares their mechanistic conclusions (Her., iv.339):

Les pas que Démocrite et les autres antagonistes de la Providence faisaient dans l'investigation des effets de la nature étaient et plus rapides et plus fermes, par la raison même qu'en banissant de l'univers toute cause intelligente, et qu'en ne rapportant les phénomènes qu'à des causes mécaniques, leur philosophie n'en pouvait devenir que plus rationnelle.

Methodological and metaphysical conclusions thus coincide, each demanding and justifying the other. To a universe without God corresponds a science without finalism: to a universe in flux, philosophical relativism.

B. Presentation of materialism

In the *Encyclopédie* article 'Chaos', Diderot makes tactical use of his belief in the autonomy of scientific enquiry to demolish the Biblical account of Creation and replace it with a panorama of materialist alternatives, including his own philosophy, reiterated in its essentials from the *Lettre sur les aveugles*.

i. *Genesis discredited as an alternative to materialism*

The article 'Chaos' purports to defend the orthodox theory of Creation and offer guidance to the philosopher or scientist who wishes to work within the framework of the Biblical account. Speculation on such matters should, Diderot declares in a tone of orthodox sincerity, be severely restricted: 'il ne doit être permis aux philosophes de faire des hypothèses que dans les choses sur lesquelles la Genèse ne s'explique pas clairement' (Her., vi.363). Towards the end of the article, however, Diderot comments on the relationship between Mosaic physics and modern scientific speculation in such a way as to alert the reader to the ambiguity of what has gone before.

He undertakes, in fact, a systematic attack on scriptural authority. In the first place, he defends Moses' account of the chaos preceding Creation by stressing that belief in such a state is universal, shared by philosophies completely outside the Judaeo-Christian tradition. The special status of Biblical authority is thus undermined. The process continues with a justification of Descartes's and Newton's departures from revealed truth, which is little more than a pretext for Diderot to expound the manifest scientific errors in Genesis. He stresses the almost infinite variety of interpretations which may be placed on the scriptural texts and concludes by casting doubt on their linguistic precision.

In the light of this catalogue of Biblical inadequacy, Diderot's initial admonition hardly has the same force. Well might he conclude that, providing care is

taken, 'on peut dire du chaos tout ce qu'on voudra' (Her., vi.364). The decision is effectively left to the discrimination of the individual philosopher/scientist, and the independence of his speculations safeguarded just as surely as by the more explicit statements of the *Apologie de l'abbé de Prades*. Diderot, consequently, is free to discuss classical notions of the origins of the universe. Luppol, missing the tactical significance of Diderot's remarks, dismisses them as mere contradictions and thus concludes that the entire article 'n'est utile en rien'.[6] Vernière, too, appears to take Diderot's protestations at face value[7] – a serious misapprehension.

ii. *The concept of chaos: matter and energy*

In Diderot's account of classical views of the chaos from which the universe emerged, the essential tenets of the *Lettre sur les aveugles* reappear, together with a further principle which Diderot will shortly adopt explicitly, the heterogeneity of matter: 'Les anciens philosophes ont entendu par ce mot [chaos] un mélange confus de particules de toute espèce, sans forme ni régularité, auquel ils supposaient le mouvement essentiel, lui attribuant en conséquence la formation de l'univers.'[8] This briefly sketched system corresponds so closely to that expounded by Saunderson in the *Lettre sur les aveugles* that the article is almost certainly being used as a vehicle for Diderot's own philosophy.

a. *Inherence of movement*

'Chaos' stresses that the inherence of movement is central to materialism. There is evidence elsewhere that by 1753 it has become an integral part of Diderot's thinking after its implicit acceptance in the *Lettre sur les aveugles*.[9] The 1750 *Prospectus*, for instance, places motion in the same ontological category as extension and impenetrability.[10] The article 'Asiatiques' goes further, implying that, without motion, the other properties of matter would be inconceivable; Spinoza is compared favourably with other philosophers on account of the simplicity of his concept of matter: 'L'idée abstraite qu'il donne du premier principe n'est, à proprement parler, que l'idée de l'espace, qu'il a revêtu de mouvement, *afin d'y joindre* ensuite les autres propriétés de la matière.'[11] Without such properties as extension and impenetrability, a substance would not (in

---

6. *Diderot: ses idées philosophiques*, p.278-80.
7. *Spinoza et la pensée française*, p.578, 589.
8. Her., vi.358-89. Cf. below, 3, A.ii.a.3.
9. Cf. above, 1, D.iii.b.
10. In the extract quoted above, 2, A.i.
11. Her., v.521 (my emphasis). Lough and Proust accept Naigeon's attribution of this article to Diderot (Her., v.207).

eighteenth-century terms) be material, but spiritual. By suggesting that these are contingent upon movement, Diderot is implying, in effect, that matter itself cannot exist without energy (at least in the form of motion), that the two are nothing less than different facets of the same reality. This is a major intuition, which goes far beyond the relatively commonplace formulation of 'Chaos': 'un mélange [...] auquel ils supposaient le mouvement essentiel' (Her., vi.359).

The inherence of movement is an assumption made by Toland[12] and Priestley before him, shared by La Mettrie in 1751[13] and one which, in Szigeti's words, 'dépasse déja très nettement le matérialisme mécaniste'.[14] It provides a concept of nature more closely resembling that of the sixteenth than the seventeenth century, albeit 'une variante purifiée de tout résidu idéaliste' (Szigeti, p.49). Wartofsky argues for Leibniz's monadology as the source of this concept of self-motion on the grounds that (despite its idealism) Leibniz's philosophy possessed a far more distinctly dynamic dimension than either Spinozism or mechanism.[15] Many scholars have pointed out Leibniz's anti-cartesian assumption that monads were characterised by force rather than extension, and the ease with which this principle could be translated into materialist terms.[16] It may be true that Leibniz's philosophy rests on an eastern tradition[17] quite irrelevant to Diderot, at least in the early 1750s; that his concept of force involved the rehabilitation of scholastic substantial forms;[18] that his monads precluded physical interaction[19] and even abolished the notion of matter as

---

12. See J. A. Perkins, 'Diderot et La Mettrie', *Studies on Voltaire* 10 (1959), p.52-53, and Crocker, 'John Toland et le matérialisme de Diderot', p.290. Crocker's argument that Toland's *Letters to Serena* (1704; translated by d'Holbach and Naigeon, 1768) strongly influenced the development of Diderot's materialism (p.289) is unconvincing for, as Roger points out, Diderot's acceptance of inherent motion as early as 1749 leaves him 'rien de nouveau à tirer de Toland' (*Les Sciences de la vie*, p.653, n.357). Toland may, however, have been responsible for Diderot's materialistic interpretation of Spinoza (Vernière, *Spinoza et la pensée française*, p.357, 360).

13. 'La matière a toujours, lors même qu'elle ne se meut pas, la faculté de se mouvoir' (La Mettrie, *Traité de l'âme*, quoted in Momdzjan, 'La dialectique dans la vision du monde de Diderot', p.258).

14. *Denis Diderot: une grande figure*, p.46. N. Torrey traces the metaphysical opposition between Diderot and Voltaire to the latter's refusal to accept this principle ('Voltaire's reaction to Diderot', *PMLA* 50 (1935), p.1107-43).

15. 'Diderot and the development of materialist monism', p.289-90.

16. See for instance Perkins, 'Diderot et La Mettrie', p.58; W. H. Barber, *Leibniz in France* (Oxford 1955), p.11; P. Delaunay, 'L'évolution philosophique et médicale du biomécanisme', *Le Progrès médicale* (1927), p.1369, 1374.

17. A. Zempliner, 'Leibniz und die chinesische Philosophie', *Akten des internationalen Leibniz Kongresses 5* (Wiesbaden 1971). (D. F. Lach, 'Leibniz and China', *Journal of the history of ideas* 6 (1945), does not deal with the philosophy of nature.)

18. Tocanne, *L'Idée de nature*, p.62; L. Jugnet, 'Essai sur les rapports entre la philosophie suarezienne de la matière et la pensée de Leibniz', *Rsh* 3 (1935), p.127, 132.

19. W. H. Sheldon, 'Leibniz's message to us', *Journal of the history of ideas* 7 (1946), p.387, 390.

such, substituting 'un monisme spiritualiste', even 'un panpsychisme' (Delaunay, p.1369). Nevertheless his definition of monads in terms of force was quickly interpreted as a definition of substance in terms of its activity and hence of matter in terms of motion (Delaunay, p.1374). The extent of Leibniz's influence on Diderot has been questioned;[20] indirect influence, however, in terms of an enrichment of materialist currents, seems impossible to deny.

b. Eternity of matter

This second *sine qua non* of materialism is one of the elements Diderot integrated into his philosophy from Spinozist and classical thought. It had been proposed by the atheist in the *Pensées philosophiques*, reiterated by Oribaze and taken for granted by Saunderson. In 'Chaos', Diderot subscribes wilingly to the dictum 'ex nihilo nihil fit', calling it 'un axiome excellent en lui-même' and making only a token objection to it in the name of creationist orthodoxy (Her., vi.359).

c. Organisation of matter

1. Alternative systems

'Chaos' reviews several alternative accounts of the origin of the universe. Diderot's ostensible aim is to demonstrate disarray in the ranks of philosophers; in practice, however, this is yet another device to insinuate his own philosophy.

He distinguishes three broad accounts. The Lucretian vision, drawn from Democritus and Epicurus, which insists on the self-sufficiency of matter and motion, is the origin of his definition of chaos earlier in the article.[21] The second thesis is that of Pythagoras and Plato, which continued to posit eternal matter, but required divine intelligence to order it. The 'modern' view inverts this version, requiring God as Creator and Prime Mover, but endowing matter with unlimited powers of self-determination thereafter: 'aujourd'hui [la philosophie] consent que la matière soit créée, et que Dieu lui imprime le mouvement; mais elle veut que ce mouvement émané de la main de Dieu puisse, abandonné à lui-même, opérer tous les phénomènes de ce monde visible' (Her., vi.362).

This approach, formulated notably by Descartes and Bacon (in his 1620 *Novum organum*) and adopted by the deists, had been instrumental in Diderot's own conversion to materialism. Not surprisingly, he chooses to dwell on it, outlining its atheist and materialist implications by means of a deliberately ineffectual 'refutation' (Her., vi.362):

Un philosophe qui ose entreprendre d'expliquer, par les seules lois du mouvement, la mécanique et même la première formation des choses, et qui dit: *donnez-moi de la matière et du mouvement, et je ferai un monde*, doit démontrer auparavant (ce qui est facile) que

20. Belaval, 'Note sur Diderot et Leibniz', p.439.
21. Cf. above, introduction to section i.

l'existence et le mouvement ne sont point essentiels à la matière; car, sans cela, ce philosophe, croyant mal à propos ne rien voir dans les merveilles de cet univers que le mouvement seul n'ait pu produire, est menacé de tomber dans l'athéisme.

Diderot does not, of course, provide the 'easy' proof required to avert such a consequence. Moreover, he extends his propaganda by pointing out the qualitative distinction between ancient and modern materialism, implying that the superiority of the latter lies in its more organic concept of matter, replacing the 'mouvement fortuit des atomes' with 'une matière homogène agitée en tout sens' (Her., vi.361). Although Diderot will later insist on heterogeneity,[22] this transition from Lucretian atomism to a unified whole suffused with energy parallels his own departure from mechanism.

2. Energy

In all these accounts, movement is retained as the basic force behind both inorganic and organic phenomena. Diderot's principle of optimum organisation, introduced in the *Lettre sur les aveugles*, is reiterated here, but as in 1749 the process is ascribed simply to motion: 'jusqu'à ce qu'enfin les lois du mouvement et les différentes combinaisons aient amené l'ordre des choses qui constituent cet univers' (Her., vi.359). Nevertheless Diderot does introduce the term *fermentation*, with its organic overtones, on two occasions in 'Chaos'. In the first place, it is included in his elaboration of the cartesian picture of creation, which posits: 'que Dieu ne produisit d'abord qu'une matière vague et indéterminée, d'où le mouvement fit éclore peu à peu, par des fermentations intestines, des affaissements, des attractions, un soleil, une terre, et toute la décoration du monde' (Her., vi.360). Fermentation is presented here as an agent, or function, of motion, a qualitatively distinct manifestation of motive energy. So too is attraction. Consciously or not, Diderot has taken an important step towards the differentiation of natural forces which – together with their subsequent reintegration – will mark his later materialist speculation.

Elsewhere in 'Chaos' fermentation alone is made responsible for the emergence of order. In an attempt to 'reconcile' materialist with Biblical theory, Diderot interprets the 'waters' preceding Creation (Genesis i.1) as: 'une espèce de bourbier, dont la fermentation devait produire cet Univers avec le temps' (Her., vi.360). This is a striking notion: it has much in common with more modern visualisations of the primordial state. A similar picture will be evoked in the *Rêve de d'Alembert*, with thermal energy playing a key rôle.[23] At this early stage, of course, Diderot does not seek to distinguish between organic and inorganic organisation; the emergence of life is assumed to be of the same order

22. Cf. above, 2, B.ii.a, and below, 3, A.ii.a.3, and 4, C.iii.c.
23. See below, 5, B.i.b.

as the formation of the planets, and there is no historical dimension to his speculations.

Nevertheless, this assumption is itself a positive conceptual element: it implies quite clearly the potentiality of life within matter. Diderot boldly repeats his principle that the universe is self-sufficient and self-sustaining, making this out to be quite orthodox: 'ce que nous appelons *le globe terrestre* n'était dans son origine qu'une masse informe, contenant les principes et les matériaux du monde tel que nous le voyons' (Her., vi.359). As in the *Lettre sur les aveugles* he is content with a view which safeguards the autonomy of nature: the detailed workings of the process by which life emerges from inorganic matter do not, as yet, concern him. Confrontation with such issues will, however, be rendered inevitable by Diderot's increasing contact with biological data, as the following section will show.

C. Investigation of biology

Diderot's conviction of the special relevance of biology to the philosopher of nature demonstrates, like his atheism, the interaction between the methodology and content of his materialism. Diderot's earliest original works, the *Pensées philosophiques*, the *Promenade du sceptique* and the *Lettre sur les aveugles* were characterised by the crucial philosophical rôle they accorded to recent biological findings. It is only after the *Lettre sur les aveugles*, however, that this preoccupation could be divorced from the apologetic aims of deism.

i. *The methodological principle: defence of de Prades*

Writing in de Prades's name in the *Apologie*, Diderot is deliberately ambiguous on this, as on other subjects. The abstract metaphysicians of the seventeenth century are condemned for their lack of sensitivity to the biological world: 'J'ai seulement donné la préférence aux découvertes de la philosophie expérimentale sur leurs méditations abstraites; j'ai cru qu'une aile de papillon, bien décrite, m'approchait plus de la divinité qu'un volume de métaphysique' (Her., iv.361). Nevertheless he is aware of the rôle played by their (limited) introduction of science into metaphysics; thanks to this, he observes ironically, such thinkers 'n'ont guère lancé que des traits impuissants contre les matérialistes'.

Above all, however, in defending de Prades's use of biological data in his thesis, Diderot is concerned to attack the inflexibility of the theologians. Such is their arrogance, he asserts, that they refuse to entertain evidence from biology even when it lends support to their own beliefs. He speaks for both deist and materialist when he roundly condemns this attitude as emotionally and

intellectually unsound: 'Celui qui méprise ce que tous les autres ont estimé, et qui compte pour rien une observation d'histoire naturelle, [...] ne peut-il pas être justement soupçonné de quelque vice dans le cœur, ou du moins de quelque travers dans l'esprit?' (Her., iv.359-60). These lines play a tactical rôle in the *Apologie*: they immediately succeed Diderot's examination of spontaneous generation and thus serve to validate his implicit conclusions in that particular area of biological experimentation.

ii. *Spontaneous generation in the* Apologie

Section 14 of the *Apologie* identifies two stages in the history of attitudes towards spontaneous generation; in each case Diderot's 'orthodox' account proves to be a double-edged sword. A quotation from de Prades's thesis appears to be an objective statement of classical materialism: 'Au temps où les philosophes regardaient le monde comme un ouvrage échappé à l'aveugle nature, et croyaient que tout naissait de la corruption, la Providence était foulée aux pieds' (Her., iv.358). Diderot takes pains to point out, however, that such a system was both logically sound and consistent with the state of scientific knowledge at the time. His implicit conclusion is that metaphysical positions are dependent on scientific, especially biological research and, more specifically, that atheism is inevitably associated with a belief in spontaneous generation.[24]

This interrelationship is confirmed in Diderot's account of the historical reversal of the situation: 'quand les expériences nouvelles eurent renversé ce système dangereux, on commença à adorer où les Anciens avaient blasphémé' (Her., iv.358). Diderot's reference is to the modern period during which deism, including his own, had flourished: the years following François Rédi's experiments, whose results, published in 1688, had temporarily discredited spontaneous generation.[25] Rédi had demonstrated that insects could not be generated unless provision was made for eggs to be deposited on the experimental medium. The integrity of the general laws governing reproduction was thus maintained, and the rôle of intelligent design within matter restored.

Diderot's account is accurate, but omits to acknowledge that this stage too had been transcended. Public knowledge of Needham's contrary findings ensures that his ostensible argument is subtly distorted throughout. Protected by his token assertion that spontaneous generation has been disproved, he is able to dwell on the threat such a concept posed to orthodoxy. He repeats almost word for word the argument of the *Pensées philosophiques* that one proven

24. Cf. Winter, p.159.
25. Cf. Winter, p.155, and J. Rostand, *Les Origines de la biologie expérimentale* (Paris 1951), p.16-17.

instance of spontaneous generation would suffice to establish its potential universality and demolish both creationist and deist apologetics: 'Aux yeux du philosophe, le puceron n'est pas moins admirable que l'éléphant; [...] la production de l'un, attribuée à un mouvement intestin et fortuit des particules de la matière, semblait affaiblir la démonstration [of intelligent design] tirée du mécanisme de l'autre' (Her., iv.359). He stresses that it is in microscopic biology that the truth about such processes should be sought, knowing full well that Needham's 'proof' of spontaneous generation had been achieved in precisely this area: 'Il y a plus d'animaux au-dessous de la mouche qu'il n'y en a au-dessus; et [...] la bonne physique aperçoit les grands corps dans les petits, et non les petits dans les grands.'

By placing such emphasis on evidence he knew to be outdated, and deliberately avoiding recognition – much less refutation – of the contemporary challenge to Rédi, Diderot insinuates a message which goes far beyond the literal meaning of the text. Preceded by his declaration of methodological atheism and followed by his defence of biology, these lines are an effective reaffirmation of his belief in spontaneous generation as a manifestation of nature's creative energy, and challenge Luppol's contention that the *Apologie* is of no significance in Diderot's intellectual evolution.[26]

iii. *The biologically deviant*

This creative energy, as Diderot has acknowledged in the *Lettre sur les aveugles*, does not only produce organic perfection: it may also give rise to deviant forms. The genesis of such forms is, for Diderot, a further pointer to the spontaneity within nature's patterns.[27] Whereas in the 1745 *Essai sur le mérite et la vertu* Diderot had dismissed the philosophical significance of the existence of 'monsters',[28] by 1749 they had become a central element of his materialism.

In the *Prospectus*, Diderot raises such phenomena to an equal status with the two conventional divisions of the natural world, the 'natural' and the 'artificial'.[29] Three categories are proposed in his definition of nature: natural processes, self-modification within these processes (deviance), and finally their modification by human technology: 'Ou la nature est uniforme, et suit un cours réglé, tel qu'on le remarque généralement dans les *corps célestes*, les *animaux*, les *végétaux*, etc.; ou elle semble forcée et dérangée de son cours ordinaire, comme dans les *monstres*; ou elle est contrainte et pliée à différents usages, comme dans les

---

26. *Diderot: ses idées philosophiques*, p.155.
27. Venturi, *La Jeunesse de Diderot*, p.148.
28. Roger, 'Le déisme du jeune Diderot', p.238.
29. G. N. Laidlaw, 'Diderot's teratology', *Diderot studies* 4 (1963), p.118.

arts.[30] Nature is therefore to be considered not only as a passive medium upon which the will of God or man is imposed, but as an autonomous agent. Weinert sees the phrase 'forcée et dérangée' as evidence of Diderot's reluctance to accept an exclusively active nature.[31] Significantly, however, it is qualified by the introductory words 'elle semble': the impression of passivity is therefore to be treated cautiously. This point is made even more forcibly as Diderot summarises the definition: 'La nature fait tout, ou dans son *cours ordinaire et réglé*, ou dans ses *écarts*, ou dans son *emploi*.'[32]

Weinert has pointed out the shift of meaning[33] introduced by Diderot into the Baconian division of knowledge on which these lines are based. For Bacon had set up a logical opposition between the productions of nature and the uses of nature, with deviant forms constituting an incidental third category. In Diderot's version, however, it is uniformity and deviance which form the essential antithesis (Weinert, p.232-33). Thus is the concept of an active nature subtly underscored. Unfortunately, however, Weinert does not grasp the overall tendency of Diderot's view of nature towards a dynamic monism and therefore attributes this shift of meaning simply to a retrograde anthropomorphisation of nature.[34]

Diderot is evidently aware that his stress on *écarts* in the *Encyclopédie*'s programme of study represents a new departure, since he anticipates surprise and undertakes to justify the step: 'Si l'on nous demande à quoi peut servir l'*Histoire de la nature monstrueuse*, nous répondrons: A passer des prodiges de ses *écarts* aux merveilles de l'*art*, à l'égarer encore ou à la remettre dans son chemin; et surtout à corriger la témérité des propositions générales, *ut axiomatum corrigatur iniquitas*.'[35] The aims of research into the deviant are therefore twofold: to promote the technological goals of science, and to foster a spirit of relativism.[36] Since Diderot also considered rigid, dogmatic modes of thought an obstacle to the perception of nature's diversity and spontaneity, the methodology is self-sustaining.

30. Her., v.106. Original emphasis retained.
31. H. K. Weinert, 'Die Bedeutung des Abnormen in Diderots Wissenschaftslehre', *Festgabe Ernst Gamillscheg* (Tübingen 1952), p.238.
32. Her., v.106. Original emphasis.
33. 'Die grundlegende Wandlung der Blickrichtung' (p.233).
34. 'Allen diesen Formulierungen liegt jedoch die Vorstellung einer vermenschlichten Natur zugrunde' (p.237-38).
35. Her., v.106. For an interesting account of the philosophical overtones of eighteenth-century interest in the deviant, see G. Canguilhem, *Etudes d'histoire* (Paris 1970), 3/1/1, 'Du singulier et de la singularité en épistémologie biologique'.
36. Cf. Weinert, p.234. In addition to relativism (deviant forms indicating that nature knows few invariable laws) Diderot's statement also appeals for an approach based on empirical research rather than apriorism. I am grateful to D. E. Curtis for this amplification.

These observations confirm that, for Diderot, nature is no longer a programmed machine, but an active, autonomous entity. This conceptual shift is neatly expressed in his application of the term *prodiges*, reserved in Christian and deist apologetics for the order and purpose manifest in the universe, to nature's aberrations. It is the latter which he feels are most likely to provide the key to nature's mysteries. Weinert, on the other hand, sees this usage simply as a historical contradiction, given that neither Chambers nor Bacon had used such a term (p.231-32). He therefore remains puzzled by the coexistence of terminology based on pre-scientific concepts or religious apologetics with a complex of ideas which is both systematic and scientific (p.233, 243).

Diderot's interest in monsters, from the *Lettre sur les aveugles* to the *Rêve de d'Alembert*, is quite clearly positively motivated. We have found no evidence in support of Hill's thesis that it amounts to an 'obsession', 'a recurrent nightmare' expressing Diderot's 'fear of a lawless, capricious universe'.[37]

This shift of focus from the regular and ordered to the exceptional is accompanied by an emphasis on the specific. As early as the *Pensées philosophiques* Diderot had preferred precise biological data to vast cosmic theory: 'Songez donc que je ne vous objectais qu'une aile de papillon, qu'un œil de ciron, quand je pouvais vous écraser du poids de l'univers' (*Pensée* xx; Her., ii.28). In 1746, however, biological minutiae had been seen as microcosmic illustrations of the working out of providential schemes within nature. They were valued on account of their greater immediacy as apologetic propaganda. Now they have become potential sources of evidence to challenge such a world-view, for the individual (by virtue of its separation from an overall pattern) has a greater chance of revealing traces of diversity.

In the article 'Bois' Diderot points to the neglect of this area as a deficiency in current methodology (Her., vi.198):

La nature a ses lois, qui ne nous paraissent peut-être si générales, et s'étendre uniformément à un si grand nombre d'êtres, que parce que nous n'avons pas la patience ou la sagacité de connaître la conduite qu'elle tient dans la production et la conservation de chaque individu. Nous nous attachons au gros de ses opérations: mais les finesses de sa main d'œuvre, s'il est permis de parler ainsi, nous échappent sans cesse.

This declaration serves to justify both Diderot's concentration on the microscopic aspects of biology and his interest in the deviant. Instances of either may appear to infringe accepted physical laws, but lead in fact to a greater awareness of the complexity and diversity of natural processes.

---

37. E. B. Hill, 'Materialism and monsters in *Le Rêve de d'Alembert*', *Diderot Studies* 10 (1968), p.73. Cf. her article, 'The rôle of *le monstre* in Diderot's thought', *Studies on Voltaire* 97 (1972), where a similar line of argument is pursued.

Together these principles constitute Diderot's earliest statement of 'a method that has since become standard – the detailed examination of the aberrant in search of clues to the normal'.[38] As the later article 'Encylopédie' remarks of the natural historian: 'la dissection d'un monstre [...] lui sert plus que l'étude de cent individus qui se ressemblent' (Her., vii.242).

The methodological preoccupations of the *Prospectus* and 'Bois' are echoed in Diderot's editorial addition to another early *Encyclopédie* article, 'Arbre':

Plus on étudie la nature, plus on est étonné de trouver dans les sujets les plus vils en apparence des phénomènes dignes de toute l'attention et de toute la curiosité du Philosophe. Ce n'est pas assez de la suivre dans son cours ordinaire et réglé, il faut quelquefois essayer de la dérouter, pour connaître toute sa fécondité et toutes ses ressources.[39]

Alongside the general statement of principle is an indication of the kind of conclusion likely to emerge from such a study: the ongoing development within nature of an immanent and creative energy, for in 'Arbre' the methodology does not stand alone, but is deduced from a particular case study which has proved its worth to the materialist philosopher: vegetal regeneration.

iv. *Vegetal regeneration: the concept of latency*

'Arbre' investigates the remarkable regenerative powers displayed by trees which have undergone pruning or pollarding. Such a phenomenon is at once specific and biological and, moreover, represents an instance of deviation from naturally occurring patterns (since it is a response to external intervention). It provides Diderot with a rich intuition of nature's creative autonomy (*Enc.* i.584):

Cela montre combien sont abondants les ressources de cette sorte d'êtres vivants; car on peut dire que depuis l'extrémité des branches jusqu'au pied de l'arbre, il n'y a presque point d'endroit [...] où il n'y ait une espèce d'embryon de multiplication prêt à paraître, dès que l'occasion mettra l'arbre dans la nécessité de mettre au jour ce qu'il tenait en réserve.

These lines bring Diderot to the threshold of a major conceptual breakthrough in terms of his future philosophy of energy. The accumulation of cognate expressions – *ressources, embryon, prêt à paraître, en réserve* – reveal how close he is to applying the concept of latency to biological energy. Here it is the material manifestations of that energy, rather than the forces responsible for them, which are considered to lie dormant within the organism. Nevertheless this represents

38. Laidlaw, 'Diderot's teratology', p.105-106.
39. AT, xiii.588. Although not reprinted in the Hermann complete works, this addition is included in Lough and Proust's list of asterisked articles, and its attribution to Diderot accepted (Her., v.150).

an important extension of his thinking. Spontaneous regeneration, observed by Trembley in the animal kingdom,[40] is now shown to be a feature of the inferior kingdom of plant life[41] and a potential link established between these categories and the inanimate realm, by inviting comparison with the conceptually analagous process of spontaneous generation.

Moreover the concept of latency was already familiar to Diderot within the context of a specific energy: mechanical motion. The distinction between potential and kinetic force was an accepted part of contemporary physics. Diderot himself refers to it in his definition of mechanics for the *Prospectus*: 'La *Mécanique* a deux branches, la *Statique* et la *Dynamique*. La *Statique* a pour objet la *quantité* considérée dans les corps en équilibre, et tendant seulement à se mouvoir. La *Dynamique* a pour objet la *quantité* considérée dans les corps actuellement mus.'[42] Since he had, by now, accepted the inherence of motion, the categories of active and potential movement are effectively extended from aggregates (*corps*) to basic matter. After considerable redefinition of energy and its relationship to life, Diderot will extend latency to *sensibilité*, the concept he evolves to account for the emergence of life. Already, in 'Arbre', he has come close to an intuitive presentiment of the identity of life and energy.[43]

v. *The philosophy of flux*

The spontaneous and continuous processes initiated by biological energy had led Diderot, in the *Lettre sur les aveugles*, to a vision of universal dynamism within nature. In the early volumes of the *Encyclopédie* he takes up his concept of flux, illustrating it by reference to specific case studies drawn from the plant kingdom. The outcome of his speculations is a considerably enhanced view of the processes involved in biological change.

a. *The agent of change: nutritive assimilation*

The *Lettre sur les aveugles* had concentrated on the initial emergence of life forms: this was considered to be a somewhat random and unco-ordinated process, despite the concept of optimum organisation. In the article 'Acmella', however, Diderot envisages a completely different model of modification and renewal within biology, based on interaction between existing organisms. Such

40. See Vartanian, 'Trembley's polyp'.
41. See J. F. Leroy, 'La notion de vie dans la botanique du XVIIIe siècle', *Histoire et biologie* 2 (1969), for a brief discussion of the role played by regeneration in the development of biology.
42. Her., v.113. Original emphasis.
43. As H. Dieckmann points out, regeneration (along with assimilation and perception) was one of the key processes posing a challenge to cartesian biology, 'Bordeu und Diderots *Rêve de d'Alembert*', *Romanische Forschungen* 52 (1938), p.72. It is therefore appropriate that Diderot's alternative energetic model based on *sensibilité* should have its origins in such an example.

change is gradual and genuinely evolutionary: its agent is the process of ingestion and assimilation of new matter by an organism through nutrition.

The idea that diet could influence the characteristics of highly organised beings was commonplace in the medicine of the time and appeared in the works of both Maupertuis and Buffon.[44] Diderot's originality lies in extending the principle to plant life: 'Les substances animales prennent des qualités singulières par l'usage que font les animaux de certains aliments plutôt que d'autres; pourquoi n'en serait-il pas de même des substances végétales?'[45] This simple step is crucial to the evolution of Diderot's philosophy of life, for the concept of *sensibilité* will depend upon a chain of nutritive assimilation linking all levels of matter. The essentials of the process are already implicit in 'Acmella': through ingestion, inert matter is converted in turn to plant and animal substance. Many years later, Diderot will attribute the emergence of *sensibilité*, and life itself, to the energy transformations which accompany this process.

b. Organic variation and modification

Several important implications are made clear immediately. In the first place, the fixity of species is challenged. Ingestion allows not only spatial and temporal variation within organisms, but even their permanent modification (Her., v.271):

Si cette induction [extension of the principle to plants] est raisonnable, il s'ensuit que telle plante cueillie d'un côté de cette montagne aura une vertu qu'on ne trouvera pas dans la même plante cueillie de l'autre côté; que telle plante avait jadis une propriété qu'elle n'a plus aujourd'hui, et qu'elle ne recouvrera peut-être jamais.

The principle thus provides conceptual support on the one hand for the existence of individual differences within species, and on the other for evolutionary change. Nature's diversity and the existence of aberrant forms are both accounted for.

Another article in the first volume of the *Encyclopédie*, 'Amer', serves to confirm the conclusions of 'Acmella', pointing out that flavours cannot be adequately defined, since they are no more than subjective reactions to a reality which may be constantly evolving (Her., v.354-55):

il s'ensuit que si les substances étaient dans un état de vicissitude perpétuelle, et que les choses amères tendissent à cesser de l'être, et celles qui ne le sont pas à le devenir, les expressions dont nous nous servons ne transmettraient à ceux qui viendraient longtemps après nous, aucune notion distincte.

44. R. Mousnier, *Progrès scientifique et technique au XVIIIe siècle* (Paris 1958), p.220.
45. Her., v.271. J. Doolittle, in his article 'Robert James, Diderot and the *Encyclopédie*', *Modern language notes* 71 (1956), p.433, points out that there is no hint of these ideas in the James article which Diderot had translated for the *Dictionnaire de médecine* and on which the rest of 'Acmella' is based.

c. Methodological implication: relativism

Diderot's relativistic attitude to biological research is reinforced by this possibility. As he points out in the article 'Ablab', each generation of scientists must validate anew their predecessors' accounts: 'Il faut attendre, pour ajouter foi à cette plante et ses propriétés, que les Naturalistes en aient parlé clairement' (Her., v.227). It is for this reason that he maintains an attitude of scepticism towards classical writers' claims regarding the medicinal properties of plants. Although he is often scathingly dismissive of such claims, he prefers, quite possibly for strategic reasons, to attribute their extravagance less to credulity or deceit on the part of the Ancients than to the modification, over time, of the properties concerned (Her., v.271):

Il s'ensuit [...] que les fruits, les végétaux, les animaux, sont dans une vicissitude perpétuelle par rapport à leurs qualités, à leurs formes, à leurs éléments; qu'un ancien d'il y a quatre mille ans, ou plutôt que nos neveux dans dix mille ans ne reconnaîtront aucun des fruits que nous avons aujourd'hui en les comparant avec les descriptions les plus exactes que nous en faisons; et que par conséquence il faut être extrêmement réservé dans les jugements qu'on porte sur les endroits où les anciens historiens et naturalistes nous entretiennent de la forme, des vertus et des autres qualités d'êtres qui sont dans un mouvement perpétuel d'altération.

These lines from 'Acmella' stress the extent of biological self-modification: not only the properties but the actual constituent elements and outward forms of organisms are subject to change.

d. Universality of flux and co-ordination of change

By framing this account within the twin expressions *vicissitude perpétuelle* and *mouvement perpétuel*, Diderot suggests that flux is not an occasional, incidental feature of nature, but its very essence. Nature is not a static panorama of phenomena, but a process, a continuous deployment of energy.

In 'Agaric' he goes further, speculating that even human organisation may have evolved so that our reactions to a particular drug are no longer the same. Man, too, is engulfed in the universal flux: 'Les Anciens, qui n'avaient pas tant de purgatifs que nous, n'y [à l'agaric] étaient apparemment pas si délicats; ou bien [...] l'agaric n'a plus les mêmes propriétés qu'il avait.'[46]

The coexistence in 'Agaric' of alternative explanations for the varying effects of drugs heralds another new element in Diderot's ideas on biological change. It recognises that evolution within one organism is not necessarily isolated. Nature is a unified whole, characterised by interaction and mutual adaptation. 'Acmella' suggests two ways in which this relationship may be modified as a

46. *Enc.*, i.166. This addition to Daubenton's article bears Diderot's asterisk. Cf. Her., v.137.

consequence of evolutionary change within one part of the whole (Her., v.271):

Mais, dira-t-on, si les éléments salubres dégénèrent en poison, de quoi vivront les animaux? Il y a deux réponses à cette objection: la première, c'est que la forme, la constitution des animaux s'altérant en même proportion, et par les mêmes degrés insensibles, les uns seront toujours convenables aux autres; la seconde, c'est que s'il arrivait qu'une substance dégénérât avec trop de rapidité, les animaux en abandonneraient l'usage.

The modification of one organism thus instigates a compensatory process of adjustment by others related to it. Thus equilibrium is maintained within flux. This notion is closely linked with the concept of optimum organisation, which represents the equilibrium of component elements at any given moment.[47] It will also be incorporated into Diderot's later, more complex theory of nutritive assimilation. The latter process will be explained in terms of adaptation and the qualitative transformation of an organic whole by the addition of a new element.

The philosophy of flux adumbrated in these articles has important methodological repercussions: as Diderot will point out in the *Pensées sur l'interprétation de la nature*, a philosophy of total flux is impossible. Some unchanging point of reference, exempt from spatial and temporal variation, is essential if the philosopher/scientist's work is to have any meaning. Paradoxically, the only empirically observable constant within nature is its very state of flux. Consequently the energy of nature, the principle behind flux, becomes central to Diderot's philosophy of nature. Any materialistic account of life must seek to envisage this phenomenon also essentially in terms of energy, whatever form that energy may be considered to take.

D. Diderot and Buffon: the philosophy of life

The *Encyclopédie* article 'Animal' presents and comments on portions of Buffon's *Histoire naturelle* (1749). Diderot continues to intuit new conceptual openings in a way which prefigures his dialectic exchange with Maupertuis in the *Pensées sur l'interprétation de la nature*. His speculations on the nature of life take on a new dimension as he confronts for the first time issues which had hitherto escaped his attention. In particular, the traditional division of natural phenomena into animal, plant and mineral kingdoms raised two closely related questions, especially crucial for the materialist interpreter: the passage from inanimate to animate matter, or when and how life emerges, and the transition, within organic matter, from simple to complex levels of organisation.

Diderot's speculations on spontaneous generation had provided him with

47. Cf. above, 1, D.iv.b, and below, 3, A.ii.a.2.

only a very limited answer to the first: he had not explicitly considered the problem of abiogenesis, however, nor had he made more than a passing reference (in the *Lettre sur les aveugles*) to the question of secondary organisation and the differentiation and gradation of the organic properties and faculties associated with life. Buffon's ideas in this area prove catalytic in the extension of Diderot's philosophy of life.

i. *Definition of the kingdoms of matter: sentience as a criterion*

a. *Buffon's definitions*

In seeking to define the term *animal*, Diderot's article draws on Buffon's attempted delineation of the three kingdoms of matter. The desire to establish a valid distinguishing criterion, especially between plant and animal, was a widespread and legitimate concern of contemporary scientists.[48] The anonymous *Encyclopédie* article 'Zoophytes', for instance, reveals the distress of researchers who were constantly obliged to revise their definitions, establishing new categories or extending the old to accommodate recently discovered organisms, particularly of the marine variety (*Enc.*, xv.744). Leroy argues that this quest benefitted biology in that the discovery of intermediate forms emphasised the discontinuity between living and non-living, and the fundamental unity of the former (p.3, 7).

Buffon distinguishes plants by their faculties of growth and reproduction, and animals by the possession of mobility and sentience:

qu'est-ce que l'*animal?* C'est [...] la matière vivante et organisée qui sent, agit, se meut, se nourrit et se reproduit. Conséquemment le végétal est la matière vivante et organisée, qui se nourrit et se reproduit, mais qui ne sent, n'agit ni ne se meut. Et le minéral, la matière morte et brute, qui ne sent, n'agit, ni ne se meut, ne se nourrit, ni se reproduit. D'où il s'ensuit que le sentiment est le principal degré différentiel de l'animal.[49]

He thus follows Linnaeus[50] in establishing sentience as the key to categorising living forms.

b. *Limitations of Buffon's account of sentience*

For such a notion to prove serviceable as a criterion, however, it must be rigorously defined. After dismissing other potential criteria, Buffon himself stresses the need for precision when dealing with so nebulous a concept as sentience: 'Une différence plus essentielle pourrait se tirer de la faculté de

---

48. Cf. Leroy, 'La notion de vie dans la botanique du XVIIIe siècle', p.3-4, 7.

49. *Enc.*, i.468.; Her., v.382 (Diderot paraphrasing Buffon).

50. 'Mineralia sunt, vegetabilia vivunt et crescunt, animalia vivunt, crescunt et sentiunt', quoted in Luppol, *Diderot: ses idées philosophiques*, p.271. Leroy points out that this notion dates back to Aristotle (p.3).

sentir, qu'on ne peut guère refuser aux animaux, et dont il semble que les végétaux soient privés. Mais ce mot *sentir* renferme un si grand nombre d'idées, qu'on ne doit pas le prononcer avant que d'en avoir fait l'analyse.'[51] As he points out, the vast discrepancy between alternative concepts of sentience can lead to widely differing conclusions as to its distribution even within the animal kingdom. Empirical observation suggests that even the simplest animal forms display the basic faculty, yet its more specialised manifestations appear to be reserved for man: 'Mais est-il bien constant qu'il n'y a point d'animaux sans ce que nous appelons le *sentiment*; ou plutôt, si nous en croyons les Cartésiens, y a-t-il d'autres animaux que nous qui ayent du *sentiment*?'[52]

Despite his awareness of this confusion, however, Buffon does not escape it. The alternative definitions of sentience he offers for use in this context are both defective as criteria:

si par *sentir* nous entendons seulement faire une action de mouvement à l'occasion d'un choc ou d'une résistance, nous trouverons que la plante appelée *sensitive*, est capable de cette espèce de sentiment comme les animaux. Si au contraire on veut que *sentir* signifie *appercevoir* et comparer des perceptions, nous ne sommes pas sûrs que les animaux aient cette espèce de sentiment; et si nous accordons quelque chose de semblable aux chiens, aux éléphants, etc., nous le refuserons à une infinité d'espèces d'animaux, et surtout à ceux qui nous paraissent immobiles et sans action.[53]

Thus sentience in the form of an automatic process of reaction to physical stimuli is inadequate as a criterion, because such a phenomenon is too widespread and cannot be excluded from plants. If, on the other hand, sentience is equated with the highly developed faculties of perception and judgement, it also fails. Commonsense recoils at the universal extension of 'human' intellectual powers to the beasts.

Buffon is thwarted in two ways. In the first place he is unduly inhibited by the subjective connotations of the term *sentiment*. He rejects utterly the extension of sentience to inorganic matter, fearing the implications of such a step. He evidently believes sentience to be absolute and irreducible and concludes that, if inanimate matter were to possess this faculty, it would differ in no essential way from man himself:

Nous devons conclure [...] que la matière inanimée n'a ni sentiment, ni sensation, ni conscience d'existence; et que lui attribuer quelques-unes de ces facultés, ce serait lui donner celle de penser, d'agir et de sentir, à peu près dans le même ordre et de la même façon que nous pensons, agissons et sentons, ce qui répugne autant à la raison qu'à la religion.[54]

51. *Enc.*, i.471; Her., v.392 (Diderot quoting Buffon).
52. *Enc.*, i.468; Her., v.382 (Diderot paraphrasing Buffon).
53. *Enc.*, i.471; Her., v.392 (Diderot quoting Buffon).
54. *Enc.*, i.470; Her., v.388 (Diderot quoting Buffon).

In this literal form the proposition is indisputably absurd. Nevertheless it is a misconception that Diderot will temporarily share. During his 'vitalist phase'[55] Diderot will posit the universality and indestructibility of life, failing to distinguish the basic phenomenon from its specific manifestations within organised animal systems. Eventually, however, Diderot will overcome this problem by equating life with *sensibilité*, a term rather less evocative of human faculties than Buffon's *sentiment*.

Secondly, Buffon is unable to see beyond the contemporary scientific demand for an absolute criterion, a line of demarcation which will allow no doubt to remain as to the accurate classification of the organisms which lie on either side. He does not entertain the possibility that such a line may not exist – this despite the fact that in the introductory section of the *Histoire naturelle* he *had* entertained the idea that science might one day discover 'des choses qui soient moitié animal et moitié plante, ou moitié plante et moitié minéral',[56] that is, recognised that the traditional divisions had only practical validity. Nevertheless Buffon did continue to accept the irreducible division between living and inert matter implied by his theory of *molécules organiques*. He believed both life and thought to be absolute, a view which Diderot (here, at least) will reject in favour of full continuity.[57]

c. Diderot's extension of sentience

Diderot is at once aware of the sterility of Buffon's restricted approach to the issue. He instinctively rejects the implication that Buffon's alternative definitions necessarily exhaust the potential of sentience: 'Mais n'y a-t-il que ces deux manières de sentir, ou se mouvoir à l'occasion d'un choc ou d'une résistance, ou appercevoir et comparer des perceptions?'[58] To substantiate his objection, Diderot proposes a third category of sentience: emotion and self-awareness. This is neither simple physical reaction, nor intellectual perception: it may partake of either, but is conceptually distinct from both:

Il me semble que ce qui s'appelle en moi sentiment de plaisir, de douleur, etc., sentiment de mon existence, etc., n'est ni mouvement, ni perception et comparaison de perceptions. Il me semble qu'il en est du sentiment pris dans ce troisième sens comme de la pensée, qu'on ne peut comparer à rien, parce qu'elle ne ressemble à rien; et qu'il pourrait bien y avoir quelquechose de ce sentiment dans les animaux.[59]

As Diderot acknowledges, the existence of this form of psychological sentience

55. See below, 4, A.
56. Quoted in Ehrard, *L'Idée de nature en France*, i.191. Cf. G. Gusdorf, *Dieu, la nature, l'homme au siècle des Lumières* (Paris 1972), p.293.
57. Roger, *Les Sciences de la vie*, p.600.
58. *Enc.*, i.471; Her., v.392-93 (Diderot).
59. *Enc.*, i.471; Her., v.393 (Diderot).

in animals other than man is not proven. Apparently, then (and quite apart from the interest they hold as evidence of Diderot's concern to stress the range of phenomena embraced by the term *sentiment*), these lines are not intended to offer an alternative criterion in place of Buffon's. Their purpose is to demonstrate that the entire issue is even more complex than Buffon suggests. Diderot is arguing for a fundamental re-examination of Buffon's assumptions and a qualitative transformation of his central concept. He initiates such a transformation immediately by applying to sentience the concept of gradation.

ii. *The concept of gradation*

In an attempt to overcome the obstacles to a useful definition of sentience, Diderot stresses that he is aware both of differentials within each realm and of the possibility that such differentials might provide the key to the transition from plant to animal:

D'ailleurs, l'homme lui-même ne perd-t-il pas quelquefois le *sentiment* sans cesser de vivre ou d'être un animal? [...] Si dans cet état il est toujours un *animal*, qui nous a dit qu'il n'y en a pas de cette espèce sur le passage du végétal le plus parfait à l'animal le plus stupide? Qui nous a dit que ce passage n'était pas rempli d'êtres plus ou moins léthargiques, plus ou moins profondément assoupis; en sorte que la seule différence qu'il y ait entre cette classe et la classe des autres animaux, tels que nous, est qu'ils dorment et que nous veillons; que nous sommes des animaux qui sentent, et qu'ils sont des animaux qui ne sentent pas.[60]

Winter includes these lines in her enumeration of Diderot's anticipations of the *Rêve de d'Alembert's* central thesis and comments that Proust identified the parallel in his study of Diderot and the *Encyclopédie*.[61] For the account is couched in terms which closely resemble the principle of latency emerging in Diderot's thought at this time: *léthargiques, assoupis, dorment*. The *Pensées sur l'interprétation de la nature* will reveal the influence of 'Animal' in this respect, transposing latency from its original context of vegetal regeneration to the issue of defining organic matter.

Buffon had rejected the full application of gradation to sentience, since this would blur the distinction between kingdoms: 'Si on voulait que les huîtres, par exemple, eussent du sentiment comme les chiens, mais à un degré fort inférieur, pourquoi n'en accorderait-on pas aux végétaux le même sentiment dans un degré encore au-dessous?',[62] and he therefore failed to exploit gradation by incorporating it into a broader, more flexible definition of sentience. Diderot,

---

60. *Enc.*, i.468; Her., v.382 (Diderot).
61. Winter, p.31, n.1; J. Proust, *Diderot et L'Encyclopédie* (Paris 1962), p.289. Cf. Pommier, *Diderot avant Vincennes*, p.113.
62. *Enc.*, i.471; Her., v.392 (Diderot quoting Buffon).

however, transforms the principle from a hesitant compromise into a genuine intuition of the continuity of living forms. Like flux, gradation becomes a source of diversity within the organic unity of nature:

Mais une considération [...] nous est suggérée par le spectacle de la nature dans les individus, c'est que l'état de cette faculté de penser, d'agir, de sentir, réside dans quelques hommes dans un degré éminent, dans un degré moins éminent en d'autres hommes, va en s'affaiblissant à mesure qu'on suit la chaîne des êtres en descendant, et s'éteint apparemment dans quelque point de la chaîne très éloigné: placé entre le règne animal et le règne végétal, point dont nous approcherons de plus en plus par les observations, mais qui nous échappera à jamais.[63]

Diderot's belief that the validity of such a concept can never be ascertained experimentally does not restrict the scope of his thought. Paradoxically it allows him to achieve broader and more fertile intuitions, inaccessible to Buffon, who was seeking to pinpoint a literal boundary between the kingdoms. For Diderot's insertion of a qualifying *apparemment* does not refer only to the impossibility of verifying empirically the existence of sentience and thought at this level. It also betrays a deeper, possibly unconscious, reluctance to limit these characteristics to the more highly organised living forms. Even Buffon had been unwilling to deny sentience to the 'sensitive plant' (*mimosa pudica*);[64] similarly in the *Lettre sur les aveugles* Diderot had toyed with the idea that basic matter contains everything necessary for thought.

Indeed modern biology has been obliged to recognise that the distinction sought by Buffon does not exist. Certain organisms such as bacteria cannot be definitively classified as either plant or animal. Buffon's suspicion: 'qu'entre les animaux et les végétaux le créateur n'à pas mis de terme fixe'[65] has today been vindicated. Diderot will eventually resolve this issue to his own satisfaction by means of *sensibilité*, linking all three kingdoms in a single sequence of energetic processes.

iii. *Inorganic matter*

Already, unhampered by Buffon's reservations on the universal application of such concepts as latency and gradation, he takes an important step towards this solution. Disturbed by the irrevocability of Buffon's declaration that the minerals 'n'ont aucune sorte de vie ou de mouvement',[66] he attempts to incorporate inorganic matter into an overall scheme based on gradation.

Buffon had invoked a separate criterion, that of interaction with the environ-

---

63. *Enc.*, i.470; Her., v.388-89 (Diderot).
64. See above, 2, D.i.a.
65. *Enc.*, i.474; Her., v.399 (Diderot quoting Buffon).
66. *Enc.*, i.469; Her., v.386 (Diderot quoting Buffon).

ment, to place minerals in the lowest class of natural phenomena. Diderot, however, sees that this concept of *rapports* is potentially more flexible, permitting of variation even within inorganic matter: 'Observez encore que rien n'empêche que ces rapports ne varient aussi, et que le nombre n'en soit plus ou moins grand, en sorte qu'on peut dire qu'il y a des minéraux moins morts que d'autres.'[67] Diderot will not in fact use gradation in this form in his eventual philosophy of matter. Nevertheless the idea proves to be important as a conceptual stepping-stone, both for the extension of latency to inorganic matter and for the elaboration of *sensibilité*. For not only will gravitational force be interpreted in terms of *rapports* in the *Pensées sur l'interprétation de la nature*, the function of *sensibilité* will be precisely that of establishing relationships between organisms; the exact nature of these interactions, infinitely variable, will determine the faculties enjoyed by each living system.

Diderot's words are indicative also of his concern to achieve a consistent materialism by integrating all matter, organic and inorganic, into a single account. Although this aspect of his philosophy of nature will be among the last to be satisfactorily elaborated, he is already aware of its importance. In a striking passage which prefigures his 1759 letter to Sophie Volland,[68] Diderot implicitly rejects Buffon's concept of a special organic matter by quoting a contradictory statement from the *Histoire naturelle*. Life is not, speculates Buffon on this occasion, an abstract metaphysical concept, but simply a physical attribute of matter – of all matter: 'Plus on fera d'observations, plus on se convaincra [...] qu'enfin le vivant et l'animé, au lieu d'être un degré métaphysique des êtres, est une propriété physique de la matière.'[69]

It will be many years before Diderot can develop this bold conjecture. Nevertheless his encounter with Buffon's ideas has served to pose the central questions which are to provide a focus for his speculations in later works, together with a large proportion of the raw materials which he will use to construct his answers. Thanks to the twin concepts of sentience and gradation he is now in a position to see the twin issues of materialism – the emergence of life and its differentiation into advanced faculties – as two facets of the same process, and thus potentially admitting of a common solution. For if life is to be defined as the possession of (varying degrees of) sentience, and if sentience is to embrace (again by means of gradation and hence diversification) the ambitious range of phenomena touched on in 'Animal', from reactive physical

67. *Enc.*, i.469; Her., v.386 (Diderot).
68. See below, chapter 4.
69. *Enc.*, i.474; Her., v.399-400 (Diderot quoting Buffon). Roger has pointed out this discrepancy within Buffon's thought (*Les Sciences de la vie*, p.549).

behaviour to the most sophisticated intellectual and emotional faculties of man, the two problems become one.

'Animal' offers evidence of Diderot's instinctive belief in the unity underlying all natural phenomena, organic and inorganic, his acquisition of the principle of gradation to account for heterogeneity within these phenomena and his realisation that the faculty of sentience, rigorously defined, holds the conceptual key to life. These three elements will merge with the other conceptual gains of this transition period, catalogued in the earlier part of the present chapter (anti-finalism, confirmed atheism, inherence of movement in matter, the flux of nature, *fermentation*, biological deviance, latency and nutritive assimilation), and together they will undergo investigation, clarification and modification during the years ahead, and emerge in 1769, fused and transformed into a coherent energetic materialism.

With a confident and consistent methodology, from which all traces of metaphysics have been eliminated, and a deepened sense of the complexity, dynamism and creativity of nature, Diderot is well equipped to set down his *Pensées sur l'interprétation de la nature*. His reflections will take on a new cohesion and sense of direction as a result of the enhanced conceptual background acquired since the dramatic conjectures of the *Lettre sur les aveugles*. For, as Fabre has so astutely remarked: 'Diderot ne s'arrête jamais. Pour lui les certitudes ne se vérifient qu'à condition qu'il les dépasse et s'engage sur les chemins qu'elles lui ont ouverts.'[70]

70. 'Le chemin de Diderot', p.3.

3. *Pensées sur l'interprétation de la nature*

By the middle of the eighteenth century, the content and methodology of mechanical science had been seriously called into question, and the domain of 'natural science' considerably expanded both by the emergence of an embryonic biology, physiology and chemistry, and by startling new discoveries in biology, magnetism and electricity. It was in this context, explains Dieckmann, that Diderot 'ventured to pursue the wider implications of the new discoveries and to push some of the new theories to their ultimate conclusions'.[1] The field of research was, as Dieckmann puts it, 'wide open to imagination and conjecture'. The fruit of Diderot's imagination, on this occasion, was his *Pensées sur l'interprétation de la nature*, published first at the end of 1753 and re-edited, in their more widely known form, a few weeks later in 1754. Only one copy of the original edition is extant. The variants are extensive and have been published by Varloot in his edition of the *Interprétation*,[2] after their initial revelation by Dieckmann.

For Venturi, the *Interprétation* represents the culmination of a first period in Diderot's intellectual evolution, 'un nœud essentiel'.[3] Of even greater importance, however, is its contribution to the *future* development of Diderot's materialism. Within the essentially threefold structure – curiously akin to Diderot's other outstanding philosophical work, the 1769 *Rêve de d'Alembert* – a wealth of new intuitions unfolds.[4]

In the first part of the work, after an introduction devoted largely to questions of scientific methodology (sections 1-31), Diderot investigates a series of contemporary scientific issues under the title of *conjectures* – originally *rêveries* (sections 32-38). Further methodological reflections (39-49) are followed by two sections devoted to an analysis of Maupertuis's recently published *Dissertatio inauguralis metaphysica de universali naturae systemate*. A third sequence of miscellaneous points of methodology (52-57) leads to the final section of the work, which traces a programme for the future speculative interpretation of nature.

With the exception of the methodological sections which, although original

1. H. Dieckmann, 'The first edition of Diderot's *Pensées sur l'interprétation de la nature*', *Isis* 46 (1955), p.251-52.
2. J. Varloot (Paris 1953); cf. Her., ix.15.
3. *La Jeunesse de Diderot*, p.283.
4. Cf. Ehrard, who sees the *Interprétation* as both 'point d'arrivée' and 'point de départ' (*L'Idée de nature*, i.244-45).

and perceptive,[5] make little direct contribution to the subject of the present study, each phase of the *Interprétation* adds another refinement to Diderot's philosophy of matter and energy. Even his more general remarks contribute an important reaffirmation of his belief in the fundamental unity of natural phenomena. In the *conjectures*, the analysis of Maupertuis's thesis and the concluding *questions*, he investigates multiple aspects of the organisation and energy of matter, organic and inorganic, and the relationship between them.

The outcome of the work is a heady mixture of conceptual materials which will commit Diderot more firmly than ever to the pursuit of a coherent materialist synthesis in the years which follow.

A. *Conjectures* and *Questions*

i. *From the unity of nature to the unity of energy*

a. *The importance of unity*

Diderot had first expressed his belief that nature is a unified whole at the very outset of his philosophical career, in the *Essai sur le mérite et la vertu*.[6] The same conviction had been implicit within much of his subsequent speculation as he evolved from deistic dualism to a monist conception of the universe. Venturi goes so far as to call it an *acte de foi* on Diderot's part, a logical and emotional necessity.[7] His reaffirmation of unity in the *Interprétation* seems to be prompted by partly conceptual, partly methodological requirements.

Buffon had thrown up the disturbing question of the apparent breach between the organic and the inorganic: this had to be denied if monism was to be preserved. Moreover, as Diderot points out on several occasions, the interpretation of natural phenomena presupposes their interrelation in a single, coherent system: 'L'indépendance absolue d'un seul fait est incompatible avec l'idée de tout; et sans l'idée de tout, plus de philosophie.'[8] The point is reiterated in the closing pages: 'Si les phénomènes ne sont pas enchaînés les uns aux autres, il n'y a point de philosophie.'[9] Several alternative formulations of the principle of unity coexist within the *Interprétation*, with Diderot apparently unaware of the need for further clarification.

5. And also, incidentally, the only area in which even minimal influence of Bacon may be detected, despite the work's title (H. Dieckmann, 'The influence of Francis Bacon on Diderot's *Interprétation de la nature*', *Romanic review* 34 (1944), p.304, 305; cf. Casini, *Diderot 'philosophe'*, p.189-93).
6. See above, i, A.
7. *La Jeunesse de Diderot*, p.284.
8. *OPhil.*, p.186; Her., ix.35.
9. *OPhil.*, p.240; Her., ix.94.

b. First formulation: chain of being

The first is little more than a vague expression of the 'chain of being' concept so commonplace in the eighteenth century, and in Diderot's case probably taken from Buffon. 'La grande chaîne qui lie toutes choses',[10] an essentially static conception, was generally associated with a hierarchical model more appropriate to the classifications of Linnaeus (which Diderot rejects as sterile)[11] or to Buffon's attempts to delineate the natural kingdoms than to Diderot's intuitions of the dynamic, organic dimension of nature.

Two other formulations are rather more promising.

c. Second formulation: causal unity

On the one hand, Diderot seeks to embody unity within the infinite chain of cause and effect: 'Supposez une molécule déplacée; elle ne s'est point déplacée d'elle-même; la cause de son déplacement a une autre cause, celle-ci une autre et ainsi de suite. [...] Supposez une molécule déplacée, ce déplacement aura un effet; cet effet un autre effet, et ainsi de suite.'[12] The underlying determinism of nature is valuable as a source of unity since it takes not only matter, but also energy into account.[13] For it is natural forces which determine the present state of the universe: 'Les êtres n'étant jamais, ni dans leur génération, ni dans leur conformation, ni dans leur usage, que ce que les résistances, les lois du mouvement et l'ordre universel les déterminent à être.'[14] Thus energy does at least contribute to unity, even if it does not as yet constitute it.

d. Third formulation: dynamic unity

A third formulation, on the other hand, suggests that Diderot is prepared to take even this step. For if phenomena are envisaged as matter-in-action rather than as the static end-results of individual processes, then the whole of nature is a unified, organic manifestation of a single, energetic causal principle. Such a supposition would, Diderot suggests, obviate many of the obstacles to interpretation: 'L'étonnement vient soudain de ce qu'on suppose plusieurs prodiges où il n'y en a qu'un; de ce qu'on imagine, dans la nature, autant d'actes particuliers qu'on nombre de phénomènes, tandis qu'elle n'a peut-être jamais produit qu'un seul acte.'[15]

It is only after careful consideration that I use the label 'organic' of this concept of unity. Crocker denies that the world constitutes an organism for

10. *OPhil.*, p.182; Her., ix.32.
11. *OPhil.*, p.222-23; Her., ix.76.
12. *OPhil.*, p.234; Her., ix.88.
13. Cf. Crocker, *Diderot's chaotic order*, p.19.
14. *OPhil.*, p.199; Her., ix.51.
15. *OPhil.*, p.186; Her., ix.35.

Diderot on the grounds that its 'parts do not act in concord towards the realisation of a single, common purpose', that fermentation prevents the maintenance of a constant, identifiable structure, and that, if it were an organism, 'the Whole could not survive the disappearance of its constituent parts or organs'.[16] I accept that there is some truth in these points, particularly where Diderot's later thought is concerned,[17] but not that they invalidate the use of the term 'organic' to distinguish Diderot's world view at this time from that of the mechanists. As will be made clear, Diderot will posit (in 1759) a universal principle of life which together with his concept of dynamic unity heralds a flirtation with vitalism characterising his interpretation of nature for several years. When he does come to reject vitalism, and with it universal organic unity, it will not be for the reasons outlined by Crocker.[18]

e. Implications for the unity of energy

This issue is, however, subsidiary to the implications of his third formulation for his developing theory of energy. For, according to these lines, unity lies not within matter so much as within the forces which shape it.[19] The forces themselves must therefore be homogeneous in some way[20] and Diderot faces up to this consequence squarely, speculating that all energetic phenomena will one day prove to be ultimately linked:

dans la nature, on reconnaîtra, lorsque la physique expérimentale sera plus avancée, que tous les phénomènes, ou de la pesanteur, ou de l'élasticité, ou de l'attraction, ou du magnétisme, ou de l'électricité, ne sont que des faces différentes de la même affection. [...] Il y a peut-être un phénomène central qui jetterait des rayons, non seulement à ceux qu'on a, mais encore à tous ceux que le temps ferait découvrir, qui les unirait et qui en formerait un système.[21]

Although motive energy is not included in Diderot's enumeration, it should be remembered that 'Chaos' had identified such phenomena as attraction as manifestations of this basic energy source,[22] thus establishing motion as the first link in the energetic chain. These prophetic lines therefore represent another step in the integration of energy forms which will later receive such a strikingly modern expression.

16. *Diderot's chaotic order*, p.19-20.
17. Though the first is refuted to some exent by the concept of optimum organisation, or in Crocker's terms resistance to entropy (cf. below, ii.a.2, and Crocker's own statements, p.31), and the third by empirical observation (the phenomenon of regeneration is but one instance).
18. Cf. below 5, D.iii.b.
19. For Wartofsky this principle, like that of self-motion within matter (cf. above, 2, B.ii.a), is drawn from Leibniz ('Diderot and the development of materialist monism', p.289, 290).
20. But see below, ii.a.3 for the importance of heterogeneity.
21. *OPhil.*, p.220; Her., ix.73.
22. Cf. above, 2, B.ii.c.2.

Of the particular phenomena mentioned here, weight and elasticity will be linked as functions of attraction in 1761[23] and magnetism and electricity are examined immediately.[24] Indeed a large proportion of the *Interprétation* is devoted to the examination of natural forces: not only magnetism and electricity, but also attraction, the special energy of organic phenomena, and the new, potentially energetic concepts introduced by Maupertuis to account for certain vital functions. Diderot's concern for synthesis and unity will be evident throughout.

ii. *The organisation of matter: attraction*

The *cinquièmes conjectures* are devoted to an analysis of attraction, seen primarily as the agent of combination and organisation within matter. Diderot investigates the way it works and, in the interests of unity, the subsidiary phenomena which may be attributed to it.

a. Attraction: general features

1. Its operation in simple aggregates

The workings of attraction are shown to involve an adaptive process within matter akin to that described in the context of nutritive assimilation. In the first place, the effect of attractive energy is determined by the physical configuration of the matter upon which it is exercised. Thus a two-way process of interaction is involved from the start: 'Si deux molécules s'attirent réciproquement, elles se disposeront l'une par l'autre selon les lois de leurs attractions, leurs figures, etc.'[25] Secondly, its effects are cumulative. The addition of further matter, also endowed with attractive force, to an existing interactive system, leads to a transformation of the whole: 'Si ce système de deux molécules en attire une troisième dont il soit réciproquement attiré, ces trois molécules se disposeront les unes par rapport aux autres, selon les lois de leurs attractions, leurs figures, etc.'[26] Thus a purely quantitative change – the transition from two to three energetic molecules – gives rise to a qualitatively distinct aggregate. No new type of property emerges, but the character of the whole is altered insofar as its arrangement and interrelationships are concerned. This is an important intuition, conceptually analogous to the conclusions Diderot had drawn from ingestion.

2. Complex aggregates: optimum organisation

The principle of optimum organisation is also applied in the context of

23. Cf. below, 4, C (*Sur la cohésion des corps*).
24. Cf. below, iv.
25. *OPhil.*, p.207; Her., ix.60.
26. *OPhil.*, p.207; Her., ix.60.

attraction. Within larger accumulations of molecules, the interplay of attractive forces brings about a state of equilibrium which provides maximum viability for the resultant whole. Capable of surviving minor, temporary external disturbance, the 'system' also has sufficient flexibility to adopt a new arrangement to accommodate new elements of matter or energy. The principle of optimum organisation ensures order and adaptability rather than anarchy or instability within matter:

Elles [les molécules] formeront toutes un système *A*, dans lequel [...] elles résisteront à une force qui tendrait à troubler leur co-ordination, et tendront toujours, soit à se restituer dans leur premier ordre, si la force perturbatrice vient à cesser, soit à se co-ordonner relativement aux lois de leurs attractions, à leurs figures, etc., et à l'action de la force perturbatrice, si elle continue à agir.[27]

Each new combination of energetic matter will have its own point of optimum organisation. Moreover, this co-ordinating function of attraction is operative at all levels of organisation, from the molecular to the cosmic. The self-stabilisation of matter is universal:

Ce système *A* est ce que j'appelle un corps élastique. En ce sens général et abstrait, le système planétaire, l'univers n'est qu'un corps élastique: le chaos est une impossibilité; car il est un ordre essentiellement conséquent aux qualités primitives de la matière.[28]

In no way does this invalidate Diderot's concept of flux or even his belief in the historical reality of a state of chaos as examined in the article of that name. It is only the subjective notion of chaos which Diderot rejects. Historical chaos, the state preceding organisation, is in itself a perfectly balanced system. So too is flux, taken at any point in time. Matter is tending constantly towards a state of optimum organisation, but through an infinite and continuous series of interactions which ensures permanent dynamism. Order is not necessarily a static phenomenon.

Crocker interprets this vision (as in the *Lettre sur les aveugles*) in terms of entropy, contending that Diderot's account expresses an essential tendency within any system to resist entropy, to seek stable formations and maintain them against counterforces tending to decompose existing, viable structures. He points out, however, that Diderot's concepts diverge from the modern theory of entropy in that, for Diderot, order is synonymous with stability ('organised matter and energy in highly structured forms') and both are counter-entropic, whereas for a modern scientist they are incompatible, entropy entailing minimum order but maximum stability.[29]

27. *OPhil.*, p.207; Her., ix.60.
28. *OPhil.*, p.208; Her., ix.60.
29. Crocker, *Diderot's chaotic order*, p.15-16 and p.16, n.

3. Attraction and heterogeneity

Diderot's account of attraction allows for heterogeneity within matter. The organisation of a compound, or *corps élastique mixte* (as opposed to the *corps élastique simple*, which corresponds to what we would call the element), establishes heterogeneity on an energetic basis:

J'entends, par un corps élastique mixte, un système composé de deux ou plusieurs systèmes de matières différentes, de différentes figures, animées de différentes quantités et peut-être mues selon des lois différentes d'attraction, dont les particules sont co-ordonnées les unes entre les autres, par une loi qui est commune à toutes, et qu'on peut regarder comme le produit de leurs actions réciproques.[30]

Each type of matter (or element) therefore has its own distinct quantity of attractive energy, which determines the nature of its relationships both with other particles of the same element and with aggregates of other elements. This account is remarkably analogous to the modern theory of valency laws governing the structure of molecules and chemical compounds.

The extension of attraction to chemical phenomena was a subject of considerable debate in the early eighteenth century. Newton himself had argued for the universal application of attraction,[31] though he accepted a distinction between chemical and gravitational attraction in that the second was a force dependent only on mass and distance, whereas the first was selective and depended on the nature of each substance involved.[32] It was Huygens, however, who had argued that attraction was not universal, but exercised only by the globe as a mass, and therefore capable of explaining planetary motion, but not of serving as a general scientific principle, for instance in chemistry.[33] Rouellian chemistry gave this argument a new twist, accepting newtonian attraction in the context of an ideal, homogeneous basic matter, but declaring it invalid in the real world of interacting heterogeneous bodies. Rouelle and his pupil Venel proposed instead a principle of affinity based on the work of E.-F. Geoffroy.[34] Thus Venel's *Encyclopédie* article 'Chymie' put forward a principle of affinity working not by attraction but by the joining of similar parts present in both bodies involved in a chemical combination.[35] D'Alembert, on the other hand (in his article 'Attraction'),

30. *OPhil.*, p.209-10; Her., ix.62.
31. Mousnier, *Progrès scientifique et technique*, p.17-18.
32. M. Crosland, 'The development of chemistry in the eighteenth century', *Studies on Voltaire* 24 (1963), p.382.
33. Mousnier, *Progrès scientifique et technique*, p.51.
34. J.-C. Guédon, 'Chimie et matérialisme', *Dix-huitième siècle* 11 (1979), p.190-92. Geoffroy had published the first table of affinities in 1718, using the term *rapport* rather than *attraction* so as not to offend cartesian orthodoxy (Crosland, 'The development of chemistry', p.383-84; cf. H. Metzger, *Les Doctrines chimiques en France*, Paris 1969, p.418).
35. M. Daumas, 'La chimie dans l'*Encyclopédie*', *Revue d'histoire des sciences* 4 (1951), p.339.

outlined the theories of Newton's English contemporaries Keill and Freind, where chemical reactions *were* explained in terms of attraction at the corpuscular level, and the tables of Geoffroy and others were generally ignored in the *Encyclopédie* (Daumas, p.339-40). Maupertuis, finally, equated Geoffroy's affinities with attraction, despite the latter's rejection of such a link, but went beyond this to propose a form of 'instinct' as an explanatory device.[36]

It is difficult to situate Diderot precisely within this debate. Certainly he was an admirer of Rouelle, attending his lectures from 1754-1757[37] and later recommending his notebooks in the *Plan d'une université* (Rappaport, p.79). Rouellian chemistry did offer a real alternative to mechanistic deism,[38] particularly in its belief that physical properties are transient and dependent upon the type of chemical interrelationships in which the bodies are engaged (Guédon, p.197), an attitude close to the one expressed by Diderot here.

On the other hand, both here and in his 1761 paper *Sur la cohésion des corps*, Diderot seems to attach considerable importance to Newton's own methodological principle that 'Les effets du même genre doivent toujours être attribués, autant qu'il est possible, à la même cause.'[39] This would imply the reduction of all cognate physical processes to attraction, an important step in the unification of material phenomena[40] and one which Diderot will defend in 1761.

Nevertheless, the overall tenor of Diderot's remarks certainly seems to invalidate Lefèbvre's contention that the issue of heterogeneity presents an insoluble problem for Diderot, 'devant lequel sa pensée hésite et fléchit'.[41] Lefèbvre suggests that Diderot has only three options open to him: homogeneity, infinite qualitative diversity, or a finite number of elements, and that, by opting for the third, Diderot fails to recognise the realtionship between quality and quantity. Since Diderot's formulation: 'J'appellerai donc *éléments* les différentes matières hétérogènes, nécessaires pour la production générale des phénomènes dc la nature'[42] accords with modern chemical theory, at which Lefèbvre would presumably not level the same criticism, this judgement can mean only one of

36. Roger, *Les Sciences de la vie*, p.478, 479.

37. J. Ehrard, 'Matérialisme et naturalisme', *CAIEF* 13 (1961), p.197; R. Rappaport, 'G.-F. Rouelle', *Chymia* 6 (1960), p.78, 87.

38. Guédon, 'Chimie et matérialisme', p.188.

39. Quoted from Mme Du Châtelet's 1756 translation, in M. Paty, 'Matière, espace et temps selon Newton', *Scientia* 107 (1972), p.1020.

40. Paty, p.1014. For a further account of the development of newtonian concepts in France, see Ehrard, *L'Idée de nature*, p.125-77.

41. Lefèbvre, *Diderot*, p.151. Cf. Lerel, who devotes a considerable proportion of his work to a rather abstruse analysis of the apparent duality between Diderot's concepts of, on the one hand, natural unity and, on the other, heterogeneous matter, before acknowledging that unity is based on 'die konstante Dynamik des Alls' (*Diderots Naturphilosophie*, p.45).

42. *OPhil.*, p.239; Her., ix.93.

two things. Either Lefèbvre is reproaching Diderot for not having intuited the findings of twentieth-century subatomic physics (namely that the qualitative distinctions between elements are determined by the number and arrangement of certain types of particle within their atoms) or he has overlooked the contribution which energy makes to Diderot's concept of heterogeneity (namely that diversity within nature, qualitative variety, can be produced by purely quantitative variations of energy).

Diderot is aware that the multiplicity of natural forms must be explained in the simplest terms possible if unity is to be preserved. It is for this reason that he will eventually reject the possibility of alternative laws of attraction tentatively suggested here. Nevertheless he wholeheartedly subscribes to the general principle of heterogeneity widely accepted by his contemporaries: 'Il me paraît aussi impossible que tous les êtres de la nature aient été produits avec une matière homogène, qu'il le serait de les représenter avec une seule et même couleur.'[43] Diderot has put an original construction on the principle by attributing heterogeneity, in part at least, to the energy of matter. Eventually this transfer will be total, as the relationship between matter and its forces is radically redefined.[44] In the meantime, the interests of unity are served by attributing the largest possible number of phenomena to this quantitatively variable force of attraction.

b. Attraction: subsidiary phenomena

Diderot gives attraction a broad field of reference. In the first place, the physical state of matter (solid, liquid or gas) is presented as a function of attraction. Such an association is, he claims, possible in the abstract, ideal world of total vacuum, and may therefore be assumed to hold good in the plenum of the observable world. Here attraction cannot be presumed to act alone, as it is part of a broader, energetic whole. Nevertheless the intervention of other forces serves only to alter, in quantitative terms, the basic relationships between material particles established by attraction:

Sans prétendre donc que l'attraction constitue dans le plein la dureté et l'élasticité, [...] n'est-il pas évident que cette propriété de la matière suffit seule pour les constituer dans le vide, et donner lieu à la raréfaction, à la condensation, et à tous les phénomènes qui en dépendent? Pourquoi donc ne serait-elle pas la cause première de ces phénomènes dans notre système général, où une infinité de causes qui la modifieraient feraient varier à l'infini la quantité de ces phénomènes [...]?[45]

Phenomena such as evaporation and condensation, that is the transition of

43. *OPhil.*, p.239; Her., ix.92; cf. Varloot (ed.), *Le Rêve de d'Alembert*, p.10.
44. See below, 4, C.
45. *OPhil.*, p.208; Her., ix.61.

matter from one state to another, are shown to be dependent on the quantitative variation within relationships between elements, and thus ultimately on attraction itself.[46]

Similar mechanisms are invoked to explain other physical processes in terms of attraction. The rupture of a body under strain, for instance, or its shattering on impact with another body, may be accounted for by the destruction of the cohesive bonds of attraction between its component parts: 'Elles [les parties] n'auront plus d'action sensible les unes sur les autres par leurs attractions réciproques.'[47]

Finally, Diderot seeks to extend attraction to a variety of chemical phenomena. Chemical reactions where a portion of the matter involved appears to be detached, such as vaporisation, or combustion as it was then understood, seem to be less easily attributable to attraction, which is essentially an agent of addition and combination. Nonetheless Diderot is aware of the conceptual dangers involved in seeking an alternative solution: 'Des attractions, selon les lois différentes, ne paraissent pas suffire dans ce phénomène; et il est dur d'admettre des qualités répulsives.'[48] Such an explanation had been proposed in the *Encyclopédie* article 'Air': 'Quand par la chaleur et quelque autre agent, la force attractive est surmontée, et les particules du corps écartées au point de n'être plus dans la sphère d'attraction, *la force répulsive* commençant à agir, les fait éloigner les unes des autres.'[49] Rather than have recourse to occult qualities, Diderot applies the same principle used earlier to account for the physical disintegration of bodies. Attractive bonds are weakened, and eventually destroyed, in this case by the impact of particles of other elements involved in the reaction.[50]

Attraction, then, is shown to be capable of extension to a wide range of physical processes. Although it provides Diderot with no special intuitions regarding the workings of what is uniquely organic, his examination has confirmed a number of important general principles which will contribute to his eventual synthesis of energy: the rôles of adaptation, optimum organisation and heterogeneity in the interactions of matter.

Although at first sight Diderot's reflections on attraction seem to be universally applicable, it becomes clear towards the end of the *Interprétation* that this

---

46. Cf. above, A.ii.a.3.
47. *OPhil.*, p.208-209; Her., ix.61.
48. *OPhil.*, p.210; Her., ix.63.
49. My emphasis. Quoted in Vassails, 'L'*Encyclopédie* et la physique', p.307.
50. This was not in itself a new idea. Galileo had argued that melting was due to the decomposition of 'cohesive force' when particles of fire interpenetrated those of, for instance, a metal (M. Boas, 'The establishment of mechanical philosophy', *Osiris* 12 (1952), p.435).

conclusion was less evident to Diderot himself. For one form of interaction continues to disturb him: that which characterises living matter and its relationship with inorganic substance.

iii. *Organic matter: its relationship to the inorganic*

a. *The distinction between organic and inorganic*

Diderot's concern to seek unity within nature accentuates the dilemma provoked by Buffon concerning the division of natural phenomena into animate and inanimate categories. Physical evidence suggests that the division is irreducible, yet philosophical consistency requires unity of substance. Diderot's series of questions which closes the *Interprétation* points up the nature and the implications of this conflict.

The basic issue is simply stated: 'il est évident que la matière en général est divisée en matière morte et en matière vivante. Mais comment se peut-il faire que la matière ne soit pas une, ou toute vivante ou toute morte?'[51] There appear to be only two solutions to the dilemma: dualism, admitting an external principle to account for the animation of matter, or vitalism. The first Diderot has already rejected; the second will preoccupy him for several years until he succeeds in elaborating a third formula (based on latency) to transcend the impasse. The origin of what I shall call his 'vitalist temptation' during the years leading up to the *Rêve de d'Alembert* lies here in the *Interprétation*.

Diderot remains unsure as to the exact basis of the distinction between animate and inanimate matter. He makes no attempt to introduce either Buffon's criterion of sentience or the new concept offered by Maupertuis (which he has just discussed) and restricts the difference to organisation plus spontaneity of movement:

Y a-t-il quelque autre différence assignable entre la matière morte et la matière vivante, que l'organisation, et que la spontanéité réelle ou apparente du mouvement?

Ce qu'on appelle matière vivante, ne serait-ce pas seulement une matière qui se meut par elle-même? Et ce qu'on appelle une matière morte, ne serait-ce pas une matière mobile par une autre matière?[52]

Despite its gesture towards the self-sufficiency of living things, there is little to choose between this and the equally mechanistic accounts which have previously dissatisfied Diderot. It leads, in fact, to a particularly sterile form of dualism, as Diderot himself recognises. If life is equated simply with motion, there can be no guarantee that it continues when movement is not apparent: 'Si la matière

51. *OPhil.*, p.242; Her., ix.95-96.
52. *OPhil.*, p.242; Her., ix.96.

vivante est une matière qui se meut par elle-même, comment peut-elle cesser de se mouvoir sans mourir?'[53]

This particular weakness can be overcome only by applying the concept of latency. Eventually Diderot will substitute *sensibilité* for motion and equate potential energy with potential life. Although the necessary concepts are already available to him,[54] Diderot does not apply them to this issue and the problem remains unresolved.

b. The interaction between organic and inorganic

Consequently he is also unable to elaborate an adequate account of the manner in which organic and inorganic matter interact, even separately: 'La matière vivante se combine-t-elle avec de la matière vivante? Comment se fait cette combinaison? [...] J'en demande autant de la matière morte.'[55] Diderot's two substances may be resolutely material, but they are no more capable of being integrated into a common system than the spiritual and material substances rejected by Oribaze in the *Promenade du sceptique*: 'dans la nature, si une molécule de matière vivante s'applique à une molécule de matière morte, le tout sera-t-il vivant ou sera-t-il mort?'[56] The problem is exacerbated by the fact that Diderot envisages such combination only in terms of contiguity (*s'applique*), not continuity.[57]

In future years this obstacle will be overcome by reference to the conversion of matter through nutritive assimilation, a process involving continuity between the constituent parts of an organism. At present, however, Diderot formulates no alternative and is obliged to concede that this dualistic view of matter remains unconvincing as an account of the totality of natural phenomena: 'S'il y a une matière vivante et une matière morte par elles-mêmes, ces deux principes suffisent-ils pour la production générale de toutes les formes et de tous les phénomènes?'[58]

The only positive intuition on this issue lies in Diderot's speculation that, despite the apparent irreducibility of the two categories, one may be convertible to the other. Interaction through qualitative change is not, therefore, wholly ruled out: 'La matière vivante est-elle toujours vivante? Et la matière morte est-elle toujours et réellement morte? La matière vivante ne meurt-elle point? La matière morte ne commence-t-elle jamais à vivre?'[59] He even goes so far as to

53. *OPhil.*, p.242; Her., ix.96.
54. Cf. latency, above, 2, C.iv, and *sensibilité*, below, B.iii.b.
55. *OPhil.*, p.243; Her., ix.98.
56. *OPhil.*, p.242-43; Her., ix.97.
57. Cf. Szigeti, *Denis Diderot: une grande figure*, p.70.
58. *OPhil.*, p.242; Her., ix.96.
59. *OPhil.*, p.242; Her., ix.96.

envisage the possibility that such conversion may be a continuous process, thus anticipating his own principle of the circulation of matter: 'les molécules vivantes, ne pourraient-elles pas reprendre la vie, après l'avoir perdue, pour la reperdre encore; et ainsi de suite, à l'infini?'[60] In its present formulation, however, the suggestion is tentative and limited, since there is no attempt to identify the process underlying such a conversion.

c. The energy of organic matter

Diderot's questions are more fruitful in their investigation of the forces characterising living matter. His speculation suggests the existence of a special complex of forces responsible for the organisation and development of organic forms. Buffon had attributed this process to internal 'moulds', performing a similar function to Aristotelian Forms. Diderot strips this concept of its scholastic associations and reduces it to the action of an intrinsic, material power: 'Est-ce [la moule] un être réel ou préexistant? ou, n'est-ce que les limites intelligibles de l'énergie d'une molécule vivante unie à de la matière morte ou vivante; limites déterminées par le rapport de l'énergie en tout sens, aux résistances en tout sens?'[61]

Form, then, is determined by the relationships within matter established by the energy each portion manifests. *Energie*, in its eighteenth-century sense of effective force (*force vive*), refers here to the complex of forces involved; the individual energetic components are not isolated and identified. Despite its imprecision, such a concept of the forces active at the organic level makes a significant contribution to Diderot's thought. It shows that he is prepared to consider all forms of energy as essentially analogous in their workings. In later speculations it is precisely this awareness of common structural features which will enable Diderot to extrapolate concepts from one force to another and arrive at so strikingly modern a view of energy.[62] As Chouillet has pointed out, the subsequent association of energy and *sensibilité* has its roots in this concept of molecular energy: 'Toute la genèse du Rêve est là: rendre évidente et palpable cette "énergie de la molécule" sans laquelle aucune explication correcte des origines de la vie ne peut être avancée',[63] an aim which he will succeed in fulfilling by means of an extended, imaginative use of analogy: 'Diderot sait très bien qu'il ne peut pas rendre son objet saisissable, autrement que par une série d'analogies, de métaphores, de présomptions.' Moreover, his proposed account anticipates a central feature of *sensibilité*, the phenomenon to which the organis-

---

60. *OPhil.*, p.244; Her., ix.98.
61. *OPhil.*, p.243; Her., ix.97.
62. See below, 4, C.
63. *Diderot poète de l'énergie*, p.46.

ation of animate matter will later be ascribed, in that the workings of molecular energy are defined in terms of action and reaction ('le rapport de l'énergie en tout sens, aux résistances en tout sens'). In such an account, material form is not determined by pre-defined patterns, be they Aristotelian Forms, Buffon's *moules intérieurs*, or the deist's *germes*. Nor is it the result, as Venturi has pointed out, of an extrinsic process of random combinations, but of an internal law.[64] It is established automatically through the interplay of matter's own forces, working inexorably towards their point of optimum organisation. The function of *sensibilité* will be precisely that of co-ordinating such a process, through a network of dynamic, reciprocal relationships within matter.

Finally, Diderot remains aware of the need for an element of heterogeneity. He suggests two alternative forms which this may take within organic matter: 'L'énergie d'une molécule vivante varie-t-elle par elle-même, ou ne varie-t-elle que selon la quantité, la qualité, les formes de la matière morte ou vivante à laquelle elle s'unit?'[65] Diderot is not prepared to state whether the heterogeneity of molecular energy is intrinsic and absolute, or whether it is simply contingent upon the nature of the matter involved. In 1761 he will resolve this particular issue by speculating that the manifestations of a force vary according to the conditions under which it is deployed.[66] As early as 1753, however, he evidently feels that a variability factor of some kind is as essential to organic molecular energy as to attraction.[67]

Although a composite phenomenon, therefore, molecular energy is discussed in much the same terms as Diderot uses for the examination of a single force. This is in accordance with his own declaration earlier in the *Interprétation*: 'Par le principe de la décomposition des forces, on peut toujours réduire à une seule force toutes celles qui agissent sur un corps.'[68] His evolution towards a fully unified concept of energy is thus furthered by these lines[69] and will be given

64. *La Jeunesse de Diderot*, p.288.
65. *OPhil.*, p.243; Her., ix.97.
66. See below, 4, C.
67. See above, A.ii.a.3.
68. *OPhil.*, p.207; Her., ix.59.
69. These sections of the *Interprétation* are rarely discussed by scholars. Only Delaunay, as far as I can ascertain, has acknowledged the importance of Diderot's speculations on attraction and molecular energy, and his conclusion bears repetition: 'De même que, dans l'univers brut, les phénomènes se réduisent en dernière analyse à des gravitations et attractions moléculaires, les formes animales ne sont que les limites de l'énergie d'une ou plusieurs molécules vivantes, limites déterminées par le rapport de l'énergie aux résistances; que toutes les fonctions organiques tant cérébrales que viscérales ne sont qu'une suite d'actions et de réactions. Et voilà le monisme matérialiste constitué, démentant ses origines (Leibniz), dépassant ses précurseurs (La Mettrie) et trahissant ses alliés (sensualisme)' ('L'évolution philosophique et médicale du biomécanisme', p.1377). Although Delaunay commits the common error of confusing chronologically distinct elements of Diderot's philosophy, he does capture the special relevance of the *Interprétation*.

additional impetus by his reflections on electricity and magnetism.

iv. *Electricity and magnetism*

Several pages of the *Interprétation* are devoted to an examination of electrical and magnetic phenomena, highly topical at the time, as a result of the recent publication in France of Franklin's work.[70] Although the bulk of Diderot's speculations are of relevance only to a more specialised study of his scientific thought, several points are worthy of note for their contribution to his overall conception of energy in matter.

a. *Common source of electricity and magnetism*

In the first place, electricity and magnetism are relevant to his quest for energetic unity. Diderot shares with Franklin and Buffon the view (subsequently confirmed by scientific research)[71] that the phenomena have a common origin: 'Il y a grande apparence que le magnétisme et l'électricité dépendent des mêmes causes.'[72] Moreover, these causes are themselves exclusively energetic. Meteorological and geological processes, along with the inherent forces of each particle of matter, conspire, at both the cosmic and the elemental levels, to bring about magnetic and electrical phenomena:

Pourquoi ne seraient-ce pas des effets du mouvement de rotation du globe et de l'énergie des matières dont il est composé, combinée avec l'action de la lune? Le flux et le reflux, les courants, les vents, la lumière, le mouvement des particules libres du globe, peut-être même celui de toute sa croûte entière sur son noyau, etc., opèrent d'une infinité de manières un frottement continuel.[73]

The general eighteenth-century tendency was to view electricity as a special, subtle form of matter, rather than as a force.[74] Diderot himself refers to it most frequently as 'la matière électrique'[75] and on one occasion as 'le feu électrique'.[76] Magnetism, on the other hand, was accepted as a force after the manner of attraction. To identify the two was therefore to take a step in the direction of identifying matter with energy, although no-one at the time seems to have been aware of the significance of this implication. Buffon's *Traité de l'aimant* (1778),

---

70. I. B. Cohen, 'A note concerning Diderot and Franklin', *Isis* 46 (1955), p.268-69.
71. Cf. Winter, p.119.
72. *OPhil.*, p.201; cf. p.202, n.1, and Varloot edition, p.61, n.1; Her., ix.53.
73. *OPhil.*, p.201; Her., ix.53.
74. Vassails, '*L'Encyclopédie* et la physique', *Revue d'histoire des sciences* 4 (1951), p.311. Vassails points out that, for several thinkers, this matter is identified with ether or with fire.
75. *OPhil.*, p.201, 202; Her., ix.52, 54.
76. *OPhil.*, p.203; Her., ix.54.

for instance, refers to magnetism as a modification of electricity[77] and character-ises both as forces[78] without any attempt to reconcile this interpretation with the alternative contemporary view of electricity as 'une matière très fluide et très subtile'.[79] In Diderot's case, however, the implication is something more than an interesting anomaly, since the identity of matter and energy will become an implicit principle of his philosophy.

b. Electricity as a possible source of energy transformation

1. Inorganic matter

Already it is clear that Diderot is thinking in terms of energy transformation – the conversion of one force into another under appropriate physical conditions. This is the unspoken assumption behind both his and Buffon's accounts of the origins of electromagnetic forces. Diderot takes his speculation further in this direction by suggesting that electricity may be capable of 'energising' otherwise inert substances, that is to say creating in them a form of energy which they did not previously possess.

His first application of this notion is to medicinal substances. In the eighteenth century, the effective power of a drug was frequently considered as a form of *force vive* or *énergie*. The chemist Venel, for instance, refers in the *Encyclopédie* to 'l'énergie de certains purgatifs'[80] and to 'les remèdes plus énergiques'.[81] Diderot proposes that this particular force may be brought into existence or intensified by the application of electrical energy: 'On a essayé si ce feu extraordinaire ne porterait point quelque vertu dans les remèdes, et ne rendrait point une substance plus efficace, un topique plus actif.'[82] Neither Vernière nor Varloot have found evidence of the experiments to which these lines refer, and Diderot himself mentions that they were not extensively pursued. Nevertheless, the conceptual value of such a proposal is considerable.

2. Organic matter

In the 1753 edition, Diderot had taken this idea further still, applying it not only to the mineral and vegetal substances involved in medicine, but to organic,

77. 'Il me paraît donc démontré que le magnétisme, qu'on regardait comme une force particulière et isolée, dépend de l'électricité, dont il n'est qu'une modification occasionnée par le rapport de son action avec la nature du fer', quoted by Varloot in his edition of the *Interprétation*, p.61-62, n.1.
78. 'Nous ne pouvons plus douter que la force particulière du magnétisme ne dépend de la force générale de l'électricité', quoted by Vernière, *OPhil.*, p.202, n.1.
79. Le Monnier, 'Electricité', *Enc.*, v.469.
80. Venel, 'Correctif', *Enc.*, iv.272.
81. Venel, 'Dose', *Enc.*, v.60.
82. *OPhil.*, p.203. The 1753 version referred to 'cette qualité extraordinaire de la matière' rather than 'ce feu', an alternative indicative of Diderot's hesitation as to the exact ontological status of electricity (Her., ix.55).

animal matter. His contemporaries had experimented with the use of electric shock treatment in cases of paralysis;[83] Diderot makes a radical application of this principle to the problem of animal sterility, speculating that electricity could act as a vitalising force in these cases: 'Qui sait si la matière électrique [...] n'animerait pas une matière spermatique froide et languissante, et ne la disposerait pas à la combinaison et au mouvement, dont l'organisation animale est le résultat?'[84] Electricity is considered as a means of operating a transition from one level of organisation to another – from organic but inert to organic and active. The process involved again seems to imply energy transformation. Electricity produces heat and movement, and these in turn, through a combinatory process, bring about the special organisation characteristic of active life. Although Diderot will go beyond the attribution of life to movement and organisation alone, he will remain concerned to redefine, rather than totally replace such an account. His speculative introduction of electricity is an original and striking intuition which prefigures his use of *sensibilité* as one element in a chain of energetic transformations leading to life. Although he refers here only to one highly particularised phenomenon, Diderot remarks elsewhere that electricity is a widespread and potent force, calling it 'un des ressorts les plus généraux et les plus puissants de la nature'.[85] It could so easily have been made into a universal principle of life, a step which was taken by several English thinkers, for instance John Freke (1688-1756), who identified electricity with *vis vitae*,[86] and William Stukely, who declared in 1750: 'all motion, voluntary and involuntary, generation, even life itself, all the operations of the vegetable kingdom, and an infinity more of nature's works, are owing to the activity of this electric fire, the very soul of the material world.'[87]

Why then was the idea eliminated not only from the 1754 edition of the *Interprétation*, but also from the whole of Diderot's subsequent thought? It seems probable that under the impact of his encounter with Maupertuis, Diderot was immediately – and permanently – convinced of the superiority of *sensibilité* as the key to life. With this concept available to him, Diderot no longer felt a need to broaden the scope of electricity. It was, after all, difficult to do so without recourse to unacceptably occultist models of nature: as Ritterbush has shown, such theories were generally couched in terms either of newtonian ether or of

83. Daumont reports these experiments in his article 'Electricité médicinale' (*Enc.*, v.477-78); cf. Her., ix.55, 107 (note 99).
84. Varloot edition, p.64 (1753 version); Her., ix.55 (note).
85. *OPhil.*, p.205; Her., ix.56.
86. C. Ritterbush, *Overtures to biology* (New Haven 1964), p.47.
87. Quoted in Ritterbush, p.33.

an igneous world soul.[88] Thus the turning point in Diderot's philosophy represented by his initial intuition of *sensibilité* is demonstrated even within the work in which it appears.

For it is this which constitutes the major contribution of the *Interprétation* to his lasting philosophy. Important though Diderot's reflections on electromagnetic forces, molecular energy, attraction and the unity of nature are, they are outweighed by the fact that, in the pages devoted to Maupertuis, he is led to formulate an embryonic version of the concept of *sensibilité*, on which his entire philosophy of life will ultimately rest.

B. Diderot and Maupertuis

Sections 50 and 51 of the *Interprétation* are devoted to the discussion of a major work by Maupertuis, first published in Latin under the pseudonym of Dr Baumann in 1751. Although this did not appear in French until 1754, Diderot seems to have had earlier access to it through the good offices of either d'Alembert or the author himself (*OPhil.*, p.171). Its successive titles are indicative of its likely relevance to Diderot's own speculations at this time: *Dissertatio inauguralis metaphysica de universali naturae systemate*, *Essai sur les corps organisés*, and *Système de la nature*.[89] Indeed, his sympathy with Maupertuis's aims is expressed immediately, in the opening lines of section 50: 'Son objet est le plus grand que l'intelligence humain puisse se proposer; c'est le système universel de la nature.'[90]

Like Diderot, Maupertuis is dissatisfied with previous interpretations of nature and speculates on the possibility of finding a new, material principle to account for the special characteristics of life. Diderot's examination is therefore twofold: he scrutinises both the *Système de la nature*'s account of the inadequacy of previous systems and the conceptual alternative it proposes. In doing so he is able not only to reaffirm the general principles of his own materialism (partly under cover of an ostensible refutation of Maupertuis) but also to reformulate Maupertuis's central thesis in the form of *sensibilité*. These pages thus constitute

88. p.14, 33. The exact nature of electricity was not to be clarified until the 1780s, when Coulomb succeeded in quantifying it and demonstrating that the newtonian principle of gravitation held for electrical attraction and repulsion (Mousnier, *Progrès scientifique et technique*, p.332-34), a possibility which Diderot does not consider.

89. Respectively: original version (1751); French translation (1754); definitive title given by Maupertuis when he incorporated it into the 1756 edition of his works. It is this edition to which I shall refer, as it contains the text of Maupertuis's responses to Diderot's objections in the *Interprétation*.

90. *OPhil.*, p.224; Her., ix.77.

both a partial *mise au point* of Diderot's philosophy and a source of valuable new intuitions.

i. *Common rejection of previous systems*

Diderot makes it clear from the start that he considers Maupertuis's ideas to represent a break with existing philosophies of nature. The *Système de la nature* is, he approvingly points out, 'rempli d'idées singulières et neuves'.[91] Maupertuis's misgivings about previous thinkers and 'l'insuffisance de leurs principes pour le développement général des phénomènes' are shared by Diderot, who reports the account carefully.[92]

The evolution within philosophies of nature from Descartes on is shown to stem from an increasing awareness of the complexity of nature. The tensions resulting from the incompleteness of early mechanism were resolved by the introduction of new properties and forces, culminating in the newtonian theory of attraction. This in turn came to require extending to accommodate the data of corpuscular physics and chemistry:

> Les uns n'ont demandé que l'*étendue* et le *mouvement*. D'autres ont cru devoir ajouter à l'étendue, l'*impénétrabilité*, la *mobilité* et l'*inertie*. L'observation des corps célestes, ou plus généralement la physique des grands corps, a démontré la nécessité d'une force par laquelle toutes les parties tendissent ou pesassent les unes vers les autres selon une certaine loi, et l'on a admis l'*attraction*. [...] Les opérations les plus simples de la chimie, ou de la physique élémentaire des petits corps, a fait recourir à des *attractions* qui suivent d'autres lois.[93]

It was precisely this latter concern which informed Diderot's earlier pages on attraction, and which will give rise to his 1761 *Essai sur la cohésion des corps*.

Diderot presents Maupertuis's thesis as a further step in this cumulative process, indicative of the historical dynamism of scientific explanation. Just as the development of cosmic and corpuscular physics required an enlarged conceptual framework, so the growth of biology has justified the elaboration of a futher principle: 'L'impossibilité d'expliquer la formation d'une plante ou d'un animal, avec les attractions, l'inertie, la mobilité, l'impénétrabilité, le mouvement, la matière ou l'étendue, a conduit le philosophe Baumann à supposer encore d'autres propriétés dans la nature.'[94] Maupertuis himself had been aware of the particular logic behind his thesis, expressing succinctly the dynamism involved: 'Plus on a eu de phénomènes à expliquer, plus il a fallu

---

91. *OPhil.*, p.224; Her., ix.77.
92. Cf. Winter, p.231.
93. *OPhil.*, p.224-25; Her., ix.77-78.
94. *OPhil.*, p.225; Her., ix.78. Cf. Winter, p.29.

charger la matière de propriétés.'[95] Like Diderot, he is certain that the workings of organic matter must be accounted for by reference to a purely physical principle. Previous, metaphysical attempts to transcend the inadequacies of mechanism are dismissed by Maupertuis as misguided and sterile. Diderot reports his dissatisfaction with such theories as Cudworth's 'plastic natures', continuous creation and preformation, described by Maupertuis as 'systèmes désespérés'.[96]

Omitting Maupertuis's extensive aprioristic refutations, Diderot stresses only those points of the original account relevant to his own materialistic monism, notably the fact that such artificial schemes stem from theologians' fears of reducing the sphere of direct divine action. As both he and Maupertuis point out, the alternative course of attributing further properties or forces to matter was seen as a dangerous step in the direction of materialism. Diderot's dismissal of these fears as ungrounded is no doubt somewhat less sincere than Maupertuis's; nevertheless they agree that ignorance of the essence of matter should not stand in the way of constructive speculations on its observable forms and characteristics:

[Maupertuis] a pensé que tous ces systèmes peu philosophiques n'auraient point eu lieu, sans la crainte mal fondée d'attribuer des modifications très connues à un être [la matière] dont l'essence nous étant inconnue, peut être par cette raison même, et malgré notre préjugé, très compatible avec ces modifications.[97]

Biological organisation, therefore, even in the view of the relatively orthodox Maupertuis, may safely be attributed to the intrinsic workings of matter. Maupertuis is confident that his theories avoid the drawbacks of both mechanistic and metaphysical alternatives,[98] whilst remaining compatible with Christian theology as he sees it. Indeed he will be outraged by the materialist implications Diderot draws from them, accusing the latter, not entirely without reason, of misrepresentation and distortion.

ii. *Maupertuis's system: Diderot's exposition*

a. The basic principle

According to Diderot, Maupertuis postulates four basic modifications of matter: desire, aversion, memory and intelligence. These correspond to the sentient

95. Maupertuis, *Œuvres*, ii.146-47, section 14.
96. Maupertuis, *Œuvres*, ii.141, section 5. See Roger, *Les Sciences de la vie*, for detailed accounts of these systems.
97. *OPhil.*, p.225; Her., ix.78.
98. As Ehrard puts it, he had tried to trace 'une voie moyenne entre un mécanisme trop simpliste et le renoncement à une explication purement naturelle' (*L'Idée de nature*, i.218).

and intellectual faculties observed in advanced organisms. Consequently, if their existence is made essential to matter, no further principle need be invoked at the organic level: basic matter contains all that is necessary for its development into organised forms. Diderot's account appears to be an objective report of Maupertuis's thesis:

Mais quel est cet être? quelles sont ces modifications? Le dirai-je? Sans doute, répond le docteur Baumann. L'être corporel est cet être; ces modifications sont le *désir*, l'*aversion*, la *mémoire*, l'*intelligence*; en un mot, toutes les qualités que nous reconnaissons dans les animaux, que les Anciens comprenaient sous le nom d'*âme sensitive*, et que le docteur Baumann admet, proportion gardée des formes et des masses, dans la particule la plus petite de matière, comme dans le plus gros animal.[99]

In fact, however, these lines contain a distinct element of overstatement of Maupertuis's position, and thus anticipate Diderot's reworking of the principle.[100] Maupertuis does not advocate the acceptance of four new properties within matter, as Diderot implies. He posits only a single additional concept, characterising this by reference to those animal faculties to which it seems most closely analogous: 'Il faut avoir recours à quelque principe d'intelligence, à quelquechose de semblable à ce que nous appelons désir, aversion, mémoire' (*Œuvres*, ii.147). This distortion goes unnoticed in the accounts of both Casini (*Diderot 'philosophe'*, p.204, 205) and Winter (p.232).

Apart from this initial misrepresentation, whose value will become apparent later,[101] Diderot's main concern at this point is to put forward, with dubious sincerity, Maupertuis's self-defence against anticipated objections from the upholders of orthodoxy. Maupertuis states that his proposal poses no greater threat to orthodoxy than does the attribution of a degree of intelligence to the beasts, a principle accepted by contemporary, anti-cartesian theologians: 'S'il y avait, dit-il, du péril à accorder aux molécules de la matière quelques degrés d'intelligence, ce péril serait aussi grand à les supposer dans un éléphant ou dans un singe, qu'à les reconnaître dans un grain de sable.'[102] For Diderot, however, this association implies the value of Maupertuis's thesis as a tool against metaphysical dualism: if intelligence is accepted as a material property, at any level, the self-sufficiency of matter is guaranteed. It is therefore with heavy irony that he concurs with Maupertuis's assessment of the orthodoxy of his speculation: 'Il est évident qu'il ne soutient son hypothèse, avec quelque chaleur, que parce qu'elle lui paraît satisfaire aux phénomènes les plus difficiles,

---

99. *OPhil.*, p.225-26; Her., ix.78-79.
100. See below, iii.b.
101. See below, B.iii.b.1.
102. *OPhil.*, p.226; Her., ix.79.

sans que le matérialisme en soit une conséquence.'[103]

In fact he will go on to reverse his apparent acceptance of both the substance and the implications of Maupertuis's theory. In the meantime, however, he puts this issue on one side in favour of an exposition of certain specific aspects of the theory less subject to ambiguity of interpretation. Diderot's own philosophy of life will require an adequate account of animal reproduction, transformism and the emergence of consciousness from basic matter, and on these issues, Maupertuis's ideas serve as a valuable catalyst.

b. Reproduction and transformism

1. Basic theory

Maupertuis's account of the processes involved in heredity is a consistent development of his basic principles. As such it is reported objectively by Diderot. The sentience and intelligence possessed by matter produce a form of molecular memory which is responsible for the transmission of characteristics from one generation to the next. Germ cells are considered to be a kind of essence distilled from all parts of the body and therefore containing within their memory patterns, details of the entire organism: 'L'élément séminal, extrait d'une partie semblable à celle qu'il doit former dans l'animal, sentant et pensant, aura quelque mémoire de sa situation première; de là, la conservation des espèces et la ressemblance des parents.'[104] Although modern theory has rejected Maupertuis's version of the origin of germ cells, the remainder of his account bears a striking resemblance to present-day genetics, which often expresses the storage and transmission of genetic data by means of an analogy with memory.

2. Sterility and deformity

This theory allows Maupertuis to account for sterility and congenital malformations – examples of the deviant forms in which Diderot had shown so keen an interest in earlier years.[105] Sterility results quite simply from the breakdown of the memory mechanism; deformity from an imbalance of seminal elements or, again, memory malfunction:

Il peut arriver que le fluide séminal surabonde ou manque de certains éléments; que ces éléments ne puissent s'unir par oubli, ou qu'il se fasse des réunions bizarres d'éléments surnuméraires? de là, ou l'impossibilité de la génération, ou toutes les générations monstrueuses possibles. [...] Quand l'impression d'une situation présente balancera ou éteindra la mémoire d'une situation passée, en sorte qu'il y ait indifférence à toute situation, il y aura stérilité; [...][106]

103. *OPhil.*, p.226; Her., ix.79.
104. *OPhil.*, p.226-27; Her., ix.79.
105. See above, 2, C.iii.
106. *OPhil.*, p.227; Her., ix.80. Cf. Laidlaw, 'Diderot's teratology', p.117-18 and *passim*.

It is quite possible that Maupertuis's account of sterility was instrumental in persuading Diderot to abandon his notion of an electrical cure, as the two models are scarcely compatible.[107]

3. Mutation and transformism

Maupertuis invokes the same principle to account for the mutation of species. Any aberration or variation within the organisation of an individual creature may arise through the malfunctions outlined above; it is then perpetuated by the normal process of molecular memory. Maupertuis saw this as an important principle of diversity within nature;[108] Diderot is more interested, however, in the potential unity such a process offers. It appears to corroborate his own intuition earlier in the *Interprétation* of a uniquely dynamic form of unity within nature:

Qui empêchera des parties élémentaires, intelligentes et sensibles de s'écarter à l'infini de l'ordre qui constitue l'espèce? de là, une infinité d'espèces d'animaux sortis d'un premier animal; une infinité d'êtres émanés d'un premier être; un seul acte dans la nature.[109]

Maupertuis's psychic properties may appear to bear little resemblance to the molecular energy based on movement and attraction which Diderot seeks to integrate into a vision of unity. Nonetheless, the fact that organic diversity, together with a materialist account of the development (if not the origin) of life forms, can be shown to derive from Maupertuis's principles, makes Diderot's eventual reformulation of the thesis into a more recognisably energetic form all the more crucial.

4. Biogenesis and regeneration

The orthodox Maupertuis is able to account even for the apparently spontaneous phenomena of biogenesis and regeneration with equanimity. He assumes that they result from particular processes of molecular memory operating within matter which is in some way pre-programmed, and does not therefore feel obliged to explain the initial organisation of the elements involved. His ideas are essentially a reworking of the germ theory, and do not appear to recognise fully the implications of Needham's and Trembley's discoveries in this area.[110] Diderot's exposition, drawing on several sections of the *Système de la nature*, makes no attempt to clarify matters:

Certains éléments auront pris nécessairement une facilité prodigieuse à s'unir constam-

---

107. Cf. above, A.iv.b.
108. Maupertuis, *Œuvres*, ii.148*-149*, section 45.
109. *OPhil.*, p.227; Her., ix.80. Cf. above, A.i.
110. Cf. above, 1, D.i.b.

ment de la même manière; de là, s'ils sont différents, une formation d'animaux microsco-
piques variés à l'infini; de là, s'ils sont semblables, les polypes, qu'on peut comparer à
une grappe d'abeilles infiniment petites, qui n'ayant la mémoire vive que d'une seule
situation, s'accrocheraient et demeureraient accrochées selon cette situation qui leur
serait la plus familière.[111]

Spontaneous generation, then, involves the cohesion of heterogeneous material elements; regeneration, the cohesion of homogeneous elements. In neither
case is it clear under what physical conditions the cohesion occurs, nor where
the necessary memory of a previous, analogous situation originates. Diderot
must have felt the inadequacy of an account which failed to investigate the
origin of life and organisation, and perhaps intends the obscurity of his version
to reflect the weaknesses of the original.

Nevertheless, even this aspect of Maupertuis's thesis is not without its value
for Diderot's philosophy. On the one hand, memory seems to perform a similar
rôle in these phenomena to that which Diderot had ascribed to the principle of
optimum organisation. It serves as a directing element, establishing a viable
pattern and channelling the energies of matter into the realisation of that pattern.
Both function as intrinsic, materialist alternatives to the final causes rejected by
Diderot and Maupertuis alike. When *sensibilité* is elaborated in place of molecular
memory, transfer of the latter's directive purpose to *sensibilité* will be facilitated
by this initial analogy with optimum organisation.

Of almost equal significance is the fact that Diderot borrows from Maupertuis
the image of the swarm of bees, which is play so central a rôle in the *Rêve de
d'Alembert*. There too it will be associated with optimum organisation and the
special characteristics of combination within aggregates of organic matter. As
yet, however, it is treated literally, as an illustration of mere contiguity between
molecules ('s'accrocheraient') rather than of true organic continuity.[112]

The absence of a concept of continuity is common to Maupertuis and Diderot
at this time, and is reflected in their examination of the emergence of organic
consciousness.

c. Corporate consciousness

Maupertuis's explanation of the emergence of a corporate consciousness from
the fragmented psychic properties of basic matter is straightforward. His assumption of molecular intelligence enables him to envisage the development of
higher intellectual faculties as a purely cumulative process. A strictly materialist
philosophy (such as Diderot's is to become) has to account for the emergence

---

111. *OPhil.*, p.227; Her., ix.80. Cf. Maupertuis, *Œuvres*, ii.146* (section 40), p.149*-150*
(section 46), p.151*-152* (section 47), p.154*-155* (section 51).
112. Cf. above, A.iii.b.

of sentience and intelligence *ab initio*; for Maupertuis, however, these faculties are intrinsic even to the most basic levels of matter. Moreover, they are considered to be absolute and irreducible: the element may possess quantitatively less of each than the aggregate, but this is purely on account of its relative size. There is no suggestion of gradation or potentiality within the distribution of these qualities. Consequently their combination is a purely mechanical process: corporate consciousness is nothing more than a multiplication of elemental consciousness:

Mais chaque élément perdra-t-il en s'accumulant et en se combinant, son petit degré de sentiment et de perception? Nullement, dit le docteur Baumann. Ces qualités lui sont essentielles. Qu'arrivera-t-il donc? Le voici. De ces perceptions d'éléments rassemblés et combinés, il en résultera une perception unique, proportionnée à la masse et à la disposition; et ce système de perceptions dans lequel chaque élément aura perdu la mémoire du *soi* et concourra à former la conscience du *tout*, sera l'âme de l'animal.[113]

The inadequacies of such a thesis are evident, though it was to be some years before Diderot himself became aware of them. In the first place, it enables no discrimination to be made between the sentient and intellectual faculties of organisms except on grounds of size. The largest organism possesses the greatest amount of intelligent matter, and consequently the most advanced faculties: no allowance is made for specialisation within organic material. This amounts to a denial of heterogeneity which Diderot will later consider unacceptable.

There is also a parallel lack of discrimination between sentience, perception, memory and consciousness. Even for the sensualist, these faculties represented distinct stages of the intellectual process: Maupertuis's account makes no attempt to establish a hierarchy or progression from one to another. This is a direct result of his literal treatment of molecular intelligence without reference to a principle of latency or gradation.

Nevertheless, this important issue has at least been raised by Maupertuis. It is perhaps no accident that Diderot's reformulation of Maupertuis's thesis will take him in the direction of a concept which will ultimately enable him to resolve the particular difficulties associated with a materialist account of consciousness. It will be 1769 before an explicit solution is elaborated, yet already the conceptual materials with which Diderot will construct his account are present in his thought in a rudimentary form.

iii. *Maupertuis's system: Diderot's interpretation and reformulation*

Diderot immediately realises that, despite Maupertuis's protestations to the contrary, his reduction of consciousness to a function of the inherent properties

---

113. *OPhil.*, p.228; Her., ix.81. Cf. Maupertuis, *Œuvres*, ii.155*-159*, sections 52-56 and *passim*.

of matter has a valuable contribution to make to a monist materialist philosophy of nature. He wastes no time in ensuring that the reader shares this realisation. The latter part of section 50 is devoted to a highly ambiguous interpretation of the implications of Maupertuis's thesis; section 51 presents an alternative version supposedly free of any taint of materialism, but in fact far more rigorously materialist than the original.

a. Interpretation: the issue of natural unity

1. The method of Diderot's interpretation

Diderot's interpretation of Maupertuis is presented as an illustration of the methodological priniciple advocated earlier in the *Interprétation*: that the validity of a hypothesis should be tested by developing and examining its furthest implications: 'Pour ébranler une hypothèse, il ne faut quelquefois que la pousser aussi loin qu'elle peut aller.'[114] As he moves from exposition to analysis of Maupertuis's ideas, Diderot indicates that this is the method he intends to adopt. He will reveal to the reader certain consequences of Maupertuis's thesis incompatible with orthodoxy, and thereby show it to be unacceptable: 'C'est ici que nous sommes surpris que l'auteur, ou n'ait pas aperçu les terribles conséquences de son hypothèse, ou que, s'il a aperçu les conséquences, il n'ait pas abondonné l'hypothèse. C'est maintenant qu'il faut appliquer notre méthode à l'examen de ses principes.'[115] Diderot is, of course, quite insincere. He will indeed demonstrate unacceptable aspects of Maupertuis's ideas, but with the requirements of materialism, not orthodoxy, in mind. Moreover, he will be guilty, on more than one occasion, of deliberate confusion and misrepresentation.

2. Selection of the issue of natural unity

Diderot selects the issue of unity, by which the *Interprétation* has already set great store, as the vehicle for his examination of Maupertuis. The initial question he poses to Maupertuis appears innocent enough: 'Je lui demanderai donc si l'univers, ou la collection générale de toutes les molécules sensibles et pensantes, forme un tout ou non.'[116] In fact the terms of this question, as Maupertuis will quite rightly point out in his *Réponses*, are lacking in proper definition. Unity is not the simple, monolithic concept Diderot seems to imply. The alternatives he will lay before Maupertuis are not, therefore, exhaustive. He suggests that Maupertuis must answer this opening question in either the affirmative or the negative, and allows no scope for qualification.

If Maupertuis denies the existence of unity within nature, Diderot claims,

114. *OPhil.*, p.224; Her., ix.77.
115. *OPhil.*, p.228-29; Her., ix.82.
116. *OPhil.*, p.229; Her., ix.82.

neither philosophy nor theology can be satisfied. If there is no continuity between phenomena, there can be neither coherent interpretation nor evidence of a co-ordinating, ordering God: 'S'il me répond qu'elle ne forme point un tout, il ébranlera d'un seul mot l'existence de Dieu, en introduisant le désordre dans la nature; et il détruira la base de la philosophie, en rompant la chaîne qui lie tous les êtres.'[117] If on the other hand Maupertuis is prepared to accept the unity of nature, there is, according to Diderot, only one form this unity can take. The process of cumulative development outlined to account for the transition from element to organism would continue to operate up to the cosmic level: the sum of elementary perceptions or intelligences would amount to nothing less than a world soul:

S'il convient que c'est un tout où les éléments ne sont pas moins ordonnés que les portions [...] le sont dans un élément, et les éléments dans un animal, il faudra qu'il avoue qu'en conséquence de cette copulation universelle, le monde, semblable à un grand animal, a une âme; que, le monde pouvant être infini, cette âme du monde, je ne dis pas est, mais peut être un système infini de perceptions, et que le monde peut être Dieu. Qu'il proteste tant qu'il voudra contre ces conséquences, elles n'en seront pas moins vraies.[118]

The final implication drawn by Diderot, then, is that Maupertuis's thesis leads to a philosophy indistinguishable from spinozist pantheism.

3. The validity of Diderot's conclusions

Maupertuis himself, however, hotly disputed the conclusion that the only alternatives open to him were discontinuity or vitalistic pantheism. He claimed Diderot's argument to be invalid in that it depended upon two quite different senses of *tout*: as general, physical unity and as a specific form of psychic unity.[119] He also objected to Diderot's analogy between the universe and an animal (p.166*-174*). Both objections are justified;[120] at the same time, however, the individual stages of Diderot's argument are logically tenable and reveal something of his genuine reservations.

Firstly, it is true that Maupertuis's account gives an excessive degree of autonomy to the individual particles of matter, to the extent that the unity of nature is threatened. Although the *Système de la nature* envisages organic

---

117. *OPhil.*, p.229; Her., ix.82.
118. *OPhil.*, p.229; Her., ix.82-83.
119. Maupertuis, *Œuvres*, ii.172*-176*.
120. Cf. Venturi, *La Jeunesse de Diderot*, p.302-303. As Venturi points out, what Maupertuis really objected to was Diderot's application at a metaphysical level of what had been intended as purely scientific notions. Cf. Wartofsky, 'Diderot and the development of materialist monism', p.296-97.

combination as a process subject to divine direction,[121] the fact remains that molecular intelligence and independence is equivalent to that possessed by highly developed organisms. There is therefore no reason to assume that the elements are in any way bound to follow the requirements of an imposed pattern, external or intrinsic. Each is an individual agent.

It is also true that universal consciousness is the logical outcome of molecular psychism, if the universe is assumed to be a continuum (a point Diderot denies, incidentally, in the *Rêve de d'Alembert*).[122] Diderot could not be expected to concur with a principle which appeared to lead directly back to the spinozism he had clearly abandoned by 1753. Venturi makes the mistake of taking Diderot's criticism of Maupertuis in this respect as an insinuation of the *philosophe*'s own vitalism.[123] It is Maupertuis rather than Diderot whose philosophy deserves Venturi's label *panthéisme vitaliste* (p.285). A similar misconception is evident in Greenwood's thesis.[124] Greenwood claims that the *Interprétation* fixes Diderot's metaphysical position after the experimentation of the *Pensées philosophiques* and the *Lettre sur les aveugles*, and that that position is pantheistic.[125]

In both respects, therefore, Maupertuis's thesis is unacceptable to Diderot in its original form; the revised version he proposes will tend to eliminate both psychism and excessive molecular autonomy.

Maupertuis's objections fail to recognise that the real distortion of his argument lies elsewhere. For Diderot introduces a more important conceptual confusion over the term *âme*. It is this which enables him to extrapolate from psychism at the molecular level, via corporate organic consciousness, to a world soul. Maupertuis's account of the first two stages of this process had referred to a *perception élémentaire* at the molecular level,[126] from which arise a *perception unique* (p.157*, section 54) and eventually a *faculté intellective* in the organism. He is at considerable pains to distinguish this *faculté intellective* from the immortal, spiritual soul of man (p.160*-161*, section 57). Diderot, on the other hand, knows no such scruples, applying the term *âme* unhesitatingly to corporate consciousness (organic or cosmic). Maupertuis's use of the term in the context

---

121. 'Les éléments eux-mêmes doués d'intelligence s'arrangent et s'unissent pour remplir les vues du créateur' (Maupertuis, *Œuvres*, ii.168, section 67).

122. See below, 5, D.iii.b.

123. *La Jeunesse de Diderot*, p.301. Cf. Vernière, *Spinoza et la pensée française*, p.598.

124. T. Greenwood, 'The philosophy of nature of Denis Diderot', *Revue de l'Université d'Ottawa* (1947), p.169-86. Cf. also L. J. Forno, 'The cosmic mysticism of Diderot', *Studies on Voltaire* 153 (1975), p.134, and Ehrard, *L'Idée de nature*, i.244.

125. 'Diderot himself experienced both deism and atheism, ultimately finding mental rest by merging both in an uncompromising pantheism' (p.172).

126. Maupertuis, *Œuvres*, ii.155*, section 52; p.156*, section 54.

of organic consciousness had been limited to the analogy he drew between his properties and the Ancients' *âme sensitive*.

It is this intentional confusion of the psychological with the spiritual soul which allows Diderot to insinuate the need for a reformulation of Maupertuis's principle, in section 51. The entire development devoted to the theme of unity will then prove to have been little more than a smokescreen for Diderot's real intentions: to expose the materialist potential of Maupertuis's ideas, their true *terribles conséquences*.

4. Diderot's praise of Maupertuis

For, despite the misgivings noted above, Diderot is well aware of the valuable, original content of Maupertuis's work. Section 50 of the *Interprétation* closes with an extensive tribute to Maupertuis. The particular value of his speculation is shown to lie within the very issue which preoccupies Diderot during these years: the organisation of living matter. Moreover, its only serious drawbacks are declared to be its inability to account adequately for unity within nature and for the existence of an ordering God:

L'hypothèse du docteur Baumann développera, si l'on veut, le mystère le plus incompréhensible de la nature, la formation des animaux, ou plus généralement celle de tous les corps organisés; la collection universelle des phénomènes et l'existence de Dieu seront ses écueils.[127]

The latter, however, is of no relevance to Diderot[128] and the former will be overcome by his reformulation. The way is therefore open for explicit praise:

Mais, quoique nous rejetions les idées du docteur d'Erlang, nous aurions bien mal conçu l'obscurité des phénomènes qu'il s'était proposé d'expliquer, la fécondité de son hypothèse, les conséquences surprenantes qu'on en peut tirer, le mérite des conjectures nouvelles sur un sujet dont ne se sont occupés les premiers hommes dans tous les siècles, et la difficulté de combattre les siennes avec succès, si nous ne les regardions comme le fruit d'une méditation profonde, une entreprise hardie sur le système universel de la nature et la tentative d'un grand philosophe.[129]

Profond – hardi – grand; this trio of epithets[130] leaves little doubt as to the positive impression the *Système de la nature* has made on Diderot. Section 51, too, despite its apparent tone of disapproval, is based on the assumption that Maupertuis's approach is essentially sound.

127. *OPhil.*, p.230; Her., ix.83.
128. Despite Rostand's claim that Diderot is still, in 1754, a deist (a claim made, it seems, on the strength of this extract, with no reference to Diderot's earlier writings), in 'La molécule et le philosophe', p.7. Cf. his *Biologie et humanisme*, p.217.
129. *OPhil.*, p.230; Her., ix.83.
130. Reinforced by Diderot's triple substantives: *fécondité – conséquences surprenantes – mérite*.

b. *Reformulation: sensibilité*

Section 51 of the *Interprétation* is remarkable for its density and richness. Subtle distortion of Maupertuis blends with Diderot's original thought, which is itself so concisely stated and yet so far-reaching that it is little wonder Maupertuis was unable to do more than protest feebly at the use Diderot had made of his ideas.

1. Initial misrepresentation

Consciously or unconsciously, Diderot manipulates the original material provided by Maupertuis in such a way that his own proposal stands out in all its originality and potential. In the first place he again conveniently ignores the fact that Maupertuis's speculations on corporate consciousness had referred to a *faculté intellective* and the *Interprétation*'s *conséquences* to a spiritual soul. This enables him to declare Maupertuis's ideas over-ambitious:

Si le docteur Baumann eût renfermé son système dans de justes bornes et n'eût appliqué ses idées qu'à la formation des animaux, sans les étendre à la nature de l'âme, d'où je crois avoir démontré contre lui qu'on pouvait les porter jusqu'à l'existence de Dieu, il ne se serait point précipité dans l'espèce de matérialisme la plus séduisante, en attribuant aux molécules organiques le désir, l'aversion, le sentiment et la pensée.[131]

For Szigeti, the irony of these lines lies in the fact that Maupertuis's concepts are actually far from materialistic, despite the use Diderot makes of them.[132] He makes no comment, however, on the distortions introduced by Diderot. For it must be recalled that Maupertuis has not posited desire, aversion, sentience and thought at the molecular level, but only a single principle analogous to these four faculties,[133] another distinction which Diderot chooses to ignore.[134]

He implies that since it is not the scientist's job to explain the soul, Maupertuis's multiplicity of terms may be abandoned. In fact Maupertuis had been no less concerned about economy of explanation than Diderot, and had stressed that the additional principle he was proposing was essential for an adequate account of organic phenomena, just as attraction had proved necessary at the cosmic level:

Dans l'explication de ces phénomènes, nous n'avons plus qu'une règle à observer; c'est que nous y employions le moins de principes et les principes les plus simples qu'il soit possible. [...] Une philosophie qui n'explique point les phénomènes ne saurait jamais passer pour simple, et celle qui admet des propriétés que l'expérience fait voir nécessaires, n'est jamais trop composée.[135]

131. *OPhil.*, p.230; Her., ix.83-84.
132. Szigeti, *Denis Diderot: grande figure*, p.70-71.
133. And in fact had specified *mémoire* and *intelligence*, rather than *sentiment* and *pensée*.
134. Cf. above, B.ii.a.
135. Maupertuis, *Œuvres*, ii.152-53.

Nevertheless, Diderot's insistence that Maupertuis ascribes four additional properties to basic matter makes it appear that the principle of economy has been contravened. His proposed amendment will therefore have the character of a simplification.

2. Diderot's alternative

Substitution of 'sensibilité': Maupertuis had made it clear that his proposals were purely speculative and open to modification, should some adequate alternative be put forward. [136] Diderot responds to this invitation by suggesting that the only additional property needed is *sensibilité*: 'Il fallait se contenter d'y supposer une sensibilité mille fois moindre que celle que le Tout-Puissant a accordée aux animaux les plus voisins de la matière morte.' [137] As an alternative to desire, aversion, sentience and thought, this formulation represents a useful quantitative reduction; it is here that its superficial attraction lies. As an alternative to what Maupertuis had actually proposed, however, its value is less immediately apparent. *Sensibilité* is a single property, capable of accounting for the phenomena of desire, aversion, sentience and ultimately thought (at least within the sensualist framework accepted by Diderot and Maupertuis alike). As such it appears to differ in no essential respect either from the Ancients' *âme sensitive* or its modern counterpart, Maupertuis's own *principe d'intelligence*.

This, indeed, is the interpretation laid on it by various critics, from Janet, who speaks of 'ultra-spiritualisme', [138] to Crocker, who reproaches Diderot for 'a metaphysical acrobatics that attempted in some way to spiritualise matter without giving the impression of so doing'. [139] Mayer, too, considers that Diderot universalises intelligence here, [140] and Szigeti conflates *perception* with *sensibilité*, claiming that Diderot has simply bypassed the issue of the duality of organic and inorganic matter and left himself open to idealism. [141] This is an observation which is correct to a certain extent, [142] but nor for the reasons Szigeti gives.

Maupertuis dismisses Diderot's substitution of *sensibilité* for molecular perception as a mere linguistic trick, arguing that sentience and perception are identical: 'Il ne veut pas que la perception puisse appartenir à la matière; et croit que la sensation peut lui appartenir [...] Est-ce sérieusement que M.

136. ii.146, section 13 and p.164, section 61. Cf. *Réponse aux objections de M. Diderot, Œuvres*, ii.183.
137. *OPhil.*, p.230-31; Her., ix.84.
138. 'La philosophie de Diderot', p.698.
139. *Diderot the embattled philosopher*, p.142.
140. *Diderot homme de science*, p.215.
141. *Denis Diderot: une grande figure*, p.71.
142. Cf. below, 4, A.

Diderot propose cette différence?', [143] and again: 'lorsqu'il propose de substituer à la *perception élémentaire* du docteur Baumann, *une sensation semblable à un toucher obtus et sourd*, c'est un vrai jeu de mots pour gagner ou surprendre le lecteur, une sensation étant une vraie perception' (ii.182).

Certainly, given the ambiguities of section 50, it is possible to conclude that Diderot is indulging in wordplay to disguise a genuine support for Maupertuis's thesis – that his suggested alternative is indeed meaningless, and deliberately so. At the same time, however, such an interpretation is less tenable in the light of Diderot's apparent misgivings about Maupertuis's thesis.

Conceptual advantages of 'sensibilité': It appears, in fact, that Maupertuis has once again failed to appreciate the import of Diderot's criticism. For the *Interprétation*'s elaboration of *sensibilité* reveals that far from merely tinkering with the *Système de la nature*'s concept, as Maupertuis thought, Diderot is attempting to put forward a qualitatively distinct alternative. Having demonstrated – and exaggerated – the dangers inherent in Maupertuis's molecular psychism, Diderot suggests *sensibilité* as a concept which avoids both the sterility of mechanism and the unacceptable excesses of molecular consciousness and self-determination. He seeks to reduce organic activity to a more mechanistic level (despite the overall anti-mechanistic tendency of his early thought) in order to maintain the coherence and unity of nature which Maupertuis had threatened.

Thus the operation of *sensibilité* is presented as an essentially automatic (non-conscious) process:

En conséquence de cette sensibilité sourde et de la différence des configurations, il n'y aurait eu pour une molécule organique quelconque qu'une situation, la plus commode de toutes, qu'elle aurait sans cesse cherchée par une inquiétude automate, comme il arrive aux animaux de s'agiter dans le sommeil, lorsque l'usage de presque toutes leurs facultés est suspendu, jusqu'à ce qu'ils aient trouvé la disposition la plus convenable au repos. [144]

In the first place, *sensibilité*, unlike Maupertuis's principle, is not absolute and irreducible. Its effects are subject to modification by physical circumstances beyond those of sheer size ('la différence des configurations'). [145] Secondly, Diderot stresses that this property cannot be equated with consciousness. The analogy he draws between the *molécule sensible* and a sleeping animal makes it clear that the former's intellectual faculties are in a state of suspension: the molecule is not actively intelligent or conscious. The accumulation of terms associated with potentiality – *sourde, en sommeil, usage ... suspendu* – indicates

143. Maupertuis, *Œuvres*, ii.180.
144. *OPhil.*, p.231; Her., ix.84.
145. Cf. above, B.ii.c.

how close Diderot comes, as early as 1753, to considering *sensibilité* dormant at the molecular level, active within the organism.

Diderot comes equally close to taking the complementary step of envisaging *sensibilité* as a force rather than a property, by means of the implicit parallel he establishes between *sensibilité* and attraction. In the first place, the account quoted above reveals that the special function of *sensibilité* in organic matter is that of bringing about a state of optimum organisation, the rôle fulfilled for Maupertuis by memory and for Diderot, at the inorganic level, by attraction.[146] A further analogy between the processes of organic and inorganic interaction lies in the susceptibility of both attraction and *sensibilité* to modification in their effects by physical conditions, and the participation of both in an energetic complex of action, reaction and adaptation.

This correspondence renders Diderot's failure to extend *sensibilité* to the inorganic world less serious. For whereas Maupertuis had shown no hesitation in extending his thesis not only to plants but even to metals and other minerals,[147] Diderot is wary of following suit. Indeed, such a step would lead him directly back to the very animism he is seeking to avoid. For the time being, attraction appears to offer an adequate account of inorganic interaction; the gap between animate and inanimate matter will eventually be bridged in terms of, firstly, the energetic parallel and, secondly, the concept of potentiality.

At the organic level, however, *sensibilité* provides a satisfactory account of the phenomena which had troubled Diderot since his earliest speculations. Biological diversity and apparent purpose can both be explained, since *sensibilité* involves principles both of heterogeneity and of co-ordination (through optimum organisation). Diderot is therefore able to recommend his alternative whole-heartedly to Maupertuis's readers: 'Ce seul principe eût satisfait, d'une manière assez simple et sans aucune conséquence dangereuse, aux phénomènes qu'il se proposait d'expliquer, et à ces merveilles sans nombre qui tiennent si stupéfaits tous nos observateurs d'insectes.'[148] *Sensibilité* does indeed satisfy the criterion of economy and has the ambiguous merit of offending neither orthodoxy nor materialism: whether divinely imparted or intrinsic to matter, it avoids the animism distasteful to theologian and Diderot alike.

Semantic advantages of sentience: The definition with which Diderot closes his reformulation not only reiterates the essential features of *sensibilité*, but sheds

146. Cf. above, A.ii.a.2 (Diderot); B.ii (Maupertuis).
147. Maupertuis, *Œuvres*, ii.150*, 151*, section 47. Cf. the comment of Maupertuis's French editor, the abbé Trublet, in 1754: '[Il] donne l'instinct à chaque partie la plus petite de la matière, et forme tout avec cela, sans cette distinction de M. de Buffon entre matière brute et matière organisée' (quoted in Venturi, *La Jeunesse de Diderot*, p.313).
148. *OPhil.*, p.231; Her., ix.84.

additional light on the reasons behind Diderot's decision to retain sentience (after his encounter with Buffon) as the key to organic matter. Although these final lines refer to *sensation* rather than *sensibilité*, the term which Diderot will adopt permanently in later works, there is no contradiction between the two. For both suggest a purely physical sentience in diametrical opposition to the psychic overtones of Maupertuis's thesis:

[Maupertuis] eût défini l'animal en général, *un système de différentes molécules organiques, qui, par l'impulsion d'une sensation semblable à un toucher obtus et sourd que celui qui a créé la matière en général leur a donné, se sont combinées jusqu'à ce que chacune ait rencontré la place la plus convenable à sa figure et à son repos.*[149]

The analogy of touch (to be contrasted with Maupertuis's 'semblable à ce que nous appelons *désir, aversion, mémoire*')[150] suggests the process of contact and bonding which will be *sensibilité*'s major function, together with its essential mode of operation: action and reaction. Dieckmann gives a rather different interpretation of Diderot's choice of terminology, treating Diderot's scientific philosophy of life as an expression of his general sensitivity to the natural scene,[151] a view shared by Trahard, Hazard and even Varloot,[152] but emphatically rejected by Winter (in part, ironically, on account of evidence provided by another of Dieckmann's articles[153] that *sensibilité* was already a crucial *biological* concept in the eighteenth century).[154] She concludes (p.38):

Die 'sensibilité générale' als Grundhypothese der Diderotschen Naturerklärung ergibt sich also nicht nur notwendig als Basis einer einheitlichen Naturphilosophie, wenn man wie Diderot die Eigengesetzlichkeit und Unableitbarkeit der Lebensphänomene erkennt, sondern ist darüber hinaus eng mit der naturwissenschaftlichen Problematik seines Jahrhunderts verknüpft.

Implications and sources of 'sensibilité': Lefèbvre considers that Diderot has attempted here to unite mechanism and idealism into a coherently materialist synthesis, and failed. For him, Diderot posits an elementary material version of Leibniz's monad, which combines the disadvantages of both the alternatives Diderot had sought to transcend: 'c'est une particule mécanique, chargée cependant d'une ébauche de conscience et de finalité métaphysique' (*Diderot*, p.149). It would appear from the foregoing that neither of these criticisms holds

149. *OPhil.*, p.231; Her., ix.84-85.
150. Cf. above, B.ii.a.
151. 'Diderots Naturempfinden und Lebensgefühl', p.57-83.
152. P. Trahard, *Les Maîtres de la sensibilité française* (Paris 1932), ii.150; P. Hazard, *La Pensée européenne au XVIIIe siècle* (Paris 1946), ii.154; Varloot, 'Diderots Philosophie im *Rêve de d'Alembert*', p.710, n.2.
153. 'Théophile Bordeu und Diderots *Rêve de d'Alembert*', p.55-122.
154. Winter, p.36. Cf. also below, B.iii.b.2, section four, *Implications and souces of 'sensibilité'*.

water. *Sensibilité* is not conscience, and the finalism admitted by Diderot is of a strictly physical kind. The criticism may be validly applied to Maupertuis's thesis – Niklaus, for example, judges Maupertuis's attempt to bring together monad and matter as an impossible compromise between two opposed conceptions of the world[155] – but rather less so to Diderot's reworking of it. Dieckmann argues that Maupertuis had given the molecule the psychological content of Leibniz's monads without their metaphysical connotations; that Diderot's concept of the sentient molecule goes back to this as well as to Buffon and ultimately Aristotle's entelechy, and that despite his denial of metaphysics Diderot's idea of *sensibilité* is thus associated with the persistent current of hylozoism within western thought.[156] It needs to be made clear, however, that this association is of the loosest kind, since it is precisely the 'psychological content' adopted by Maupertuis which Diderot's version eliminates. In any case, Diderot's mention (in his closing definition quoted above) of *impulsion*, with its connotations of movement and the activation of potential energy, makes it tempting to envisage *sensibilité* as an essentially dynamic (that is, energetic) phenomenon.

Sensibilité, then, involves rather more than the mere *jeu de mots* perceived by Maupertuis. It is a rich and detailed concept, wholly different from Maupertuis's in its materialistic content, if not yet comfortably integrated into Diderot's maturing philosophy of nature.

Scholars have proposed a host of sources for Diderot's concept of *sensibilité*, ranging from Hobbes, Colonna and Leibniz to Glisson, Whytt and Haller. It seems probable that in 1753 the most direct influence on Diderot would have been that of La Mettrie, who had conflated Haller's concepts of irritability (muscular contractility) and sensibility (an analogous function, but exclusive to nerve tissue) into a single general property of living substance. Generally, however, there was a wide variation in both terminology and philosophical content of systems drawing on such concepts, making it virtually impossible to trace their precise relationship to Diderot's earliest formulation of *sensibilité*.

Moreover, what might be termed the philosophical and the physiological strands of this particular web of ideas (the first operating primarily through Colonna and later Robinet, but traceable to classical thought via alchemy and theosophy; the latter through the neurophysiological researches of Glisson, Whytt and later Haller) merge to some extent in the work of the Montpellier school (which itself, incidentally, claimed Hipprocrates and Stahl as its intellectual ancestors) whose most notable exponent, Bordeu, together with his pupils Ménuret and Fouquet, exercised a far more clearly demonstrable influence on

---

155. Niklaus (ed.), *Rêve de d'Alembert*, p.xxii, n.
156. Dieckmann, 'Bordeu und Diderots *Rêve de d'Alembert*', p.110.

the *later* development of Diderot's thought, an influence which for reasons of chronology could not be operative in the *Interprétation*.

Sensibilité cannot, in 1753, be pinned down to any particular source or movement: for all its suggestive resonances it is really no more (one might, in view of its future destiny in Diderot's thought, be entitled to say 'no less') than an intuition entirely of Diderot's own making.[157]

iv. *Postscriptum*

Diderot's provocative speculations on Maupertuis's *Système de la nature* are followed by a section whose title, *Des instruments et des mesures*, appears to mark a complete break with the subject matter of the preceding few pages. On closer analysis, however, section 52 proves to be of considerable relevance to *sensibilité*. It contains two apparently casual observations which serve to prolong the reflections associated with Diderot's analysis of Maupertuis.

The section opens with a declaration of sensualist principle: 'Nous avons observé que, puisque les sens étaient la source de toutes nos connaissances'.[158] In itself a commonplace, this takes on a fresh significance in the present context. *Sensibilité* has been explicitly related to the operation of the senses ('un toucher obtus et sourd'); Diderot is now implying that advanced intellectual faculties may derive ultimately from this elementary molecular principle. This is a conclusion which will be drawn explicitly in later years. Already it is a more refined concept than Maupertuis's assumption of a literal molecular intelligence, or Diderot's own earlier references to the presence of thought in matter.[159] The materialist reader would be unlikely to miss the subtle echo of the previous section.

In the final sentence of the section Diderot implicitly defends *sensibilité* by cutting short a likely objection to his (and indeed Maupertuis's) hypothesis. Common sense would be inclined to protest that such a property cannot be proved to exist, since it cannot be directly detected and measured, that is to say,

157. Further details of this historical background may be found in: Callot, *Six philosophes français*, p.112-13; Crocker, 'John Toland et le matérialisme de Diderot', p.294; Delaunay, 'L'évolution philosophique et médicale du biomécanisme', p.1370, 1373, 1377; Dieckmann, 'Bordeu und Diderots *Rêve de d'Alembert*', p.67-117; Ehrard, *L'Idée de nature*, i.52-53, 238-39; Ehrard, 'Matérialisme et naturalisme', p.190-95; P. Hazard, *Quatre études* ('Les origines philosophiques de l'homme de sentiment') (New York 1940), p.138; P. Hoffmann, 'L'idée de liberté dans la philosophie médicale de Bordeu', *Studies on Voltaire* 88 (1972), p.773-74; F. Laplassotte, 'Quelques étapes de la physiologie du cerveau', p.601-10; Moravia, 'Dall' "Homme machine" all' "homme sensible"', p.641-42; Perkins, 'Diderot and La Mettrie', p.52-57; Roger, *Les Sciences de la vie*, p.632-51; Thielemann, 'Diderot and Hobbes', p.255-56; Vartanian, *La Mettrie's L'Homme machine*, p.18-23, 74-75, 32-89; Vernière, *Spinoza et la pensée française*, p.601.

158. *OPhil.*, p.231; Her., ix.85.

159. Cf. above, 1, D.iii.b.

subjected to the procedures of quantitative science. Diderot challenges the view that the essence of scientific advance lies in such procedures: 'Combien d'industrie, de travail et de temps perdus à mesurer qu'on eût bien employés à découvrir!'[160]

These lines confirm Diderot's elevation of the intuitive interpretation of nature to a status of respectability (expressed earlier in the work) and validate not only the specific concept of *sensibilité* but his entire philosophical approach. They herald a range of speculations which will occupy the years between the *Pensées sur l'interprétation de la nature* and the *Rêve de d'Alembert*, leading Diderot from his first formulation of *sensibilité* to its full integration in a philosophy of energy, life and unity.

Conclusion

In many ways the bold introduction of *sensibilité* in the *Pensées sur l'interprétation de la nature* was ahead of its time, insofar as the internal evolution of Diderot's thought was concerned. With no clear idea as yet of the exact relationship between organic and inorganic matter, Diderot is faced with two equally unpalatable alternatives. He must either acknowledge that the qualitative differences between dead and living matter present an insuperable obstacle to their interaction, or accept a philosophy of vitalism. Without applying the principle of latency there is no satisfactory way in which he can extend *sensibilité* to all matter; thus it remains a partial concept only, in conflict with his quest for unity within nature.

Several other inconsistencies and tensions prevent him from realising the full potential of *sensibilité*. In the first place, he remains unsure as to whether it should be considered a property of matter, or a force. This reflects his analogous uncertainty over the nature of electricity and points up the abundant hints of ideas yet to be elaborated: the possibility of a specifically organic form of energy, the tentative identification of energy and matter, and the related suggestions that one form of matter, or indeed one form of energy, may be convertible into another.

Furthermore, he speculates that energy may hold the key to natural unity, only to confuse the issue by proposing it subsequently as the possible source of heterogeneity within material forms, at the molecular level.

On more than one occasion he implies that quantitative change may lead to qualitative transformation, yet at the same time persists in seeing molecular interaction in terms of contiguity rather than the continuity which alone could effect such a process.

160. *OPhil.*, p.231; Her., ix.85.

93

Finally, his reaction against Maupertuis's molecular psychism remains at a largely instinctive level. He evidently fears its vitalistic implications, yet fails to see that these derive as much from the absence of any discrimination, in Maupertuis's account, between the various psychic faculties concerned as from his use of the concept of *un principe d'intelligence* at molecular level. Diderot himself will pass through a phase where he tends to overlook the need for an element of gradation between sentience, intelligence, and their various manifestations in higher beings. Nor has he explained here how *sensibilité* obviates vitalism, and this is another problem which will recur frequently in his future writings.

None of this, however, must be allowed to detract from, on the one hand, the major development represented by Diderot's introduction of the concept – however rudimentary as yet – of *sensibilité*, and, on the other, the host of minor conceptual advances made within this complex and fascinating work.

4. Transition: from the *Pensées sur l'interprétation de la nature* to the *Rêve de d'Alembert* (1754-1769)

THE evolution of Diderot's thought during this second transition period can be traced in both public and private writings, but his intuitions are expressed increasingly within the privacy of his own correspondence, the limited circulation of the *Correspondance* edited by Grimm, or the semi-anonymity of the *Encyclopédie*. Consequently, chronology becomes uncertain, and it is no longer possible to trace clear linear developments from one writing to another.

Nevertheless there is a definite sense of progress in the years which separate the hesitancies of the *Interprétation* from the masterly declarations of the *Rêve de d'Alembert*. It is essentially a period of transition, in which Diderot comes gradually to terms – not always systematically, and sometimes, it seems, not even consciously – with the philosophical issues which needed to be resolved before the hastily intuited concept of *sensibilité* could be given full expression.

It is also a period invariably neglected by scholars. Even Winter devotes only a few lines to acknowledging its importance and gives the sketchiest of indications as to where the significant developments lie (p.24, 133). When she does invoke works from this period in some detail, it is, ironically, in an anti-evolutionary sense.[1]

As far as Diderot's letters are concerned, I concur with Benot's contention that 'elles doivent être considérées comme de véritables œuvres, et non comme une correspondance privée'.[2] For on several occasions they constitute, as he puts it, 'une sorte de laboratoire intellectuel permanent' where fruitful philosophical ideas are first tried out. Proust has made a similar observation on the subject of Diderot's *Encyclopédie* articles, labelling them 'le jalon qui nous manquait jusqu'ici entre les *Pensées sur l'interprétation de la nature* et le *Rêve de d'Alembert*'[3] and explaining the relationship in terms which complement the evolutionary character of Diderot's thought: 'Il y a un saut *qualitatif* [...] de l'*Interprétation de la nature* au *Rêve de d'Alembert* [...]. Mais ce saut se fait après une longue et lente évolution *quantitative*, et c'est l'*Encyclopédie* qui l'a préparé' (p.110; Proust's emphasis). Nevertheless, it is undoubtedly, as Varloot stresses

---

1. p.230-31. Cf. also p.29-30, 31 n., and below, 5, D.iii.a.
2. Y. Benot, 'Diderot épistolier: de ses lettres à ses livres', *Pensée* 99 (1961), p.99.
3. 'L'*Encyclopédie* dans la pensée et dans la vie de Diderot', *Europe* 405-406 (1963), p.115.

in his review of Proust's *Diderot et l'Encyclopédie*, the letters of 1759 and 1765 which must take precedence in this rôle.[4]

A. The temptation of vitalism

i. *Letter to Sophie Volland, 15 October 1759*

Almost six years after the completion of the *Pensées sur l'interprétation de la nature*, Diderot writes to Sophie Volland of a philosophical discussion at Le Grandval. In the course of a lighthearted exchange on the subject of a famous contemporary who claimed to have discovered the secret of eternal life,[5] Diderot turns to the more serious question of actually defining life. He concludes a shrewd and witty argument with the proposition that life is an indestructible property of organic matter. He calls this a *paradoxe*, a term he reserves for his more outrageous theories, for example the *Paradoxe sur le comédien*. Remarks in the later *Réfutation d'Helvétius* imply that such propositions require extraordinary care in their manner of presentation (AT, ii.272):

Il n'y a rien qui veuille être prouvé avec moins d'affectation, plus dérobé, moins annoncé qu'un paradoxe. Un auteur paradoxal ne doit jamais dire son mot, mais toujours ses preuves: il doit entrer furtivement dans l'âme de son lecteur, et non de vive force.

Winter points out further instances of the significance Diderot attaches to the term in *Pages contre un tyran* (p.230). The lines: 'Le paradoxe n'est donc qu'une proposition contraire à l'opinion commune; or, l'opinion commune pouvant être fausse, le paradoxe peut être vrai' (Lew., ix.683) seem particularly relevant to this instance.

In many ways this reported conversation reads like a first draft of the *Entretien avec d'Alembert* of a decade later. The same questions are posed, similar solutions offered, albeit in far cruder form, and similar objections parried. Varloot's account of Diderot's materialism quotes this letter at length, as a preliminary sketch of the *Rêve de d'Alembert*'s themes, but does not analyse it, save to comment that Diderot does not as yet deny the existence of inanimate matter.[6] Winter calls it the key to understanding the *Rêve de d'Alembert*'s central tenet (p.29) but accords it only a brief examination (p.29-30, 230), mistakenly implying that its conclusions are identical with those of the *Rêve de d'Alembert*.

---

4. 'Sur Diderot et l'*Encyclopédie*', *Pensée* 3 (1963), p.93.
5. A swindler who styled himself comte de Saint-Germain and enjoyed a decade of success in Paris and Versailles before fleeing to pursue his deceptions in London (*Corr.*, ii.281).
6. 'Diderots Philosophie im *Rêve de d'Alembert*', p.711. The implication that such a denial later occurs will not be borne out by my interpretation. See below, p.102, and 5, D.iii.b.

4. Transition: 1754-1769

a. Diderot's paradox: the eternity of life

'Dites-moi, avez-vous jamais pensé sérieusement ce que c'est que vivre? Concevez-vous bien qu'un être puisse jamais passer de l'état de non-vivant à l'état de vivant?' (*Corr.*, ii.282). Diderot's opening challenge recalls instantly one of the major issues raised in the *Pensées sur l'interprétation de la nature*: the nature of living matter. In 1753 he had attempted to distinguish the animate from the inanimate by two criteria, organisation and mobility, but ultimately left the question unresolved. Now, however, he rejects explicitly both the possibilities he had previously entertained.

He concedes that certain physical signs of life may be attributed to the mechanical principles of organisation and motion. Growth and decay, together with alternating motion and rest, constitute evidence that life is present; they are not, however, responsible for its creation. Life is, quite simply, of a qualitatively distinct order: 'Un corps s'accroît ou diminue; se meut ou se repose; mais s'il ne vit pas par lui-même, croyez-vous qu'un changement, quel qu'il soit, puisse lui donner de la vie? Il n'en est pas de vivre comme de se mouvoir; c'est autre chose.' The difference between mobility and life appears to lie in the fact that life cannot be produced where it did not previously exist, whereas motion can:

Un corps en mouvement frappe un corps en repos et celui-ci se meut. Mais arrêtez, accélerez un corps non-vivant, ajoutez-y, retranchez-en, organisez-le, c'est à dire disposez-en les parties comme vous l'imaginerez. Si elles sont mortes, elles ne vivront non plus dans une position que dans une autre.

This attack on the relevance of cartesian motion to vital phenomena makes explicit misgivings which had been implicit in Diderot's thinking since his earliest works.[7] The need for an alternative model is based partly on the quest for unity, for the mechanists' concept of motion was neither materialistic nor monistic; not only did it have to be imparted from outside,[8] it operated by means of external causal interconnections, rather than internal dynamism (p.286, 301). Here Diderot's ideas are rather closer in spirit to Leibniz than to Descartes, despite Vartanian's arguments for a parallel between cartesian physics and Diderot's materialism.[9] For, as Barber has pointed out, not only did Leibniz substitute motion for extension as the essential characteristic of matter, he also redefined movement as an energy form involving mass, that is the entirety of

---

7. Cf. above, 1, B.ii.b.2 and 1, D.iv.a: Diderot's use of *fermentation*.
8. Wartofsky, 'Diderot and the development of materialist monism', p.288, 301.
9. *Diderot and Descartes*, p.97-98, 118-19, 123, 204.

substance rather than simply the surface, extrinsic form of movement to which the cartesian dynamics referred.[10]

Such is Diderot's concern to deny the identity of mobility and life that he overlooks the analogy which will later become central to his theory of *sensibilité*. For Diderot was well aware that motion is not created *ab initio* by the collision of two bodies, but merely activated, and in future writings the principle of activation is transposed from motion to life. In addition he fails, as in the *Pensées sur l'interprétation de la nature*, to distinguish between contiguity and continuity in the combination of matter. His rejection of organisation as a means to the creation of life is thus unwittingly strengthened: 'Supposer qu'en *mettant à côté* d'une particule morte, une, deux, ou trois particules mortes, on en formera un système de corps vivant, c'est avancer, ce me semble, une absurdité très forte, ou je ne m'y connais pas' (*Corr.*, ii.282; my emphasis). Considered in such terms (of contiguity only) the proposition is indeed absurd, not that this prevented its appearance in the writings of materialist thinkers less sophisticated than Diderot, for instance Jean Meslier's declaration in 1718 that 'Tout [...] n'est qu'une suite ou effet naturel des parties de la matière et de la différente constitution ou construction des corps organiques qu'elles composent.'[11] Furthermore, by concentrating here on the process of creating life from exclusively inanimate matter, Diderot omits to acknowledge that the rôle of organisation might be rather different where the combination of mixed matter – some living, some not – is concerned. This initial restriction will prove to have an important bearing on his overall conclusion.

A further limitation implicit in Diderot's analysis of life lies in the fact that he fails to discriminate between basic life and the more highly developed animal faculties such as awareness of self. A similar confusion obtains between life and sentience. This leads to an overstatement of the weaknesses inherent in any theory based upon the mere juxtaposition of inert molecules, and lends an air of irrefutability to Diderot's argument (*Corr.*, ii.282):

Quoi! la particule *a* placée à gauche de la particule *b* n'avait point la conscience de son existence, ne sentait point, était inerte et morte; et voilà que celle qui était à gauche mise à droite et celle qui était à droite mise à gauche, le tout vit, se connaît, se sent? Cela ne se peut.

This *reductio ad absurdum* of the mechanistic approach to life may help Diderot

---

10. Barber, *Leibniz in France*, p.14. Cf. C. I. Iltis, 'Leibniz' concept of force', p.144. It must be acknowledged, however, that Leibniz recognised only mechanical force (motion), not gravitation or chemical force, so that his importance as a direct source is somewhat limited. Belaval, 'Note sur Diderot et Leibniz', p.445-46.

11. Quoted in Wade, *Clandestine organisation*, p.72. Similar ideas were expressed in his *Testament*, which circulated in the 1740s (p.73, 92).

to score a debating point, but it hinders his development of an adequate alternative, lacking as it does any suggestion of a qualitative (or indeed at this point even quantitative) difference between molecular and corporate levels of biological organisation.

For the provocative proposal which follows – that life and sentience are irreducible and indestructible properties of a certain type of matter – will lead Diderot directly to the kind of molecular psychism he had been seeking to avoid in his encounter with Maupertuis:[12]

Ce qui a ces qualités [la vie et le sentiment] les a toujours eues et les aura toujours. Le sentiment et la vie sont éternels. Ce qui vit a toujours vécu, et vivra sans fin. La seule différence que je connaisse entre la mort et la vie, c'est qu'à présent vous vivez en masse, et que dissous, épars en molécules, dans vingt ans d'ici, vous vivrez en détail.[13]

Here indeed is a paradox: when corporate life ceases, life at the molecular level, and with it sentience and consciousness of self, continues. Diderot thus sees only that the phenomena of life cannot be attributed to simple mobility and organisation,[14] not that the phenomena themselves are ill-defined.

b. Nutritive assimilation

1. Introduction and limitations

Diderot seeks to render his paradoxical theory more credible by reference to the process of nutritive assimilation in animals. Addressing himself to Mme d'Aine, he challenges her to deny that the diet of her dog Tisbé consists of anything other than living matter (*Corr.*, ii.283):

Attendez. Tisbé vit, n'est-il pas vrai? – Si ma chienne vit? Je vous en réponds; elle pense, elle aime; elle raisonne; elle a de l'esprit et du jugement. – Vous vous souvenez bien d'un temps où elle n'était pas plus grosse qu'un rat? – Oui. – Pourriez-vous me dire comment elle est devenue si rondelette? – Pardi, en se crevant de mangeaille, comme vous et moi – Fort bien; et ce qu'elle mangeait, vivait-il, ou non? – Quelle question! Pardi non, il ne vivait pas. – Quoi! une chose qui ne vivait pas appliquée à une chose qui vivait est devenue vivante, et vous entendez cela?

The growth of a developed organism is shown to result from the assimilation of new matter through the processes of ingestion and digestion. This assimilation is presented in terms of contiguity ('appliquée'), which Diderot has declared incapable of generating life and which does, indeed, preclude the possibility of total incorporation and hence qualitative transformation of the matter assimilated. The organism nevertheless remains wholly living. Consequently, Diderot implies, and contrary to all appearances, the foodstuffs themselves must be alive.

12. See above, chapter 3.
13. *Corr.*, ii.283.
14. Cf. Winter, p.230.

This passage raises several important issues indicative of the tensions and confusions still inherent in Diderot's speculations. The concept of nutritive assimilation will eventually provide the answer to this question of the creation of life, but for the moment it raises more problems than it solves.

In the first place it introduces an unconscious logical inconsistency into Diderot's argument. He had previously contended that the movement or rearrangement of two *inert* particles could not produce life. His exchange with Mme d'Aine, on the other hand, refers to a mixed system, in which part of the matter is already animated. If like is to be compared with like, it is this process which should be considered analogous to the transmission of motion from a moving body to one at rest. It will be some time before Diderot realises this discrepancy and draws the parallel correctly.

The passage also confirms Diderot's somewhat simplistic conception of vital functions. Mme d'Aine cites the highly developed emotional and cognitive powers displayed by her dog as evidence that it is alive. Diderot makes no attempt to rebut the absurd anthropomorphism of her attitude, and thus allows its implications to pass unchallenged: if life in the organism is equated with its manifestations in the form of affective and rational faculties, the same equation must apply at the molecular level, since life has been posited as an absolute, irreducible property of organic matter.

This recurring lack of definition is compounded by Diderot's failure, in this necessarily brief exposition of his views, to consider the place of inorganic matter in the process of nutritive assimilation.

2. The inorganic kingdom: vitalism

Despite the absence of any explicit reference in this letter or the conversation it reports, to what we would call the mineral kingdom, inorganic matter clearly has a part to play in the growth of animal organisms. For eighteenth-century biologists believed the ingestion of food in plants and animals to be essentially analogous: 'Les plantes prennent leur nourriture par la suction des racines et des feuilles, comme les animaux par la bouche ou par les suceoirs qui leur servent de bouche; il se fait dans les plantes des digestions, des sécrétions, des évacuations,' etc.'[15] Diderot's acceptance of this belief is confirmed by his observations in the article 'Acmella'.[16] Inorganic elements are thus necessarily involved in a single food-chain linking mineral to plant to animal. Since Diderot's

15. In the anonymous *Encyclopédie* article 'Histoire naturelle' (viii.228). It is interesting to note that several elements in this article (notably the attitudes towards botanical classification and the respective roles of the *observateur* and the *génie* in scientific investigation) recur in Diderot's own writings.
16. See above, 2, C.iv.

paradox requires that plant matter eaten by animals be living, it follows that the minerals ingested by plants are, in their turn, alive. Consequently they must also share all the faculties which have not yet been differentiated from their underlying vital principle – sentience, emotion and reason.

There is a certain amount of evidence in the letter that Diderot was unaware of these vitalistic consequences of his paradox. In the first place he gives no sign that he considered the omission of minerals from his speculations on nutritive assimilation as a flaw. Might he not, therefore, simply have been oblivious of the logical necessity of including them? The remainder of the Grandval conversation also appears to limit itself to the subject of organic matter only. For instance, the ridicule of Diderot's friends is directed at the principle – outrageous enough at the time – of endowing plants with the same class of vital faculties as animals: 'Le reste de la soirée s'est passé à me plaisanter sur mon paradoxe. On m'offrait de belles poires qui vivaient, des raisins qui pensaient' (*Corr.*, ii.283). In 1769 the fictional d'Alembert will object not to living pears or thinking grapes, but to feeling stones, which appear to present a far more paradoxical philosophical problem, especially if Diderot shares the belief expressed in the article 'Histoire naturelle' that the animal and plant kingdoms are rather more closely analogous to each other than either is to the minerals: 'Les animaux et les végétaux ont beaucoup plus de rapports les uns aux autres, qu'ils n'en ont aux minéraux' (*Enc.*, viii.228). This would imply that it was not until 1769 that Diderot gave minerals their proper place in his theory of life.

Critics have therefore claimed that this conversation concerns only a special organic matter, similar to Buffon's *molécules organiques*. This is, for instance, the interpretation of Roger, who asserts that these lines reinforce the concept of a qualitatively distinct living matter.[17] Further evidence in support of this thesis emerges when Diderot returns to the question of the survival of molecular life after the death of an organism.[18] The matter involved here is again strictly organic since, although it appears inert, it has been part of an organised life form.

Nevertheless, other points militate against the viewpoint that Diderot has simply chosen to ignore the minerals here. His continuing concern with the issue of inorganic versus organic matter makes it improbable that he would have overlooked their involvement in nutritive assimilation (unlike the situation in the *Pensées sur l'interprétation de la nature*, where it was valid to consider *sensibilité* as a property unique to organic matter).

17. *Les Sciences de la vie*, p.617.
18. Examined in detail in the following section.

At the same time, too much significance should not be attached to the exclusively biological illustrations of his paradox. For Diderot's undefined concept of life at this time renders him incapable of accounting adequately for its presence in either a grape or a stone. The fact that he mentions only the former does not therefore mean that he feels one is fully elucidated and the other not. Consequently I must conclude that Diderot did in fact acquiesce to the vitalistic implications of declaring life eternal.

In the light of this interpretation it appears that 1769 will see not so much the extension of a concept (the inclusion of minerals in the nutritive chain) as a wholesale redefinition of its terms. Far from being the source of Diderot's vitalism, as critical opinion has frequently asserted,[19] universal *sensibilité* (with its active and inert categories) will prove to be the means by which Diderot eliminates vitalism.[20]

Despite the fact that Diderot appears to be moving away from materialism in 1759, his temporary deviation into vitalism is not without its advantages. It plays a crucial part within the dialectic of his thought.

c. Positive contribution of vitalism

As the Grandval conversation continues, Diderot applies his paradox to another specific case. If, as he has claimed, organic molecules retain their vital qualities after the 'death' of the organism to which they belonged, it may be that human remains should be looked upon in a new light:

Ceux qui se sont aimés pendant leur vie et qui se font inhumer l'un à côté de l'autre ne sont peut-être pas si fous qu'on pense. Peut-être leurs cendres se pressent, se mêlent et s'unissent. [...] Peut-être n'ont-elles pas perdu tout sentiment, toute mémoire de leur premier état? Peut-être ont-elles un reste de chaleur et de vie dont elles jouissent à leur manière au fond de l'urne froid qui les renferme.[21]

This rather startling idea is tempered to some extent by Diderot's hesitant introduction of an element of gradation: 'pas [...] tout', 'un reste', 'à leur manière'. He is, after all, aware of the need to distinguish quantitatively, if not qualitatively, between the life of the organism and that of the molecule. These lines are strongly reminiscent of Maupertuis's account of corporate consciousness: he too had posited the retention of psychic qualities at molecular level when an organism breaks down.[22]

Diderot goes beyond a mere paraphrase of Maupertuis, however, to speculate that there may even be qualitative differences between the two forms of life.

19. Cf. below, 5, D.iii.b
20. Cf. above, n.6.
21. *Corr.*, ii.283-84. The extension of this passage is studied later in the chapter, section ii.d.2.
22. See above, chapter 3.

Just as the sections of a polyp are clearly not identical with the whole creature, yet retain the potential to develop into whole polyps, so molecular life in general may be actually distinct from, yet potentially identical with the life of the organism (*Corr.*, ii.284):

Nous jugeons de la vie des éléments par la vie des masses grossières. Peut-être sont-ce des choses bien diverses. On croit qu'il n'y a qu'un polype; et pourquoi la nature entière ne serait-elle pas du même ordre? Lorsque le polype est divisé en cent mille parties, l'animal primitif et générateur n'est plus; mais tous ses principes sont vivants.

The term *principes* recalls the intuitions of the *Encyclopédie* article 'Arbre';[23] once again, as with *sensibilité* in the *Pensées sur l'interprétation de la nature*, Diderot comes very close to applying the concept of latency to life.

It is in this respect that vitalism makes a positive contribution. For his reference to 'la nature entière' is quite unambiguous. All matter, animate or inanimate, may be capable of participating in vital processes. Strictly speaking, the division between organic and inorganic is abolished. Diderot is not claiming, as he had earlier appeared to do, that all organic matter (and only organic matter) is living. He is making the far bolder assertion that all matter is organic and *therefore* living.

This is a fine distinction, but one which is crucial – paradoxically, in view of its vitalistic character – to the further development of Diderot's materialism. For it represents an incvitable and long-prepared reaction against the sterility of mechanism: by setting aside, temporarily, the reservations he had displaycd in the *Pensées sur l'interprétation de la nature*, and embracing vitalism, Diderot has acquired a position from which to reassess the whole range of issues involved in a monist, materialist account of life. Vitalism will thus prove to have been not an inconsistency within his thought, nor a passing weakness precipitated by the conflict of head and heart, but an indispensable dialectic stage.

The 'paradox' of external – and by implication universal – life which Diderot outlines to his Grandval audience directly reflects certain aspects of his public writings from this period. The exact chronological relationship between his letter to Sophie and the *Encyclopédie* articles which demonstrate similar lines of thought is difficult to ascertain. In the same month as Diderot reported his Grandval conversation to Sophie, he was working on the history of philosophy article 'Sarrasins' (*Corr.*, ii.294). The majority of articles concerned precede 'Sarrasins' alphabetically and, since he had completed his revision of the *Encyclopédie* by September 1761 (*Corr.*, iii.299), it is clear that Diderot wrote them considerably in advance of their eventual publication date of 1765. Chronologically, then, they are close to the letter. *Le temps de l'histoire* is not,

23. See above, chapter 2.

however, the same as *le temps de l'esprit*, as Chouillet has pointed out in his study of the evolution of Diderot's aesthetic philosophy,[24] and conceptually the articles are often closer to later writings.

'Naître' contains a more carefully phrased version of Diderot's 'paradox', but also takes the step of distinguishing explicitly between active and potential life, and thus looks ahead to another of his private writings, the crucial 1765 letter to Duclos; 'Inné' (and the closely related 'Toucher') examine the issue of gradation within animal sentience, indicating the means by which Diderot will transcend his vitalistic paradox in the *Rêve de d'Alembert*. Finally 'Locke' seeks to define more closely the relationship between *sensibilité* and life, anticipating the approach adopted by Diderot in his 1761 paper *Sur la cohésion des corps*.

A strictly chronological presentation has therefore been rejected in favour of an order which demonstrates more clearly these conceptual links.

ii. *'Naître'*

To a large extent, this article[25] repeats the substance of the Grandval conversation of 1759. Indeed Winter merely quotes a passage from the article as confirmation of the conclusions expressed in the letter (p.230-31). By virtue of its context, however, it is more comprehensive in its approach to the same issues.

a. Organisation and motion rejected as sources of life

Once again, Diderot is at pains to stress that neither the combination nor the motion of inert matter is sufficient to animate it. His rejection of organisation as the means by which life is initiated leads him, as in the letter, to the conclusion that life is an eternal property (*Enc.*, xi.10; Her., viii.47-48):

La vie ne peut être le résultat de l'organisation; imaginez les trois molécules *A*, *B*, *C*; si elles sont sans vie dans la combinaison *A*, *B*, *C*, pourquoi commenceraient-elles à vivre dans la combinaison *B*, *C*, *A* ou *C*, *A*, *B*? Cela ne se conçoit pas. [...] La vie est une qualité essentielle et primitive dans l'être vivant; il ne l'acquiert point; il ne la perd point.

An illuminating point, not evident in the letter, emerges from this version of the argument: it is clear that Diderot envisages organisation in terms of rearrangement, not of greater complexity. ABC is transposed to become BCA or CAB rather than elaborated into an entire alphabet (which would then have the potential of being converted into something 'organic' – words, and ultimately

---

24. *La Formation des idées esthétiques de Diderot*, p.10.
25. Lough and Proust accept Naigeon's attribution of this article to Diderot (Her., v.12, 208). In any case, as Winter has pointed out (p.231 n.), its textual similarity to the letter to Sophie leaves little doubt as to its authorship.

sentences). Little wonder, then, that it strikes him as a somewhat sterile concept.

Motion is dismissed on account of its qualitative disparity with life: living matter may be mobile, but mobile matter is not necessarily living: 'Il n'en est pas de la vie comme du mouvement; c'est autre chose: ce qui a vie a mouvement: mais ce qui se meut ne vit pas pour cela.'

b. A new departure: active and potential life

1. The concept stated

In elaborating this point, however, Diderot hits upon a major intuition. His main contention is still that neither motion nor organisation can produce life, but within this argument arises an implicit statement of the relationship between motion and organisation themselves. In the *Pensées philosophiques*, motion had been declared responsible for the development of organised *germes*, but incapable of bringing about the initial organisation.[26] By the time of the *Pensées sur l'interprétation de la nature*, Diderot had revised this view: organisation was held to result from combination and motion.[27] Now he offers a third formulation: that motion *results* from the combination of basic elements – the latter process having already effectively been equated with organisation (the ABC argument): 'Si l'air, l'eau, la terre, et le feu viennent à se combiner, d'inerts qu'ils étaient auparavant, ils deviendront d'une mobilité incoercible, mais ils ne produiront pas la vie' (*Enc.*, xi.10; Her., viii.48).

In this account, motion is not created (since Diderot believed it to be a universal property)[28] but activated. This is the first time he has juxtaposed the concept of active and potential motion – itself mentioned in his writings as early as the *Prospectus*[29] – with the question of motion's rôle in life. Thus at the same time as he denies motion a direct rôle in the passage from inanimate to animate matter, he is able to use it in a rather different and more positive way, as a source of analogy.

For life, too, may be visualised as a form of energy rather than as a static property of matter. Needham's philosophy, for instance, implied just such a conclusion, though reached via a somewhat different route from that of Diderot. As Roger explains, Needham made 'vitality' depend on complexity of organisation, itself governed by energetically determined chemical phenomena, so that 'la vie elle-même, au moins dans ses aspects élémentaires, n'est qu'une forme de l'affrontement des forces qui animent l'univers matériel'.[30] In Diderot's case,

---

26. See above, chapter 1.
27. See above, chapter 3.
28. Cf. above, chapter 1, and below, 5, A.i.
29. Cf. above, chapter 2.
30. Roger, *Les Sciences de la vie*, p.505-506.

the way is then open for extrapolation, at a structural level, from one form of energy to another. Just as there is both latent and kinetic motion – or indeed any force – there may be a potential and an active form of life: 'Il faut distinguer une vie inerte et une vie active: elles sont entre elles comme la force vive et la force morte: ôtez l'obstacle, et la vie inerte deviendra vie active.'[31] Later, Diderot will redefine this concept and view life more specifically as the effect, or manifestation, of a particular form of energy, and it is to the latter (*sensibilité*) that latency will be applied.[32] Nevertheless it is already an important refinement of his 1759 paradox.

2. Sources of the concept in Diderot's writings

This striking application of the latency principle to life is drawn directly from an analogy with motion. It is sustained, however, by a range of kindred concepts available to Diderot.

Within the biological sciences, several phenomena, notably the regenerative powers of both plant[33] and animal[34] afforded evidence of a potential for spontaneous growth and development within organic matter. Of even greater relevance is Diderot's long-standing belief in biogenesis,[35] which presupposes a capacity for organisation and animation at the most basic levels of matter. (The concept of *a*biogenesis had not yet been explicitly considered – nor could it be until the issue of organic versus inorganic was satisfactorily resolved.)

An alternative origin of Diderot's application of latency to the life force lies within the Aristotelian notion derived from Plato[36] of the triple faculties of the soul. This involved a belief in a hierarchy of vital faculties, each latent within its predecessor. Diderot's history of philosophy articles for the *Encyclopédie* show that he was familiar with both the basic principle and its corollary; it is mentioned in his account of the Eclectics' philosophy of soul transmigration ('Eclectisme'; Her., vii.98):

L'âme séparée du corps reste dans ses révolutions à travers les cieux ce qu'elle a le plus été pendant cette vie, ou rationnelle, ou sensitive, ou végétale. La fonction qui la dominait dans le monde corporel la domine encore dans le monde intelligible; elle tient ses autres puissances inertes, engourdies et captives

and, in simpler form, in the article 'Péripatéticienne': 'L'âme a trois facultés: la

31. *Enc.*, xi.10; Her.,viii.48. Winter quotes these lines as an anticipation of the *Rêve de d'Alembert*, but without further analysis (p.31, n.1).
32. Cf. below, 4, D.
33. Cf. above, chapter 2, 'Arbre'.
34. Cf. above, chapter 1.
35. Cf. above, chapter 1.
36. Roger, *Les Sciences de la vie*, p.73.

nutritive, la sensitive, et la rationnelle. La première contient les autres en puissance' (Her., viii.76). Here too is conceptual support for Diderot's emphasis on the processes of nutrition ('la [faculté] nutritive') as the key to the transition from inorganic to organic.

Although at this point, as with Diderot's biological sources, only potentiality within the organic realm is concerned, such ideas will prove to have played a major catalytic rôle when they are stripped of their metaphysical terminology and re-expressed as an integral part of Diderot's monism.

A final historical source with which Diderot was equally well acquainted is the Stoics' concept of chaos, which posits a basic matter, formless, yet containing all the resources necessary for the spontaneous emergence of life forms: 'C'est sous cet état [le chaos] que se présenta d'abord la matière, qui était la somme de toutes les choses revêtues de leurs qualités, le réservoir des germes et des causes, l'essence, la nature, s'il est permis de s'exprimer ainsi, grosse de son principe.'[37] Diderot had treated the issue of chaos in essentially identical terms in the *Apologie de l'abbé de Prades*,[38] which implies his acceptance of the underlying principles.

In combination, these disparate sources have confirmed Diderot's evolution towards his own, modern version of potential life, which he will subsequently elaborate and refine, but never abandon.

c. The circulation of matter

1. The principle stated

Diderot's reflections on the eternity of life and the essentially energetic nature of this phenomenon are closely bound up with the circulation of matter, a concept which appears quite suddenly in his thought and runs through the *Encyclopédie* writings of this period like a leitmotif.

The concept is only partially stated in 'Naître' itself, but its link with the other ideas expressed here is clear. The birth of an individual is seen as a relatively insignificant event within the context of a boundless, eternally living organic substance. Foetal development is continuous with postnatal existence, growth, and ultimately the decline and death of the individual. The first three of these stages are characterised by the accretion of organic molecules – their vital energy activated as each joins the living whole – and the latter stages by the same process in reverse. At no point is life either miraculously created *ab initio* or irrevocably extinguished (*Enc.*, xi.10; Her., viii.47):

A proprement parler, on ne *naît* point, on ne meurt point; on était dès le commencement

37. 'Stoïcisme'; Her.,viii.336. Lough and Proust accept Naigeon's attribution of this article to Diderot (Her., v.209).
38. Cf. above, chapter 2.

des choses, et on sera jusqu'à leur consommation. Un point qui vivait s'est accru, développé, jusqu'à un certain terme, par la juxtaposition successive d'une infinité de molécules. Passé ce terme, il décroît, et se résout en molécules séparées qui vont se répandre dans la masse générale et commune.

This idea, of a general mass of matter in circulation throughout a variety of forms, its vital energy alternately rendered dormant and reactivated, neatly complements not only Diderot's speculations on life in matter, but also his conviction of the unity of matter, especially insofar as energy is concerned.

2. Sources of the principle in Diderot's writings

Another *Encyclopédie* article, closely related in theme to 'Naître', 'Impérissable', makes the link between Diderot's own speculations and the body of classical materialist thought on which they draw. Here the circulation of matter is shown to depend upon the twin principle of the conservation of matter and energy. Since neither can be destroyed nor created anew, all phenomena must be interrelated as functions of energetic matter (*Enc.*, viii.187-88; Her., vii.507):

Ceux qui regardent la matière comme éternelle, la regardent aussi comme *impérissable*. Rien, selon eux, ne se perd de la quantité du mouvement, rien de la quantité de la matière. Les êtres naissants s'accroissent et disparaissent, mais leurs éléments sont éternels. La destruction d'une chose a été, est et sera à jamais la génération d'une autre. Ce sentiment a été celui de presque tous les anciens philosophes, qui n'avaient aucune idée de la création.

Diderot's final disclaimer serves only to emphasise the relevance of the circulation of matter thesis to any *modern* philosopher seeking a non-creationist account of the universe.

Several other articles confirm the classical sources involved:[39] 'Epicuréisme', for instance, dwells on the relative insignificance of individual organisms within the whole:

Il [l'univers] est éternel, puisqu'il n'a point commencé, et qu'il ne finira point. Cependant les êtres s'y meuvent, des lois s'y exécutent, des phénomènes s'y succèdent. Entre ces phénomènes, les uns se produisent, d'autres durent, et d'autres passent; mais ces vicissitudes sont relatives aux parties et non au tout. La seule conséquence qu'on puisse tirer des générations et des destructions, c'est qu'il y a des éléments dont les êtres sont engendrés, et dans lesquels ils se résolvent.[40]

Thus natural forms, whether organic or inorganic, physical causality and energy (in the basic form of motion) are all part of this universal flux. The same points are made, more succinctly, in the articles 'Héraclitisme':

39. A useful survey of the classical Greek background to these articles is given in P. Gay, *The Enlightenment: an interpretation* (London 1967), esp. p.72-126.
40. Her., vii.270-71. Attributed to Diderot by Naigeon.

Rien ne naît et rien ne périt. Tout change et tout s'altère.
[...] Dans la vicissitude générale, chaque être subit sa destinée, et la génération et la destruction sont un même fait vu sous deux aspects différents[41]

and 'Stoïcisme':

Elle [la matière] n'est pas stable, elle varie sans cesse, tout est emporté comme un torrent, tout passe, rien de ce que nous voyons ne reste le même.[42]

More recent thinkers are also credited with a belief in flux as the basic pattern of the universe, from Paracelsus:

Toute corruption est cause d'une génération[43]

and Bruno, where the principle is traced back to Pythagoras:

La matière est dans un flux perpétuel; et ce qui est un corps aujourd'hui ne l'est pas demain.
Puisque la substance est impérissable, on ne meurt point, on passe, on circule, ainsi que Pythagore l'a conçu[44]

to Leibniz:

Tous les corps sont en vicissitude; des parties s'en échappent continuellement; d'autres y entrent. [...] Conséquemment il n'y a ni génération, ni mort parfaite; tout se réduit à des développements et à des dépérissements successifs.[45]

In the case of Leibniz, even his theory of created monads as the basic units of matter is shown not to be exempt from the principle of flux (Her., vii.693):

Tout être créé est sujet au changement. La monade est créée; chaque monade est donc dans une vicissitude continuelle.

3. The rôle of energy
From Leibniz too comes an explicit statement that nature's own energy is

41. Her., vii.368. Attributed to Diderot by Naigeon. Diderot's admiration for Heraclitus's theories is mentioned by Momdzjan, 'La dialectique dans la vision du monde de Diderot', p.17. Several commentators on Heraclitus's philosophy have drawn attention to its dynamic nature. Smith's 'Heraclitus and fire' (p.125, 126) argues that, unlike earlier Greek thinkers, he proposes the idea of the world as a process, rather than an edifice; W. Heisenberg's *Physics and philosophy* (London 1959, p.61), that his doctrine comes close to modern physics in that his basic element of fire corresponds both to matter and to moving force, and thus to the twentieth-century view of energy as the substance from which all things and all activities arise. Cf. also Singh, 'Herakleitos and the law of nature', p.464; B. Russell, *History of Western philosophy* (London 1979), p.61.
42. Her., viii.339. Attributed to Diderot by Naigeon. C. C. Gillispie points out that 'For the Stoics, it is always the activity, and not the matter, in things which has ontological significance' (*The Edge of objectivity*, Princeton 1960, p.182).
43. 'Théosophes', Her., viii.376. Attributed to Diderot by Naigeon (Her., v.210).
44. 'Jordanus Brunus', Her., vii.559-60. Attributed to Diderot by Naigeon (Her., v.208).
45. 'Leibnitzianisme', Her., vii.699. Attibuted to Diderot by Naigeon (Her., v.208).

responsible for this state of flux: 'En général, il n'y a point de force, quelle qu'elle soit, qui ne soit un principe de changement' (Her., vii.693). A more detailed account of this relationship is given in 'Epicuréisme'. The growth and decay of composite bodies, organic or inorganic, is seen as a function of the energy inherent in all matter. Indeed the actual processes themselves are considered as modes of the motive force, a point which will not go unheeded by Diderot:[46] 'Les vicissitudes des composés ne sont que des modes du mouvement et des suites de l'activité essentielle des atomes qui les constituent' (Her., vii.272). 'Inaltérable' confirms the rôle of various forms of energy in flux: 'Il n'y a rien dans la nature qui soit *inaltérable*, le froid, le chaud, l'humidité, la raréfaction, le mouvement, la fermentation, etc., sont des causes d'altération qui agissent sans cesse.'[47] Whilst all these forces, and effects of forces, may be considered first and foremost in the context of the part they play in the long-term changes associated with the mineral world, they are not without broader relevance. Motion and fermentation have already contributed significantly to Diderot's theories of life; attraction (of which rarefaction, a state of matter, may be considered a manifestation)[48] came under consideration in the *Pensées sur l'interprétation de la nature* and will do so again shortly in *Sur la cohésion des corps*; in 1769 thermal energy will be given a crucial rôle in the emergence of life.

Nature, then, is not so much a collective phenomenon as a process, 'un seul acte', as he had speculatively described it in 1753.[49]

4. Universality of flux

Within this vision of circulating energetic matter it becomes difficult to assign boundaries between the inorganic and the organic. Indeed it is often impossible to discern whether a particular article refers to one or the other – or even both. Individual forms lose their meaning, except as transient phenomena whose essence is their very instability: only the whole possesses any kind of permanence. The article 'Production' reiterates this: 'il n'y a proprement dans la nature aucune *production*, aucune destruction absolue, aucun commencement, aucune fin; ce qui est a toujours été et sera toujours, passant seulement sous une infinité de formes successives'[50] with no attempt at discrimination between the commonly accepted kingdoms of matter.

46. See below, section C (*Sur la cohésion des corps*). Cf. also Wartofsky, 'Diderot and the development of materialist monism', p.319.
47. Her., vii.512. Lough and Proust accept Diderot's authorship of this asterisked article (Her., v.204).
48. Cf. *OPhil.*, p.208, and above, 3, A.ii.b.
49. Her., ix.35. Cf. above, chapter 3.
50. *Enc.*, xiii.423; Her., viii.136. This article clearly belongs to the same sequence as 'Naître' and 'Impérissable'. Lough and Proust accept Naigeon's attribution of it to Diderot (Her., v.209). Cf. below, n.53.

Moreover, several contemporary articles repeatedly suggest that the minerals are not exempt from flux. An anonymous addition to d'Alembert's article 'Terraquée' declares that the erosion of the earth's surface is of essentially the same order as the constant transformations undergone by nature as a whole: 'la surface de la terre, qui est ce que nous connaissons de plus solide, est sujette, comme tout le reste de la nature, à des vicissitudes perpétuelles'.[51] This was a principle emphasised by Rouelle, whose courses Diderot attended in 1754-1757; Rouelle is quoted by one of his students as declaring 'que la surface de notre globe est dans un état continuel de destruction'.[52] The equally anonymous article 'Incorruptible' extends the conclusion in more specific terms to other mineral phenomena, challenging the general assumption that such forms are permanent and marshalling a range of inorganic chemical reactions under the banner of general flux:

Il n'y a rien dans la nature d'incorruptible. Cependant la corruption ne se dit guère que des substances animales et végétales. On regarde les sels, les pierres, les métaux, etc. comme *incorruptibles*. Les sels se dissolvent, se décomposent, les pierres tombent en poudre, les métaux se réduisent en chaux, [...][53]

This suggestion of the universality of flux, of the potential participation of all matter in all forms, helps to explain Diderot's temporary adhesion to vitalism. In turn it is strengthened by his gradual acquisition of concepts – firstly nutritive assimilation and now, in 'Naître', latency – which will enable him to retain a belief in flux even after vitalism has been discarded. The activation of *sensibilité* will involve the circulation (through nutritive processes) of matter in its entirety, and the conceptual under-pinnings of *sensibilité* (the forces enumerated in 'Inaltérable') will already have been declared instrumental in maintaining the flux of nature.

Numerous seventeenth- and eighteenth-century 'sources' have been proposed for this complex of ideas within Diderot's thought, from Bacon: 'Certain it is that matter is in a perpetual flux and never at a stay',[54] Toland: 'perpetual

51. *Enc.*, xvi.165. Such a brief addition is unlikely to have been provided by an outside contributor, and may even have come from Diderot's editorial pen, although Lough and Proust have found no evidence in support of such an assumption. The relevance of this belief to Diderot's philosophy of nature is noted only by Momdzjan ('La dialectique dans la vision du monde de Diderot', p.263), though he does not identify the article in which it occurs.

52. P. Lemay, 'Les cours de G.-F. Rouelle', *Revue d'histoire de la pharmacie* 13 (1949) p.441.

53. *Enc.*, viii.656. The anonymous articles 'Permanent' and 'Incorruptible' appear to form a trilogy with 'Invariable', which does bear Diderot's asterisk. All take the form of negative definitions: 'Il n'y a rien de *permanent* dans le monde' (*Enc.*, xii.386); 'Il n'y a rien d'*invariable* dans la nature' (*Enc.*, viii.847; Her., vii.546). Cf. also 'Inaltérable'. Their close textual resemblances point to the possibility of their common authorship. Cf. above, n.50.

54. *Of the vicissitude of things, Works*, vi.512, quoted in L. K. Luxembourg, *Francis Bacon and Denis Diderot, philosophers of science* (Copenhagen 1967), p.106.

revolution of nature',[55] and Shaftesbury: 'The vegetables by their death sustain the animals, and animal bodies dissolved enrich the earth and raise again the vegetable world',[56] to Bonnet: 'Réduit en chaux, [le caillou] passera dans la substance d'une plante, de là dans celle d'un animal.'[57] Wade also indicates their presence in an anonymous 1738 manuscript, *Dissertation sur la formation du monde*: 'Point de termes plus proches que ceux-ci dans la nature: putréfaction, génération, génération, putréfaction [...]. Sans la mort, rien ne vivrait.'[58] Clearly, the concepts of nutritive assimilation, the circulation of matter and flux were common currency. The introduction of latency and *sensibilité*, however, are very much Diderot's own.

d. Remaining problems

1. Conceptual gaps

The concept of flux is not, however, solely responsible for Diderot's vitalism, as has already been demonstrated. Its principal source lies in the absence of any notion of gradation between the various levels at which life is manifested – molecular, corporate, and that of advanced animal functions. Despite his introduction of a category of potential life, this problem remains largely untouched.

'Naître' does attempt to establish a principle of gradation but in purely quantitative terms. The account of foetal growth and organic decay examined above (c.1) implies that life is something to be computed mathematically: the total of active life in any given organism may increase or decrease according to the temporary activation or deactivation of the vital energy possessed by each of its constituent molecules. Diderot elaborates this position as the article continues, stressing the paradoxical transience of the life of the organised aggregate by comparison with the indestructibility of molecular life (*Enc.*, xi.10; Her., viii.48):

Il y a encore la vie de l'élément, et la vie de l'agrégat ou de la masse: rien n'ôte et ne peut ôter à l'élément sa vie: l'agrégat ou la masse est avec le temps privé de la sienne; on vit en un point qui s'étend jusqu'à une certaine limite, sous laquelle la vie est circonscrite en tout sens; cet espace sous lequel on vit diminue peu à peu; la vie devient moins active sous chaque point de cet espace; il y en a même sous lesquels elle a perdu toute son activité avant la dissolution de la masse, et l'on finit par vivre en une infinité d'atomes isolés.

Such an account leaves little room for the chronological or hierarchical variations such as mobility, sentience and the higher animal faculties of emotion and intellect observed within the development of an organism. In part this

55. Quoted in Crocker, 'John Toland et le matérialisme de Diderot', p.291.
56. Quoted in Niklaus (ed.), *La Lettre sur les aveugles*, p.98, n.33.
57. Quoted in Roger, *Les Sciences de la vie*, p.651.
58. Quoted in Wade, *The Clandestine organisation*, p.236.

results from Diderot's continuing conception of the combination of matter in terms of contiguity ('juxtaposition successive').[59] Qualitative transformations, whereby both part and whole are metamorphosed in a process of coalescence, are thus automatically excluded. More crucial, however, is the fact that he does not, as yet, draw any distinction between basic vital energy and life itself ('la vie devient moins active'). The force and its manifestations, the phenomena for which it is responsible, are still equated. These two conceptual gaps rob his latency theory of much of its usefulness and allow free rein to the vitalist implications of this phase of his thought.

2. Extreme expressions of vitalism

In both the letter to Sophie and 'Naître', Diderot seeks to extend his concept of eternal life on a personal, sentimental plane. The two passages are sufficiently complementary in thought to warrant joint study.

In 1759 Diderot extrapolates from his reported dialogue into a direct address to Sophie. Although this stands apart by virtue of its personal and subjective quality, and although he is at pains to stress the purely hypothetical nature of his speculation, it nevertheless represents the logical consequences of the letter's thesis.

If molecular life is indestructible, it may be, Diderot claims, that such phenomena as physical sensation, emotional response and purposeful action also survive the disintegration of the individual. Human relationships themselves might therefore continue after death (*Corr.*, ii.284):

O ma Sophie, il me resterait donc un espoir de vous toucher, de vous sentir, de vous aimer, de vous chercher, de m'unir, de me confondre avec vous, quand nous ne serons plus! S'il y avait dans nos principes une loi d'affinité, s'il nous était réservé de composer un être commun, si je devais dans la suite des siècles refaire un tout avec vous, si les molécules de votre amant dissous venaient à s'agiter, à se mouvoir et à rechercher les vôtres éparses dans la nature! Laissez moi cette chimère; elle m'est douce, elle m'assurerait l'éternité en vous et avec vous.

Whimsical though this passage appears, as long as the concept of life remains undefined, the continued existence at molecular level of its various manifestations cannot be excluded. Indeed Diderot's use of the term 'chimère' refers less to any logical inconsistency in the idea than to the likelihood of his and Sophie's molecules actually reuniting, among the myriad possible recombinations of matter.

The same principle informs the speculation which follows Diderot's proposal of eternal life in 'Naître' (*Enc.*, xi.10; Her., viii.48):

59. Cf. above, c.1.

c'est pour celui qui est fortement instruit de cette philosophie, que l'urne qui contient la cendre d'un père, d'une mère, d'un époux, d'une maîtresse, est vraiment un objet qui touche et qui attendrit: il y reste encore de la vie et de la chaleur: cette cendre peut peut-être encore ressentir nos larmes et y répondre; qui sait si ce mouvement qu'elles y excitent en les arrosant, est tout à fait dénué de sensibilité?

Certainly the notion is less extravagantly expressed here than in the letter. There is no 'loi d'affinité' which operates after death and enables the molecules of human individuals who were close in life to seek each other out again (though it is impossible to know whether this amounts to a rejection of the idea on Diderot's part or purely a sense of what is proper in an *Encyclopédie* article).

Nevertheless, the same problems arise; indeed it is more difficult here to understand how Diderot envisaged the survival of highly developed and refined emotional faculties at elemental level, since the life of such elements would be inert. To persist in seeking 'un reste de vie' is to relinquish totally the conceptual benefits of introducing a principle of potentiality, whose ostensible advantage was to exclude active life from all but the organism,

In the letter, such speculation could have been interpreted more generously. Diderot had after all, in the *Pensées sur l'interprétation de la nature*, stressed the desirability of evaluating any philosophical thesis by way of its furthest implications.[60] This extreme vitalist stand could then have been seen as a stage in his own thought akin to the dialectical treatment meted out to Maupertuis.[61] To return to the issue, however, merely serves to demonstrate the tensions within his thought during these years of transition.

In these early writings – the letter to Sophie and related *Encyclopédie* articles – the problems and confusions appear at times to outweigh the positive conceptual gains made by Diderot. Gradually, however, the balance shifts. Other *Encyclopédie* articles such as 'Inné', 'Toucher' and 'Locke' contain material which will eventually enable Diderot to transcend the limitations evident in his speculations elsewhere in the same vast work. Precise relationships remain impossible to discern, since the alphabetical and by implication chronological order of conceptually related articles is often belied by an apparent lack of cross-fertilisation between the ideas they contain.

B. *Sensibilité*

A second cluster of *Encyclopédie* articles is concerned with the subject of physical sentience – the phenomenon to which Diderot applies (at this stage) the

60. Cf. above, chapter 3.
61. Cf. above, chapter 3.

conventional contemporary label of *sensibilité*. These writings see the emergence of several important concepts which Diderot will use in elaborating his own, specialised version of *sensibilité* as the key to his scientific philosophy of life. Much of the content of these articles is little more than standard sensualism, but nonetheless provides many of the elements for a highly original philosophical synthesis.

i. *Conceptual relationship between life and* sensibilité

On just two occasions in the *Encyclopédie* it is suggested that the life remaining in organic matter after the disintegration of the organism is identical with physical sentience. The idea is touched upon in 'Naître', where the retention of organic faculties by human remains is expressed in terms of *sensibilité*: 'cette cendre peut peut-être encore ressentir nos larmes et y répondre; qui sait si ce mouvement qu'elles y excitent en les arrosant est tout à fait dénué de sensibilité?' (*Enc.*, xi.10; Her., viii.48). Similarly in the rather more 'scientific' anonymous article 'Reptiles', which discusses the kindred phenomenon of animal regeneration, the term *sensibilité* is used to identify precisely that form of vital power surviving in the constituent parts of an organism: 'il est sûr que les parties séparées conservent du mouvement et de la vie longtemps après la séparation; [...] et qu'à les examiner de près, on est porté à croire que la sensibilité est une propriété générale de la matière'.[62] These lines indicate just how easy it will be for Diderot to transfer his intuitions about the eternity of life, its universality and the possibility that it has an active and a latent form, to his new concept of *sensibilité*. Conversely, it will prove an equally simple matter to make conceptual transpositions between the development of animal sentience and the nature of life itself.

ii. *Physical sentience*

a. *Relationship between sentient and intellectual development*

Diderot's reflections on physical sentience are based on the sensualist proposition that all knowledge is derived via the senses. He outlines this position in the article 'Inné' (Her., vii.529):

Il n'y a d'inné que la faculté de sentir et de penser. Tout le reste est acquis. Supprimez l'œil, et vous supprimez en même temps toutes les idées qui appartiennent à la vue. Supprimez le nez, et vous supprimez en même temps toutes les idées qui appartiennent à l'odorat; et ainsi du goût, de l'ouïe et du toucher. Or toutes ces idées et tous ces sens

---

62. *Enc.*, xiv.10. Although the article is anonymous, it is likely that Diderot would have been aware of its content, in his capacity as editor, and a direct link with his own ideas cannot therefore be ruled out.

supprimés, il ne reste aucune notion abstraite; car c'est par le sensible que nous sommes conduits à l'abstrait.

All human faculties, therefore, including that of abstract reasoning (and thence by implication even its more specialised variants such as artistic imagination and moral awareness) derive from an innate capacity for thought. This in turn is dependent on the exact physiology of individual organisms. Quite simply, the more channels an organism possesses for the reception of sensory data, the more comprehensive its sensations and thus the more sophisticated its ideas.

This account of the relationship between physical sentience and intellectual development contains, therefore, an important element of gradation. On the one hand, it allows a straightforward distinction to be made between higher and lower animals, as Diderot points out later in the same article:

Mais après avoir procédé par voie de suppression, suivons la méthode contraire. Supposons une masse informe, mais sensible; elle aura toutes les idées qu'on peut obtenir du toucher; perfectionnons son organisation; développons cette masse, et en même temps nous ouvrirons la porte aux sensations et aux connaissances. C'est par l'une et l'autre de ces méthodes qu'on peut réduire l'homme à la condition de l'huître, et élever l'huître à la condition de l'homme.

On the other hand it will enable Diderot to declare sentience universal in matter (organic and inorganic) without risk of the psychism/animism which had resulted from his undifferentiated account of life.

b. Universal sentience

1. Universality of thought

Even without applying the concept of potentiality, Diderot is able to view the Lockean proposition that thought is inherent in matter with equanimity. For, according to his sensualist account of intellectual development, there is a vast difference of degree between the 'ideas' of unorganised matter and those enjoyed by man. Consequently, in the article 'Locke', he has no qualms about positing the universality of sentience and hence of the capacity for thought:

Locke avait dit, dans son *Essai sur l'entendement humain*, qu'il ne voyait aucune impossibilité à ce que la matière pensât. [...] Et qu'importe que la matière pense ou non? [...] Quand la sensibilité serait le germe premier de la pensée, quand elle serait une propriété générale de la matière; quand, inégalement distribuée entre toutes les productions de la nature, elle s'exercerait avec plus ou moins d'énergie, selon la variété de l'organisation, quelle conséquence fâcheuse en pourrait-on tirer? aucune.[63]

Sensibilité, it will be noted, is not equated with thought: Diderot has come a

---

63. Her., vii.714-15. Naigeon's attribution of this article to Diderot has not been disputed. Cf. Her., v.208.

long way from the rather crude formulations of the *Lettre sur les aveugles*.[64]

2. Sentience as a force

Moreover, this passage shows that Diderot is prepared to envisage *sensibilité* as a force, rather than a property – 'une *propriété* générale', but 'elle *s'exercerait*'. An identical attitude was observed in respect of life,[65] indicating once again the very close conceptual relationship between the two.

It is this point which sets Diderot apart from Helvétius, one probable source of his belief in universal sentience. Diderot had reviewed Helvétius's *De l'esprit* in 1758, and noted that: 'Il [Helvétius] paraît attribuer la sensibilité à la matière en général, système qui convient fort aux philosophes'.[66] For Helvétius, however, as for the majority of Diderot's contemporaries, *sensibilité* is essentially a passive, receptive ability: 'Nous avons en nous deux facultés ou, si je l'ose dire, deux puissances passives [...] L'une est la faculté de recevoir les impressions différentes que font sur nous les objets extérieurs; on la nomme *sensibilité physique*' (*De l'esprit*, p.71). Conceived as a force, however, *sensibilité* – like life – will be able to take on the characteristics of other forms of energy, such as potentiality. Indeed Diderot goes so far as to hint at this possibility with his apt choice of image: 'le germe premier de la pensée'.

Equally important is the notion that the precise manifestations of *sensibilité* (in the form of intellectual faculties) are determined by the conditions under which its force is deployed, that is, the physical configuration of each animal ('selon la variété de l'organisation'). This is a concept which will be outlined more explicitly in Diderot's scientific paper *Sur la cohésion des corps*[67] but whose origin, as with so much of Diderot's thought, is classical.

The history of philosophy article 'Péripatéticienne' endorses Dikaiachos's materialist alternative to the Aristotelian concept of soul: a single life force, inherent in matter and varying in its deployment according to the physical characteristics of the latter. Although for Dikaiachos himself diversity lies within the element rather than the organism, the principle is, as Diderot remarks, very close to his own ideas (Her., viii.87; Diderot's emphasis):

L'âme n'est rien; c'est un mot vide de sens. La force par laquelle nous agissons, nous sentons, nous pensons, est diffuse dans toute la matière, dont elle est aussi inséparable que l'étendue, et où elle s'exerce diversement, selon que l'être un et simple est diversement figuré. *Ce principe est bien près de la vérité.*

64. Cf. above, chapter 1.
65. Cf. above, A.ii.b.1, A.ii.d.1.
66. Her., ix.304. *Réflexions sur le livre De l'esprit par M. Helvétius.* Cf. Varloot, 'Diderots Philosophie im *Rêve de d'Alembert*', p.710, where these lines are quoted, but without comment.
67. See below, section C.

A force, finally, involves a two-way process – action and reaction: it is capable of modifying anything on which it acts. Already in 'Naître' Diderot had touched on this idea: *sensibilité* took the dual form of 'ressentir nos larmes *et y répondre*'.[68] By envisaging *sensibilité* as a force, Diderot is able to account convincingly for qualitative as well as quantitative change within the development of organisms, and for the qualitative distinctions between one organism and another. For sensualism implies that purely quantitative development, in terms of organic sophistication, results in a qualitative transformation in the nature of the ideas experienced by any composite of organised matter. It is strange that Diderot did not seek to transpose this principle into his analysis of growth through nutritive assimilation, where it would have resolved the vitalism inherent in his concept of universal life.

3. *Sensibilité* and the sense of touch

The relationship between basic sentience and its specialised forms is examined in terms which emphasise this element of qualitative change. In 'Inné', basic *sensibilité* is equated with tactile sentience: 'Supposons une masse informe, mais sensible; elle aura toutes les idées qu'on peut obtenir du toucher' (Her., vii.529). A degree of continuity is thus established in Diderot's thought between these writings and the *Pensées sur l'interprétation de la nature*, where *sensibilité* had been likened to 'un toucher obtus et sourd'.[69] A similar equation is established in the article 'Toucher', and once again a classical source is invoked:

Le *toucher* est de tous nos sens le plus grossier, mais en même temps le plus étendu, en ce qu'il embrasse plus d'objets que tous les autres ensemble: même quelques-uns réduisent tous les autres sens au seul sens de l'attouchement. Aristote dit positivement que toute sensation n'est qu'un attouchement, et que les autres sens [...] ne sont que des espèces raffinés, ou des degrés d'attouchement.[70]

The concept is repeated in 'Perception' (*Enc.*, xii.327), which is largely derivative (from Locke). Diderot's connection with this article, even as compiler, is uncertain, however, and therefore this will not be examined in detail. Indeed it is so unremarkable a view in itself that references to it can be found even in Diderot's aesthetic writings as early as 1756: 'Les sens ne sont tous qu'un toucher [...] Mais chaque sens touche [...] d'une manière qui lui est propre.'[71]

68. *Enc.*, xi.10; Her., viii.48. My emphasis. Cf. also above, chapter 3.
69. Cf. above, chapter 3.
70. *Enc.*, xvi.446. Lough and Proust include 'Toucher' in their list of articles attributable 'avec plus ou moins de vraisemblance' to Diderot (Her., v.219). Cf. 'Epicuréisme', where the same idea is attributed to Epicurus: 'Les sens ne sont qu'un toucher diversifié' (Her., vii.276).
71. *Entretiens sur le Fils naturel* (1756) (Her., x.156). Cf. *De la poésie dramatique* (1758): 'C'est par un toucher qui se diversifie dans la nature animée en une infinité de manières et de degrés, et qui s'appelle dans l'homme voir, entendre, flairer, goûter et sentir, qu'il reçoit des impressions' (Her., x.360).

The 'refinement' or 'diversification' involved (that is, a qualitative transformation) results from the increased precision and range of sentience brought about by organic development, and thus, in the context of Diderot's intuitions about the energetic nature of *sensibilité*, such remarks are far more than sensualist commonplaces.

The concept of *sensibilité* has gained considerably in philosophical weight in the course of these articles. Examined from three viewpoints – its necessary universality, its quantitative variations and its qualitatively diverse manifestations – considered as a force, and equated with life in all but name, it will re-emerge in 1765 as the keystone of Diderot's scientific philosophy.

In the meantime, however, Diderot's notions of energy in general are considerably expanded in a paper on the subject of attraction, written in 1761.

C. *Sur la cohésion des corps*: energy

The transposition of features from one energy form to another will be crucial to Diderot's philosophy of *sensibilité* in the *Rêve de d'Alembert*. Indeed he has already made use of this technique in elaborating the concept of latency.[72] It is no doubt partly rooted in his concern, expressed as early as 1753, to establish the unity of force – to attribute natural phenomena as far as possible to a single, energetic cause. This aim, stated clearly in the *Pensées sur l'interprétation de la nature* and applied there with some measure of success to electricity, magnetism and attraction,[73] is furthered in his 1761 paper *Sur la cohésion des corps*.[74] Moreover, in the course of his examination of attraction, certain general features of energy, directly relevant to *sensibilité*, are intuited.

Universal attraction and natural unity
i. *Attraction as a source of unity*

Newtonian attraction was commonly divided into two types, one governing planetary motion and gravity, and the other the cohesion of individual physical bodies.[75] Such was the range of phenomena which could be interpreted in terms of attraction that this was quite frequently held to be a universal property of matter. Diderot's paper makes it clear that he endorses this view (Her., ix.341):

72. Cf. above, A.ii.b.1.
73. Cf. above, chapter 3.
74. Published in the *Mémoires de Trevoux* with the full title *Réflexions sur une difficulté proposée contre la manière dont les newtoniens expliquent la cohésion des corps, et les autres phénomènes qui s'y rapportent*. I shall use the abbreviated title for convenience.
75. Cf. *Encyclopédie* article 'Attraction', and my discussion of the contemporary debate, above, chapter 3.

On a lieu de croire que l'attraction qui fait circuler les planètes, et qui précipite les corps pesants vers le centre de la terre, produit encore plusieurs autres effets naturels, tels que la dureté, l'adhérence des parties des fluides, les fermentations, et généralement tous les phénomènes qui naissent de la cohésion, ou qui s'y rapportent. En effet [...] si l'attraction est une propriété générale de la matière, sentiment qui, pour ne rien dire de plus, est très probable, il est naturel de lui attribuer tous les effets qui lui sont analogues; et ceux dont je viens de parler sont de ce nombre.

His readiness to accept this contemporary account was almost certainly reinforced by its virtual identity with classical materialist opinion on the issue: Diderot's own article 'Epicuréisme', for example, presents Epicurus's force of *pondération* as 'une énergie intrinsèque de la matière' (Her., vii.271), 'la cause éternelle des compositions' (vii.272), and attributes to it a wide range of phenomena: 'les cohérences, les compositions d'atomes, la formation des corps, l'ordre de l'univers avec tous ses phénomènes'. Clearly, then, attraction offered an important opportunity for synthesis, a possible key to Diderot's ideal of 'un seul acte dans la nature'.

Significantly, *fermentation* is included amongst its effects. Although the word was in general use at the time to denote chemical reactions (themselves analysed in terms of attraction in Diderot's *Pensées sur l'interprétation de la nature* and commonly by his contemporaries),[76] for Diderot it had special associations since the *Lettre sur les aveugles* had proposed it as one of the means whereby life is generated in inanimate matter. Attraction thus links the biological and the purely physical. No direct correlation is established (in either 1753 or 1761) between the rôle of attraction in chemical bonding and that of *sensibilité* in organic combination, but the capacity for cross-fertilisation between these two parallel concepts is evident.

ii. *Attraction as a challenge to unity*

Considerable contemporary debate centred on the question of whether the phenomena attributed to the two categories of attraction – the cosmic and the corpuscular – were really of the same order. The apparent disparity of the forces involved at these two levels suggested that different physical laws might be involved – a position that Diderot himself had toyed with in the *Pensées sur l'interprétation de la nature*.[77] Even now he is not prepared to reject the idea *a priori*: despite his ideal of unity he remains keenly aware of the need to account for nature's diversities (Her., ix.343):

Si l'on n'avait autre chose à objecter contre ce sentiment, sinon la variation qu'il suppose

76. Cf. *Encyclopédie* article 'Attraction', and above, 3, A.ii.
77. Cf. above, chapter 3.

dans les lois de l'attraction, il semble qu'on ne serait pas suffisamment autorisé à le rejeter. Quelques philosophes ont beau vanter la simplicité des lois de la nature, il est certain que plusieurs de ces lois souffrent des variations et des modifications considérables.

Nevertheless, Diderot points out, there is a notable lack of empirical evidence to support the supposition of twin laws, 'l'une pour les grandes distances et pour les phénomènes célestes et l'autre pour les petites distances et les cohésions' (Her., ix.343). More importantly, there is no need to have recourse to supposed variations in the laws of attraction, since the disparity can be interpreted in a quite different way; one, moreover, which presents no threat to unity.

iii. *Diderot's interpretation of attraction*

Whilst conceding that the quantitative disproportion between cohesion and gravity is considerable, Diderot reformulates the issue in such a way that the problem is transcended: he simply distinguishes attraction itself (the attractive force) from its effects (the phenomena attributed to attraction) (Her., ix.345):

Ces deux forces [cohesion and gravity] ne sont pas l'attraction même, mais des effets de l'attraction: car j'appelle attraction l'effort que fait le corps attirant pour faire mouvoir le corps attiré; et je regarde comme effet de l'attraction la force avec laquelle le corps attiré est mû en vertu de cet effort.

It is not, therefore, attraction which varies – merely the effects of this now reunified cause. Just as there are varying forms and degrees of motion, explained by the fact that a single cause, impetus, is modified in its effects by the nature of the obstacles encountered, so physical circumstances determine the precise manifestations of attraction. This principle is both stated in general terms:

Or il est certain que les effets d'une seule et même cause peuvent varier dans leurs rapports, sans que la cause elle-même varie dans sa loi. Il ne faut pour cela que le mélange de quelques circonstances particulières, qui rendent l'action de la cause tantôt plus simple, et tantôt plus compliquée, qui tantôt en prolonge et tantôt en raccourcisse la durée; qui l'applique à son effet tantôt d'une manière, et tantôt d'une autre, etc.

and applied clearly to attraction:

Pourquoi cette puissance [attraction], en suivant toujours une même loi, ne pourrait-elle pas, ainsi que l'impulsion, produire dans les corps sur lesquels elle se déploie, des effets, des forces, qui ne suivissent pas le même rapport, si, par le concours de quelques circonstances particulières, son action se trouvait diversement modifiée?

As far as attraction is concerned, therefore, unity is salvaged.

This interpretation has far broader implications, however, than its immediate context would appear to suggest. Diderot's examination of attraction places at his disposal four major principles which, in theory at least, could be extended

to *any* force. The first two can be deduced directly from what he writes here:
a. that an energetic phenomenon can be divided into two components, a basic force and its effects;
b. that the manifestations of a force vary according to the conditions of its deployment.

Two further principles are implicit in his account of attraction and only incompletely stated:
c. that energy, rather than substance, constitutes the essence of matter;
d. that one form of energy may be converted into another.

These interlinked principles contribute significantly to the conceptual background of *sensibilité*.

a. That an energetic phenomenon can be divided into two components: a basic force, and its effects

Diderot's analysis of life had encountered problems similar to that posed by attraction: the attempt to account for both molecular and corporate life in terms of a single, undifferentiated principle had been fraught with difficulties, only partially overcome in 1759 by the application of latency. Now, however, a threefold analogy is possible, which may be tabulated as follows:

force	*means of activation*	*manifestation/effect*
attraction		gravity, cohesion
potential motion	impetus (*impulsion*)	motion
sensibilité	nutritive assimilation	life

Although there is no place for latency within attraction, the structural parallels are striking. As far as *sensibilité* is concerned all the elements of this synthesis are already present in Diderot's thought: active and potential forms of life; nutritive assimilation as an activating agent; *sensibilité* identified with life at molecular level.

Thanks to his speculations here, when Diderot returns to the issue of life in 1765 and again in 1769, he will not hesitate to discriminate between *sensibilité*, the basic energy underlying vital phenomena, and life itself, the effect of this force.[78]

b. That the manifestations of a force vary according to the conditions of its deployment

1. Implications for *sensibilité*

Diderot's account of sensualism in the *Encyclopédie* opens the way for the incorporation of this principle into his concept of *sensibilité*. Already the sentient and intellectual faculties of an organism have been related to its physiological

78. See below, section D.i, and chapter 5, p.136-37.

configuration; it will be a relatively simple step to view this relationship in terms of physical circumstances determining the form in which *sensibilité* is manifested. Thus when the energetic nature of *sensibilité* is more explicitly established, in the 1765 letter to Duclos and again in 1769, the principle of variable manifestations will enable Diderot to account for organic development rather more convincingly than hitherto.[79]

2. Wider implications: causality

– monsters

This principle is also a potent ally in Diderot's quest for unity not only within attraction but also within the more specifically biological area of teratology. Monsters, it will be recalled, had been presented as exemplary demonstrations of nature's autonomous powers of creation, since they betokened an ability to produce phenomena at variance with the normal operation of universal laws.[80] As such, they tended to threaten the cause of unity. Now, however, Diderot is able to envisage monsters less as *écarts* than as the product of an unusual combination of circumstances. The article 'Naturel (métaph.)' comes close to expressing the energetic principle outlined explicitly in 1761:

> Un événement très rare pourrait venir du principe ordinaire, qui dans la suite des révolutions et des changements aurait formé une sorte de prodige, sans quitter la règle de son cours, [...]. Ainsi voit-on quelquefois des monstres du caractère le plus inouï, sans qu'on y trouve rien de miraculeux et de surnaturel.[81]

The laws involved in these deviant forms have been neither suspended by divine intervention nor infringed by natural spontaneity: it is simply that the conditions of their operation have been modified. Consequently diversity is preserved within unity.

– general causality

Elsewhere in the *Encyclopédie* Diderot relates this view of monsters to the concept of an infinite network of cause and effect. In the article 'Imparfait', for instance, he explains how natural unity, in such a causal form, makes the very concept of deviance meaningless (*Enc.*, vii.185; Her., vii.504):

> [Les] plantes *imparfaites* [sont] très improprement appelées ainsi; car il n'y a rien d'*imparfait* dans la nature, pas même les monstres. Tout y est enchaîné, et le monstre y est un effet aussi nécessaire que l'animal parfait. Les causes qui ont concouru à sa

---

79. Cf. below, esp. D.iii, and chapter 5 B.i.a.5, B.i.b, C.ii.
80. Cf. above, chapter 2.
81. *Enc.*, xi.44-45. The attribution of this article to Diderot is uncertain. Lough's *The Encyclopédie in eighteenth-century England* considers it 'may reasonably be attributed to Diderot despite the absence of Naigeon's guarantee', p.44-45, 204, although he and Proust exclude it from the more recent Hermann edition.

production tiennent à une infinité d'autres, et celles-ci à une infinité d'autres, et ainsi de suite en remontant jusqu'à l'éternité des choses.

Another article quotes Buffon in support of this purely materialist view of nature's creativity: 'Dans le nombre infini de combinaisons que peut prendre la matière, les arrangements les plus singuliers doivent se trouver, et se trouvent en effet, mais beaucoup plus rarement que les autres'.[82]

In 1749 the *Pensées philosophiques* atheist had invoked the principle of *pluralité des jets* to account for the emergence of diverse natural phenomena. Diderot's 1761 paper *Sur les probabilités* returns to an analogous concept, the interplay of energetic matter takes place on an infinite timescale: 'Comme la combinaison s'exécute sans cesse, il n'y a rien qu'elle ne puisse amener. Le temps équivaut à tout. [...] Avec le temps, tout ce qui est possible dans la nature est' (Lew., v.31). The introduction of an element of time thus allows Diderot to posit an infinite variety of conditions under which energy may be deployed, and hence an infinite number of forms, or effects.

In general terms, the conclusions I have drawn here about deviance coincide with those reached by Laidlaw,[83] although his account does not call on either the scientific papers or *Encyclopédie* articles I have used, nor does it seek to relate Diderot's treatment of deviance to his concept of energy, except in the very broadest terms. Winter's analysis of Diderot's notion of causal unity makes no mention of energy.[84]

Not only monsters, but also the concept of chaos can be reappraised in the light of this principle. Diderot touches on this in a philosophical digression in the 1767 *Salon*: a dust cloud – an apparently random phenomenon lacking any semblance of organisation – is in fact a perfectly balanced, even rigidly determined natural form, if considered within the framework of universal causality: 'Ce tourbillon qui ne vous semble qu'un chaos de molécules éparses dispersées au hasard; eh bien! [...] ce tourbillon est tout aussi parfaitement ordonné que le monde' (Lew., vii.137).

The energetic character of physical causality is confirmed a few pages later; it is, explains Diderot, the forces deployed by matter which hold the key to its configuration: 'Si toutes les forces qui animaient chacune des molécules qui formaient [ce tourbillon] qui nous a enveloppés étaient données, un géomètre vous démontrerait que celle qui est engagée entre votre œil et sa paupière, est

---

82. 'Imagination', *Enc.*, viii.563-64. These lines are attacking the belief that congenital malformations result from the effect of maternal imagination on the foetus, a point dealt with in volume iv of Buffon's *Histoire naturelle* (1754). Lough and Proust list this article as possibly attributable to Diderot (Her., v.212).

83. 'Diderot's teratology', p.111, 112, 113 and *passim*.

84. Winter, p.61-64, 183-89.

précisement à sa place' (Lew., vii.142). The same point was made in d'Holbach's *Système de la nature* – some 3 years later, which suggests Diderot as the originator of the idea.[85] For nature's molecules are not simply analogous to dice, falling into random patterns; they are *loaded* dice: 'Ce monde n'est qu'un amas de molécules pipées en une infinité de manières diverses' (Lew., vii.136). They are loaded with inherent energy, whose manifestations are as variable as the conditions under which it is deployed.

c. That energy, rather than substance, constitutes the essence of matter

As a consequence of the second principle, Diderot approaches a potential means of confirming his 1753 intuition that energy is largely responsible for the diversity within nature. A force such as attraction may in itself be invariable (as life was declared to be in 1759) but it is capable of producing an infinite variety of effects, according to the conditions under which it is deployed. These conditions in turn (the configurations of matter and the relationships between portions of matter) are themselves energetically determined (that is, by the operation and interaction of forces). Thus the classical notion of heterogeneity is tending to be transferred from matter-as-substance to matter-as-energy-system.

This is a subtle conceptual shift, so slight in presentation that it may easily be overlooked, and indeed may not even have been fully realised by Diderot himself. Although not explicity formulated, however, the notion is reinforced by remarks made in two approximately contemporaneous *Encyclopédie* articles. In 'Ignorance', Diderot refers repeatedly to the 'premiers corpuscules' of matter as 'parties actives' (*Enc.*, viii.549; Her., vii.497). Their very size renders their exact nature as substance inaccessible to human investigation; consequently the scientist can hope to analyse them only through their participation in energy systems – such as, for instance, the phenomena associated with cohesion. Interpretation is switched from attributes to action.

In 'Modification', precisely this form of interpretation leads Diderot to establish the heterogeneity of matter in predominantly energetic terms: every atom in nature is different by virtue of its involvement in a different complex of interactions: 'Il n'y a pas un atome dans la nature qui ne soit exposé à l'action d'une infinité de causes diverses, il n'y a pas une de ces causes qui s'exerce de la même manière en deux point différents de l'espace: il n'y a donc pas deux

85. 'Un géomètre qui connaîtrait exactement les différentes forces qui agissent dans ces deux cas [dust cloud, storm] et les propriétés des molécules qui sont mues, démontrerait que, d'après des causes données, chaque molécule agit précisément comme elle doit agir, et ne peut agir autrement qu'elle ne fait' (quoted in Y. Belaval, 'La crise de la géométrisation de l'univers', *Revue internationale de philosophie* 21 (1952), p.341-42).

atomes rigoureusement semblables dans la nature.'[86]

While these statements in no way indicate that Diderot considered matter and energy as equivalents,[87] they do imply that he feels the conventional eighteenth-century view of matter as extended substance to be scientifically and philosophically sterile. Crocker reaches a similar conclusion about Diderot's concept of dynamic heterogeneity, although his brief account is based on the much later *Principes sur la matière et le mouvement*, where Diderot returns to the underlying problem of matter-as-substance versus matter-as-energy.[88] In the *Rêve de d'Alembert* the consideration of heterogeneity in terms of matter's forces rather than its forms will be an important element in Diderot's concern to reconcile the unity of nature with its diversity,[89] and this time *sensibilité* (redefined as a type of energy) will have a significant role to play.

d. That one form of energy may be converted into another

This again is a principle which should not be interpreted too ambitiously. There is no suggestion that *Sur la cohésion des corps* contains a statement of energy transformation in the modern sense. Nonetheless, on two occasions Diderot does refer to the possibility that among the effects of attraction may be other forces. Gravity and cohesion are identified as 'deux forces, [...] des effets de l'attraction' (Her., ix.345); motion, similarly, may be produced by its workings.[90]

In another instance, it is suggested that impetus involves a similar process, not only bringing about the conversion of potential to active movement (as the object struck is impelled into motion) but simultaneously producing other energetic effects – unspecified, but indicated by Diderot's use of the plural form: 'Pourquoi cette puissance [attraction] ne pourrait-elle pas, *ainsi que l'impulsion*, produire dans les corps [...] des effets, des forces [...]?' (my emphasis). This implicit principle of the interrelatedness (and possible inter-convertibility) of forces will be considerably expanded in the *Rêve de d'Alembert* and form an integral part of Diderot's philosophy of *sensibilité*.

Against this enriched conceptual background Diderot is able, four years later, to venture a new account of life in a letter which clearly marks the passage from this transitional phase of his thought, with all its complexities and tensions, to the confident statements of the *Rêve de d'Alembert*.

---

86. *Enc.*, x.602; Her., viii.33. Lough and Proust accept Naigeon's attribution of this article to Diderot (Her., v.208).

87. Despite Fabre's proposal of theosophist thought as a source of this concept ('Diderot et les théosophes', p.221)! Cf. also above, chapter 3, n.19.

88. *Diderot's chaotic order*, p.11-12. Cf. below, Conclusion.

89. Cf. below, chapter 5, conclusion.

90. This also applies, of course, in the case of celestial movements.

D. Approach to the *Rêve de d'Alembert*: letter to Duclos, 10 October 1765

In 1765 Diderot takes the major step of defining explicitly the relationship between sentience, life and thought. Two strands of his thought which had hitherto followed parallel but separate courses of development: the physical sentience – sensory perception – cognition relationship (explored in the review of *De l'esprit*, 'Inné' and 'Locke') and the life – potentiality – nutritive assimilation relationship (elaborated in the letter to Sophie and 'Naître') are finally synthesised.

i. *Vital energy:* sensibilité *substituted for life*

Diderot makes it clear in his letter to Duclos that *sensibilité* is the key to the transition from inorganic to organic forms. For the first time he attributes to it a potential and an active form: *sensibilité* itself is, he declares, universal in matter;[91] it is only active, however, in living matter, where it is responsible (in true sensualist fashion) for engendering intellectual activity (*Corr.*, v.140-41):

> Si j'ai dit [...] que la pensée ne pouvait résulter de la transposition des molécules, c'est que la pensée est le résultat de la sensibilité, et que, selon moi, la sensibilité est une propriété essentielle de la matière; propriété inerte dans les corps bruts, comme le mouvement dans les corps pesants arrêtés par un obstacle; propriété rendue active dans les mêmes corps par leur assimilation avec une substance animée vivante.

The latency principle is transposed from life (to which it had been applied in 'Naître') to *sensibilité*. It is thus the latter concept which takes on the rôle of an energy form. The process of nutritive assimilation first outlined in his letter to Sophie of 1759 is redefined, so that *sensibilité* (the structural equivalent of attraction or mobility) is activated, rather than life (the manifestation of this force, corresponding to cohesion/gravity or kinetic motion). The analogy adopted by Diderot ('comme le mouvement dans les corps pesants arrêtés par un obstacle') is apt, for it draws on the whole nexus of energetic relationships: *sensibilité* is compared not simply with motion, but with motion within the context of attraction, the very area where many of his intuitions about the nature of forces in general had arisen, in both 1753 and 1761.

Furthermore, Diderot goes on to apply the label *laboratoire* to the animal

---

91. As Varloot points out, this element in itself is not particularly original – as predecessors he cites Campanella, Hobbes and Meslier, along with La Mettrie and Maupertuis – and Diderot's real originality lies in his assumption of active and potential categories ('Diderots Philosophie im *Rêve de d'Alembert*', p.712, n.14). The complex of ideas within which it arises (his overall philosophy of energy) does make Diderot's concept unique, a point which is not made in Varloot's less specialised analysis. Cf. below, chapter 5.

organisms within which nutritive assimilation takes place, implying that this process is of essentially the same order as the chemical reactions and fermentations which both the *Pensées sur l'interprétation de la nature* and *Sur la cohésion des corps* had attributed to the workings of attraction: 'L'animal est le laboratoire où la sensibilité, d'inerte qu'elle etait, devient active' (*Corr.*, v.141). Whilst the possibility of a substantive – as opposed to purely structural – relationship between attraction and *sensibilité* is not investigated here, Diderot certainly comes close to realising (in accordance, perhaps, with the rudimentary principle of energy transformation adumbrated in *Sur la cohésion des corps*) his ideal of energetic unity first expressed in 1753.

ii. *Nutritive assimilation: continuity substituted for contiguity*

A further important conceptual step towards Diderot's eventual thesis of vital energy is taken in this letter with the apparent substitution of continuity for contiguity in his account of nutritive assimilation. The term *assimilation* (as opposed to the earlier *juxtaposition*)[92] is used repeatedly. Although there is no explicit comment to indicate whether this emphasis is witting or unwitting, it is clear that the concept has taken its place within Diderot's formulation of the nutritive process, if only subliminally.

The term itself had appeared in Diderot's writings as early as 1755, in a context which establishes its association with the issue of inorganic-organic transformation. A passage from the *Encyclopédie* article 'Eclectisme' outlining the Aristotelian concept of soul comes, indeed, remarkably close (despite its metaphysical terminology) to expressing Diderot's 1765 account of *sensibilité*: 'L'âme est comme assoupie dans les êtres inanimés, mais ce qui s'allie à un autre tend à se *l'assimiler*; c'est ainsi qu'elle vivifie autant qu'il est en elle ce qui de soi n'est point vivant' (Her., vii.93; my emphasis).

A later article, 'Résurrection', represents a further possible internal source of Diderot's revised concept of nutritive assimilation. Proust (following Naigeon) attributes this article to Diderot, though Lough is less certain;[93] nevertheless, whether or not it comes from Diderot's hand, he would certainly have been acquainted with its content, and its possible rôle as catalyst is therefore undeniable.

The article examines sceptically the Christian doctrine of physical resurrection. A range of scientific objections are put forward, each of which makes it clear that the processes of nutrition and digestion irrevocably transform the

92. Cf. above, 3, A.ii.b.3, A.iii.a; 4, A.i.a and b.1.
93. Proust, *Diderot et l'Encyclopédie*, p.283; Lough, *The Encyclopédie in eighteenth-century England*, p.203, 211.

substances ingested by any organism. The resurrection of discrete individuals is impossible, for instance, in the case of cannibalism, since the matter which constituted the victim's body will have been fully assimilated. The same situation would apply if one man were consumed by a fish which was then eaten, in turn, by another man: 'On objecte que la même masse de matière et de substance pourrait faire au temps de la *résurrection* partie de deux ou de plusieurs corps. [...] Or, quand la substance de l'un est ainsi convertie en celle de l'autre, chacun ne peut pas ressusciter avec son corps entier' (AT, xvii.25).

Even where a man escapes such fates, the physical constitution of his body does not remain constant. New food is constantly ingested, assimilated and converted, to replace matter which has degenerated and been lost: 'On objecte que, selon les dernières découvertes qu'on a faites sur l'économie animale, le corps humain change perpétuellement. [...] On prétend qu'en sept ans de temps le corps éprouve un changement total, de sorte qu'il n'en reste pas la moindre particule' (AT, xvii.26). Evidently such a circulation would be impossible unless new and old matter were fully integrated so as to maintain continuity of identity within the individual.

Admittedly the rather slight manner of its presentation in Diderot's letter to Duclos ensures that the concept of assimilation is overshadowed by the central issue of *sensibilité*. Nevertheless, Diderot's far more extended treatment of the continuity principle in the *Rêve de d'Alembert* will reveal this to have been a crucial shift of thought.

iii. *Organic and inorganic*

Of equal significance is the fact that the organic and inorganic are redefined in terms which avoid both sterile dualism and vitalism. The two are not distinct in any absolute sense, and yet life need no longer be posited as universal. The question, posed in 1753, of whether inanimate matter could ever become alive, has been answered in the affirmative. Life and death are both reversible states of matter.

Nutritive assimilation and its counterpart, decay, now offer an acceptable account of the transition from inanimate to animate and the reversal of this process. They constitute the physical conditions which permit *sensibilité* to be alternately contained (inert) or deployed (active) (*Corr.*, v.141; my emphasis):

C'est ce que le phénomène de la nutrition démontre à chaque instant, phénomène par lequel un animal qui ne sentait d'abord que dans l'espace d'un pied, d'un demi-pied, d'une ligne, devient *sentant activement* dans l'espace de deux, trois, quatre, cinq, six pieds, par la digestion et l'assimilation de substances en qui la sensibilité *était inerte*, avant qu'elles fussent digérées, assimilées par l'animal.

Chouillet sees Diderot's use of nutritive assimilation (here and in the *Rêve de d'Alembert*) as a 'detour' designed to give scientific respectability to the purely speculative equation of life and energy, 'une procédure qui tient beaucoup plus du jeu sémantique que du raisonnement philosophique'.[94] The former concept, however, emerged in his thought *before* the latter was elaborated in its present form, and is much more than a post factum bid for acceptability. It is an integral part of his philosophy of energy.

Implicit in these lines, for example, is the principle already established both in the *Encyclopédie* and in *Sur la cohésion des corps* that, in general, the manifestations of a force will vary according to the conditions of its deployment, that is, that the sentient and intellectual capacities of an organism are quantitatively determined. The more actively sentient matter an organism has, the greater its potential for developing sophisticated faculties.

iv. *Remaining weaknesses*

This principle remains somewhat ill-defined, however: the confusion between quantity and quality will not be resolved until 1769, when Diderot examines the issue of specialisation within organic tissues.

A second area of obscurity concerns the exact position occupied by plants within the nutritive chain. Only animal matter is endowed with the power to activate *sensibilité* ('propriété rendue active dans les mêmes corps par leur assimilation avec *une substance animale* vivante'; '*L'animal* est le laboratoire où la sensibilité devient active', *Corr.*, v.141; my emphasis). The process described here is properly only one of animalisation. Diderot implies that any inert substance may undergo animalisation, that is, the minerals are not excluded; no account is given, however, of the growth and development, equally through nutritive assimilation, of plants. A further consequence of this omission is the failure to discriminate between the totally inert state of *sensibilité* in the mineral and its limited activity in the plant.

This lack of precision recurs in the *Encyclopédie* article 'Spinosiste', as Diderot presents a contemporary materialist view (effectively his own) of biological growth:

Le principe général de ceux-ci [modern materialists] c'est que la matière est sensible, ce qu'ils montrent par le développement de l'œuf, corps inerte, qui par le seul instrument de la chaleur graduée passe à l'état d'être sentant et vivant, et par l'accroissement de

94. *Diderot poète de l'énergie*, p.228-29. Cf. *ibid.*, 'Le couple matière/vie s'empare des virtualités sémantiques du couple force morte/force vive (qui appartient en réalité au vocabulaire de la physique) et, par cette captation de sens plus ou moins licite, se transforme en couple sensibilité inerte/sensibilité active.'

tout animal qui dans son principe n'est qu'un point, et qui par l'assimilation nutritive des plantes, en un mot de toutes les substances qui servent à la nutrition, devient un grand corps sentant et vivant dans un grand espace.[95]

Here again there is no attempt at differentiation between mineral, plant and animal. This is another issue which will be examined more thoroughly, if not fully resolved, in the *Rêve de d'Alembert*.

Clearly this letter contains only a brief and therefore necessarily incomplete statement of Diderot's concept of *sensibilité*. Those critics who have hailed it as identical in all but name and scope to the *Rêve de d'Alembert*'s thesis may therefore seem a little over-charitable in their disregard of the lack of any thoroughgoing reflection by Diderot on the details of his formula.[96] Despite the undeniable conceptual advances made in the letter, Diderot still has far to go before he achieves a fully coherent concept of *sensibilité* as vital energy.

v. *Postscriptum*

Curiously, Diderot's *Essais sur la peinture* of the following year make no mention of the ideas expressed to Duclos. He appears to subscribe here to the conventional notion of an eternally fixed division between the animate and the inanimate, with *sensibilité* attributed firmly and exclusively to the former category of phenomena. He opposes *la nature sensible* to *la nature inanimée* (Lew., vi.282) and elaborates a few pages later (vi.304):

La nature a diversifié les êtres en froids, immobiles, non vivants, non sentants, non pensants, et en êtres qui vivent, sentent et pensent. La ligne était tracée de toute éternité: il fallait appeler peintres de genre les imitateurs de la nature brute et morte; peintres d'histoire, les imitateurs de la nature sensible et vivante [...].

It seems unlikely, however, that between his letter to Duclos and the *Rêve de d'Alembert* Diderot would have reverted to a notion so at variance with the evolution undergone by his thought over the previous decade. The apparent anomaly is easily explained.

In the first place, Diderot was no doubt aware that his new ideas were not only bold, but also highly speculative and incomplete. He would therefore have

---

95. *Enc.*, xv.474; Her., viii.328. Vernière cites La Mettrie's statement that 'une seule et même matière végète, s'organise, se détruit, se régénère' as an expression of such neo-spinozism (*Spinoza et la pensée française*, p.537, 541). This seems, however, to be little more than a repetition of the commonplace belief in the circulation of matter. Cf. below, chapter 5, n.37, for the relevance of this passage to Diderot's account of heat in foetal development. Lough and Proust accept Naigeon's attribution of this article to Diderot (Her., v.209).

96. See, for example, Roger, *Les Sciences de la vie*, p.617-18; Wilson, *Diderot: the testing years*, p.559. Varloot simply states that the letter contains the 'central thought' of Diderot's philosophy, without analysing it further ('Diderots Philosophie im *Rêve de d'Alembert*', p.712). Winter's acknowledgement is equally brief (p.31).

felt fully justified in avoiding all mention of them in a work whose primary theme was, after all, an aesthetic one.

At the same time, it is perfectly reasonable to assume that the divisions referred to correspond to his own categories of active and potential *sensibilité*. To declare a certain class of beings insentient does not deny them a share in universal *sensibilité* any more than the label *immobile* denies the presence of latent motion. There was no obligation on Diderot to point out to the unsuspecting general reader the idiosyncratic principles underlying his acceptance of the traditional divisions. This aspect of his thought remains private, just as, indeed, he will choose to keep the *Rêve de d'Alembert* itself hidden.

5. *Le Rêve de d'Alembert*

Introduction

SUCH is the richness and diversity of the *Rêve de d'Alembert*[1] that it has attracted extensive critical attention almost continuously since its revelation in 1830. Much of this attention, however, has been focussed upon the psychological and moral matters treated, rather than upon the work's underlying scientific inspiration. Almost without exception, commentators have hailed the work as brilliantly intuitive and comprehensive. Thus for Wilson, it is Diderot's greatest work and for Crocker the 'supreme dialectical statement of Diderot's materialism'; Desné writes of 'l'exposé le plus hardi, le plus suggestif de la philosophie de Diderot' and Niklaus of 'unexampled dialectical brillance'; Varloot, finally, considers it 'die geschlossenste Darstellung Diderots Philosophie'.[2] Yet with similar regularity, scholars have chosen not to dwell on the underlying thesis of *sensibilité*. All too often this has been sketchily summarised and passed over rapidly in favour of a more detailed examination of other aspects of the work.[3]

This approach does Diderot's thought less than justice in two respects. In the first place, *sensibilité* is not merely an interesting preliminary to the real substance of the *Rêve de d'Alembert*, but an actual prerequisite of much that follows. In the second place, the approach entails only a cursory acknowledgement of Diderot's evident and continuous concern with the issues of matter, energy and the philosophical basis of life throughout his earlier writings.[4] On both counts, valuable evidence of the organic nature of Diderot's thought – constant and consistent in its overall direction, yet dynamic and continually evolving in its detail – is overlooked. Furthermore, many otherwise admiring scholars have felt themselves obliged to point out 'contradictions' and 'weaknesses' in Diderot's philosophy of *sensibilité*. Such flaws are then dismissed as

1. This title will be used to indicate the three dialogues together (*Entretien entre d'Alembert et Diderot; Rêve de d'Alembert; Suite de l'Entretien*); the central dialogue will be referred to simply as the *Rêve*.
2. Wilson, *Diderot: the testing years*, p.559; Crocker, *Diderot the embattled philosopher*, p.311; R. Desné, 'Sur le matérialisme de Diderot', *Pensée* 108 (1963), p.98; Niklaus, 'The mind of Diderot', p.932; Varloot, 'Diderots Philosophie im *Rêve de d'Alembert*', p.704.
3. Cf. Winter's résumé of the tendency among critics to trivialise the content of the *Rêve de d'Alembert* (p.22-23).
4. Cf. Casini, *Diderot 'philosophe'*, p.265-66; Winter, p.133-35.

historically inevitable[5] or casually excused as the excesses of an over-fertile imagination. Although charitable at first sight, this attitude often proves to be unduly negative. A more painstaking analysis of *sensibilité* shows that the materialism of Diderot's maturity, whilst in no way claiming to be a definitive system, is nevertheless built on a far more secure, consistent and meticulously worked-out foundation than much existing criticism gives him credit for.

The format of the *Rêve de d'Alembert* is sufficiently well known for the present study to dispense with a detailed introduction of the work. Similarly, in accordance with the methodological principle stated at the outset, it is not proposed to give a detailed survey of the possible influences on this work. These have been thoroughly documented elsewhere. Of particular relevance to the present study, and an indispensable source for the historical background to Diderot's concept of *sensibilité* (particularly in the field of animal physiology), is Dieckmann's 'Théophile Bordeu und Diderots *Rêve de d'Alembert*'. This study is complemented by Moravia's 'Dall' *Homme machine* all' "homme sensible"', a valuable outline of Bordeu's place in the intellectual history of the century. Wilson lists influences ranging from Lucretius, Toland and Buffon to the Montpellier school and Leibniz.[6] As Wilson himself points out, however, although Diderot reflects the speculations of his forerunners and peers, and obviously did not produce his intuitions *de novo*, it is precisely because of his acquaintance with such a range of thought currents that he was capable of this great feat of synthesis.[7] Certainly it does not imply any lack of original thought. Lemay's judgement of the *Rêve de d'Alembert*: 'C'est la réunion des idées matérialistes de l'époque. [...] Quoi qu'en aient pu dire ses panégyristes, cet écrit ne contient rien de personnel, si ce n'est la façon de traiter le sujet'[8] seems to do Diderot something of an injustice, as does Crocker's rather dismissive remark that 'Toutes ses grandes idées ont été formulées avant lui.'[9] A far sounder point is made by Casini: that the interpreter's task is not to seek to establish the provenance of each tile in the mosaic, but to evaluate the unified design which results. Diderot is influenced not by one or other current, but by all of them together: 'Nel *Rêve* confluisca infatti gran parte della cultura

---

5. See especially Crocker, *Diderot the embattled philosopher*, p.319, 323-24, and discussion of marxist criticism, below, B.i.a.4, and conclusion.

6. *Diderot: the testing years*, p.559, 561-65. Cf. I. H. Smith's survey of Lucretian influences, which he feels marked the dialogues even more deeply than did Spinozism, 'Le *Rêve de d'Alembert* and *De rerum natura*', *AUMLA* 10 (1959), p.128-34. C. A. Fusil, on the other hand, argues that Lucretius's influence on Diderot and his contemporaries was minimal, 'Lucrèce et les philosophes du XVIIIe siècle', *RhlF* 35 (1928), *passim*.

7. *Diderot: the testing years*, p.568; cf. above, 3, B.iii.b.

8. P. Lemay, 'Du nouveau sur le *Rêve de d'Alembert*', *Le Progrès médical* 15-16 (1951), p.423.

9. 'John Toland et le matérialisme de Diderot', p.294.

cosmologica e biologica del secolo XVIII, ma assimilata in una sintesi innovatrice che s'impone con forza esclusiva' (*Diderot 'philosophe'*, p.264-65).

Two final introductory points need to be made. It should be pointed out that only the first two parts of the *Rêve de d'Alembert*, the initial *Entretien* between Diderot and d'Alembert and the central *Rêve* together with its commentary, will come under consideration. The moral debates of the *Suite* fall outside the scope of this enquiry.

It has been observed that the fictional protagonists of this *sui generis* work are virtually interchangeable, particularly in the *Rêve*.[10] To attempt to identify any one character as Diderot's mouthpiece is therefore futile. Indeed, they all speak for him. This formal synthesis plays a perfect counterpoint to the philosophical synthesis (of his own and others' ideas) represented by *sensibilité*.[11]

Multiple aspects of the phenomenon Diderot calls *sensibilité* are revealed in the *Rêve de d'Alembert*, though not in a systematic fashion. Diderot draws on the wealth of intuitive and exploratory concepts introduced in his earlier writings – gradation, optimum organisation, nutritive assimilation, latency, and a host of related energetic phenomena. He considers anew many key issues raised on previous occasions – the relationship between organic and inorganic matter; living and non-living forms (including the phenomenon of spontaneous generation); unity within matter and energy; the physical origins of intellectual activity. He also resolves several questions implicit in his earlier work – whether quantitative modification can lead to qualitative change; whether matter combines in a continuous or merely contiguous fashion, the catergorisation of *sensibilité* as property or force.

These elements are fused into a single concept – *sensibilité* – which is proposed as an adequate account of life at both the physical and metaphysical levels, and which thus constitutes a focus for his entire philosophy of energy and unity.[12]

A. *Sensibilité*: the basic concept

i. Sensibilité *and energy*

In its fundamental aspects, *sensibilité* in the *Rêve de d'Alembert* is identical with the concept outlined to Duclos in 1765: a universal, intrinsic quality of matter,

10. For instance by Belaval, 'Les protagonistes du *Rêve de d'Alembert*', *Diderot studies* 3 (1961), p.52. For a rather different view, see Dieckmann, 'Théophile Bordeu und Diderots *Rêve de d'Alembert*', p.56-67, 120-22.

11. Cf. Winter, p.301. She too rejects the search to identify Diderot with a specific interlocutor, but denies that this fluidity is the expression of synthesis (either here or in the *Promenade du sceptique*). Rather, she argues, it stems from a form of positive scepticism. Her interpretation thus differs from mine in claiming that none (rather than all) of the participants speaks for Diderot.

12. Cf. Dieckmann, 'Bordeu und Diderots *Rêve de d'Alembert*', p.66.

which exists in both active and potential forms: 'une qualité générale et essen-tielle de la matière'; 'une sensibilité active et une sensibilité inerte'.[13] On this occasion, however, Diderot makes explicit the energetic analogy on which his intuition of universal *sensibilité* is based. Taking motion as his illustration, he points out to d'Alembert the distinction between active force (kinetic energy) and potential force (potential energy): 'ce que vous appelez la force vive n'est pas la force morte' (p.4; Lew. viii.56). He then draws a further distinction between a basic force (in this case, motive force) and its effect (the actual motion of a body). Motion, envisaged as a force rather than an effect, may thus be considered universal in matter, for all bodies are capable of deploying it: 'Le transport d'un corps d'un lieu dans un autre n'est pas le mouvement, ce n'en est que l'effet. Le mouvement est également et dans le corps transféré et dans le corps immobile.' In the case of a body at rest, he explains, the motive energy is simply held in check by other, opposing forces. If their action were suspended, that energy would be released: 'Otez l'obstacle qui s'oppose au transport local du corps immobile, et il sera transféré. Supprimez, par une raréfaction subite, l'air qui environne cet énorme tronc de chêne, et l'eau qu'il contient, entrant tout à coup en expansion, le dispersera en cent mille éclats' (p.4; Lew. viii.57).

The distinction between cause and effect in the classification of energy had first been used by Diderot to support his thesis on attraction in the 1761 paper *Sur la cohésion des corps*. It was not an entirely original idea. According to Crocker, both Toland and Rouelle had interpreted inertia as an expression of energy, a form of potential energy over and above mechanical energy, thus setting apart 'internal energy' and change of place.[14] For Belaval, the distinction between *transport* and motion goes back to Hobbes's notion of *nisus*, refracted through Rouelle.[15] Newton, Leibniz, Needham and d'Alembert also apparently held similar views of inertia as a real force and of the related, anti-cartesian distinction between a force and its effects. Needham, for instance, had written that 'Tous les effets produits dans l'univers ne sont que le résultat de l'action et de la réaction' and that the principle of resistance, far from being passive and inert, has 'une activité aussi réelle et aussi positive que celle du mouvement lui-même'.[16] D'Alembert had set apart 'causes motrices' from 'le mouvement qu'elles produisent'.[17] Kant had declared that motion was only the external phenomenon of force.[18] Nevertheless, Diderot's expression of it is sufficiently

13. *Rêve de d'Alembert*, ed. Varloot, p.3, 4; Lew. viii.56, 57.
14. 'Toland et le matérialisme de Diderot', p.292. Cf. Varloot (ed.), *Rêve de d'Alembert*, p.lxiii.
15. 'Note sur Diderot et Leibniz', p.446.
16. Quoted in Roger, *Les Sciences de la vie*, p.504.
17. Belaval, 'La crise de la géométrisation', p.344.
18. Belaval, 'La crise de la géométrisation', p.344. Cf. I. I. Polonoff, *Force, cosmos, monads* (Bonn 1973), p.37-38; cf. also p.9-15 (on Leibniz); Paty, 'Matière, espace et temps selon Newton', p.997-

radical for his interlocutor to remark upon its novelty: 'Cette façon de voir est nouvelle.'[19]

Diderot is breaking new ground, however, in his extension of the principle to *sensibilité*. He has d'Alembert draw a precise parallel between the two cases: to active motion (and its effect, the movement of bodies) corresponds active *sensibilité* (and its effect, physical behaviour recognised as characteristic of living forms of matter); to latent motion (setting up resistance to other forces, seeking release) corresponds latent *sensibilité* (equally seeking release in the active form) (p.4-5; Lew. viii.57):

Mais quel rapport y a-t-il entre le mouvement et la sensibilité? Serait-ce, par hasard, que vous reconnaîtriez une sensibilité active et une sensibilité inerte, comme il y a force vive et force morte? Une force vive qui se manifeste par la translation; une force morte qui se manifeste par la pression, une sensibilité active qui se caractérise par certaines actions remarquables dans l'animal et peut-être dans la plante; et une sensibilité inerte dont on serait assuré par le passage à l'état de sensibilité active?
– A merveilles, vous l'avez dit.

As in 1765, by positing active and potential modes of *sensibilité*, Diderot transcends the analogy with motion: envisaged in these terms, *sensibilité* is itself a form of energy, a force. This is confirmed by the fact that its active form is expressed as a dynamic effect ('certaines actions remarquables'). Chouillet offers a more cautious interpretation of this key move in Diderot's argument, referring to the '*quasi*-équivalence' of *sensibilité* and energy[20] and arguing that the parallel seems rather too convenient: 'la question reste ouverte de savoir si la notion de sensibilité active est ou n'est pas synonyme du concept d'énergie, et si le couple "sensibilité inerte/sensibilité active" n'est pas construit un petit peu sur mesure pour se calquer sur le couple inertie/énergie, autrement plus contrôlable et productif' (p.53). Diderot would have been the first to agree with Chouillet's contention that his idea owes more to poetic analogy than to scientific proof (p.47) but the evidence does suggest that he intended the resulting intuition to be taken seriously. The energetic nature of *sensibilité* will be acknowledged repeatedly as Diderot examines specific aspects of the concept later in the work.

ii. Sensibilité *and life*

Diderot's opening account confirms another implicit conclusion of his 1765 letter: the virtual identity of *sensibilité* and life. The distinctions between living

99 (on Newton); Varloot, 'Diderots Philosophie im *Rêve de d'Alembert*', p.708; Varloot (ed.), *Rêve de d'Alembert*, p.xcvii; above, chapter 4, p.122. We can find no evidence for Belaval's argument that Diderot's *force vive* refers to chemical/motive force rather than to the leibnizian concept of actual motion (Belaval, 'Note sur Diderot et Leibniz', p.446).
19. *Rêve de d'Alembert*, ed. Varloot, p.4; Lew. viii.57.
20. *Diderot poète de l'énergie*, p.47 (my emphasis).

and non-living matter, between a man and his statue, are reduced to two: not motion and organisation, the model frequently rejected by Diderot on previous occasions, but *sensibilité* and organisation.

It is d'Alembert who raises the issue of distinguishing between the organic and the inorganic. If *sensibilité* is indeed universal, he asks: 'Je voudrais bien que vous me disiez quelle différence vous mettez entre l'homme et la statue, entre le marbre et la chair.'[21] Diderot's reply introduces the motion/*sensibilité* analogy, which is clearly designed to resolve this very problem. Since both man and statue are material, he argues, there is no absolute difference between them; whilst evidently not identical, they are bound together as alternative facets of the same reality just as the concept of an active force implies the existence of its latent form (p.4; Lew. viii.56):

Assez peu ... On fait du marbre avec de la chair, et de la chair avec du marbre.
– Mais l'un n'est pas l'autre.
– Comme ce que vous appelez la force vive n'est pas la force morte.

The account of active and latent *sensibilité* which follows enables d'Alembert to answer his own question: 'Ainsi la statue n'a qu'une sensibilité inerte; et l'homme, l'animal, la plante peut-être sont doués d'une sensibilité active' (p.5; Lew. viii.57). By adopting this illustration Diderot makes it quite clear that inert sentience belongs to the mineral world and not, as Mayer seems to believe, simply to special categories of organism where the manifestations of life have been temporarily suspended. Mayer cites dormancy of fungal spores and the crystallisation of viruses as examples of modern discoveries which have vindicated Diderot's concept of life in the form of *force morte*.[22] Diderot would no doubt have found such cases interesting, but his concept of active and latent life as expressed here embraces something far vaster – the entirety of matter, in fact.

Living matter is quite simply, then, matter whose *sensibilité* is active. Life is the effect, or manifestation of *sensibilité* and stands in the same relationship to it as movement to motive force, or weight and gravitation to the force of attraction. It is not life which is universal (as in the paradox of 1759) but the prerequisite of life, vital energy, *sensibilité*.

Varloot sees this relationship in negative terms, as an unfortunate confusion between life and sentience. He thus misses the whole point of potential *sensibilité*.[23] A similar misapprehension underlies the thesis of Got who (apparently unaware of the evolutionary dimension of Diderot's thought) juxtaposes

21. *Rêve de d'Alembert*, p.3; Lew. viii.56.
22. *Diderot homme de science*, p.237.
23. 'Diderots Philosophie im *Rêve de d'Alembert*', p.714.

this exchange with extracts from the *Pensées sur l'interprétation de la nature* and the 1759 letter to Sophie in support of his thesis that Diderot's philosophy constitutes 'un véritable animisme'.[24] Such remarks as 'la matière, douée de sensibilité et de désir, se révèle vivante' and 'ce qui sent, à quelque degré qu'il sente, on ne peut sans contradiction le ravaler au rang d'un être tout matériel et sans vie' (p.142) reveal the extent to which he has misconstrued the *Rêve de d'Alembert*'s concept of *sensibilité*.[25]

Another paradox from the past has also been laid to rest. D'Alembert's first reaction to Diderot's proposed universal *sensibilité* had been to object that this would imply the existence of sentience in the mineral world. Initially Diderot seems unwilling (or unable) to refute such an implication:

Car enfin cette sensibilité [...], si c'est une qualité générale et essentielle de la matière, – il faut que la pierre sente.
– Pourquoi non?
– Cela est dur à croire.
– Oui, pour celui qui la coupe, la taille, la broie et qui ne l'entend pas crier.[26]

In fact, however, Diderot no more subscribes to the notion of 'feeling stones' than he did to the 'living pears' and 'thinking grapes' proposed by his Grandval audience in 1759. Whereas on that occasion he possessed no counter-argument, he is now able to call upon the concept of latency. For, as is subsequently made clear, sentience is a function only of active *sensibilité* and cannot therefore be manifested by a stone.[27] In any case, Diderot's final clause ('qui ne l'entend pas crier') points to a further objection. The stone has no organs of expression, nor indeed has it any sense organs, and sentience[28] (even in organic matter) is inoperative if there are no channels through which it can function.[29]

As at least one scholar has pointed out, Colonna reached a similar intuition of active/inert sentience:

Pour ce qui est des Pierres et des Métaux, ils ne peuvent pas en avoir [de sentiment] puisque cette matière animale est renfermée en eux sans pouvoir s'émouvoir, et par conséquent sans action sensible sur nos sens. Mais nous ne savons pas si cette âme n'a

24. M. Got, 'Sur le matérialisme de Diderot', *Revue de synthèse* 3 (1962), p.141.

25. Cf. also the arguments – equally guilty of an anachronistic approach – of J. Rostand, 'La molécule et le philosophe', *Nouvelles littéraires* (19.12.1963), p.7, and of Ehrard, 'Matérialisme et naturalisme', p.200, who equates Diderot's thesis with the 'psychisme rudimentaire' of Maupertuis; and cf. below, n.46.

26. *Rêve de d'Alembert*, p.3; Lew. viii.55-56.

27. Here Varloot's analysis coincides with my own ('Diderots Philosophie', p.717-18. Cf. Wartofsky, 'Diderot and the development of materialist monism', p.312-13).

28. Used in the sense conventionally given to *sensibilité* in the early eighteenth century: the faculty of sensory perception. For example, Richelet, *Dictionnaire françois* (1719, 1728): 'La faculté de sentir, la disposition des sens à recevoir l'impression des objets.'

29. Cf. above, chapter 4, 'Inné', and below, D.iii.

pas un sentiment douloureux d'être ainsi enchaînée dans le plus profond de ces corps, privée de toute action.[30]

Ehrard points out that Colonna also discussed the 'transmutation' of matter through nutritive assimilation, and that his ideas were available to Diderot through the work of Robinet.[31] The resemblance is, however, only superficial: Colonna's terminology ('sentiment' – 'cette matière animale' – 'cette âme') reveals the distance between his concept and that of Diderot.[32]

Diderot is well aware that organisation too plays a major rôle in the differentiation of living and non-living matter. At this stage, however, the issue merely receives a brief acknowledgement:

Il y a sans doute cette différence [of active and inert *sensibilité*] entre le bloc de marbre et le tissu de chair, mais vous concevez bien que ce n'est pas la seule. – Assurément. Quelque ressemblance qu'il y ait entre la forme extérieure de l'homme et de la statue, il n'y a point de rapport entre leur organisation intérieure.[33]

Diderot is only issuing a preliminary warning against over-simplification. The question of *sensibilité* must take precedence, since without it the animate/inanimate relationship cannot be accounted for. Organisation *alone* is an inadequate model. Nevertheless *sensibilité* is dependent on organisation for its operation, and this is an issue to which Diderot will return, elaborating it in some considerable detail.

In the meantime, however, having established that organic forms are set apart from the inanimate realm primarily by their possession of active *sensibilité*, that is, that life is essentially a mode of natural energy, his next priority is to examine the method of transition from the inert to the active state.

B. The activation of *sensibilité*

Sensibilité may be activated in two quite different contexts. Firstly there is the question of how life comes about in a system which previously has been totally non-sentient. This is the case in spontaneous generation and, for Diderot, at the moment of conception in sexual reproduction. Secondly the problem arises of how an already sentient system (the organism) assimilates to itself matter whose *sensibilité* is inert, thereby releasing its vital energy in an active form.

---

30. Quoted in Ehrard, *L'Idée de nature*, i.52, and 'Matérialisme et naturalisme', p.192 (*Les Principes de la nature*, 1731).

31. 'Matérialisme et naturalisme', p.193-94.

32. Similar, equally ill-defined ideas are expressed in an anonymous manuscript of 1738 quoted in Vartanian, *Diderot and Descartes*, p.280.

33. *Rêve de d'Alembert*, p.5; Lew. viii.57-58.

5. Le Rêve de d'Alembert

i. The non-sentient system

a. Sexual reproduction

1. The problem, and a provisional answer

The science of sexual reproduction was far from complete in 1769, with the coexistence of several alternative (and conflicting) models. Diderot himself took up no definitive position in the debate, although he did adhere fairly consistently to the view that both female and male germinal elements played a rôle in conception.[34] Believing these elements to possess no active life of their own – he refers to them respectively as 'une masse insensible' and 'un fluide inerte' – he was faced with the problem of explaining how their union could give rise to life:

Qu'est-ce que cet œuf?[35] une masse insensible, avant que le germe y soit introduit; et après que le germe y est introduit, qu'est-ce encore? une masse insensible, car le germe n'est lui-même qu'un fluide inerte et grossier. Comment cette masse passera-t-elle à une autre organisation, à la sensibilité, à la vie?[36]

This question can be answered on two levels: what actually occurs, and more importantly, how this occurrence produces its effect.

For the first answer, Diderot draws on the phenomenon of fermentation: heat produces motion within matter, which in turn brings about the reorganisation necessary for *sensibilité*, and thus life, to emerge: 'Comment cette masse passera-t-elle à une autre organisation, à la sensibilité, à la vie? Par la chaleur. Qu'y produira la chaleur? le mouvement.'[37] This line, 'Qu'y produira la chaleur? le mouvement', has frequently been misread as a statement that motion produces heat.[38] It may well be that this was the version generally held by what Kiernan has labelled the 'ferment theorists'[39] but syntax would appear to suggest the reverse procedure here.

This account, on its own, is nothing more than the ill-defined model Diderot had been putting forward as long ago as the *Lettre sur les aveugles*.[40] In effect, it answers nothing.

---

34. See *Eléments de physiologie*, ed. J. Mayer (Paris 1964), p.lxvii-lxix.

35. Diderot is taking the reproduction of birds as his example. The exact rôle of the *ovum*, or female egg, had not yet been discovered.

36. *Rêve de d'Alembert*, p.15; Lew. viii.67-68.

37. *Rêve de d'Alembert*, p.15. Cf. above, 4, D.iv, for an extract from the article 'Spinosiste' which Varloot cites as an anticipation of this passage (Lew. viii.68).

38. See, for instance Varloot, 'Diderots Philosophie', p.709; Wartofsky, p.314; and Szigeti, *Denis Diderot: une grande figure*, p.73. In this instance the question is even misprinted as 'Qui produira la chaleur?' (p.72).

39. 'Additional reflections', p.118.

40. Cf. above, i.

2. Implications of this answer

Diderot points out to d'Alembert that there are only three scientific positions logically consistent with this model: cartesian mechanism, preformationism and the dualistic belief in a separate animal soul. None of these alternatives is acceptable to the biologist-philosopher of the 1760s.

The complexities of animal behaviour militate against acceptance of the beast-machine thesis. To maintain that a bird, for instance, is a machine and man not, offends against common sense which tells even the least-educated observer that the motor skills and basic emotional faculties of bird and man are of the same order:

[le serin] marche, il vole, il s'irrite, il fuit, il approche, il se plaint, il souffre, il aime, il désire, il jouit, il a toutes vos affections, toutes vos actions, il les fait. Prétendrez-vous avec Descartes, que c'est une pure machine imitative? mais les petits enfants se moqueront de vous.[41]

The only logically tenable version of biological mechanism is to concede that both bird *and* man are mere machines: 'les philosophes vous répliqueront que si c'est là une machine, vous en êtes une autre', which would imply that they are distinguished only by the latter's more sophisticated organisation. At least this belief, in itself, raises no serious philosophical objections: 'Si vous avouez qu'entre l'animal et vous, il n'y a de différence que dans l'organisation, vous montrerez du sens et de la raison, – vous serez de bonne foi'. Nevertheless, the superior philosophical integrity of subscribing to this form of mechanism is entirely irrelevant. For the second question, of how these vital faculties (be they mechanical in operation or not) arose from inert matter, remains unanswered. The materialist philosopher is led directly back to the defective model with which he began, and is therefore still open to challenge:

vous serez de bonne foi, mais on en conclura contre vous qu'avec une matière inerte, disposée d'une certaine manière, imprégnée d'une autre matière inerte, de la chaleur et du mouvement, on obtient de la *sensibilité*, de la vie, de la mémoire, de la conscience, des passions, de la pensée.

These lines reiterate *what* happens at and after conception, but fail to explain *how* movement, heat and organisation vitalise matter. Current philosophy offered two conceptual bridges. The first of these is generally referred to as preformationism: the belief that each animal exists, preformed, in the egg (or in some versions the male seed) of its parent.[42] The second posits the introduction of a soul, or other vital principle, during the course of foetal development:

41. *Rêve de d'Alembert*, p.16; Lew. viii.68.
42. Kiernan has argued that this too was essentially a mechanistic concept ('Additional reflections', p.116).

Il ne vous reste qu'un de ces deux partis à prendre, c'est d'imaginer dans la masse inerte de l'œuf[43] un élément caché qui en attendait le développement pour manifester sa présence, – ou de supposer que cet élément imperceptible s'y est insinué à travers la coque, dans un instant déterminé du développement.[44]

Both these theories Diderot declares fraught with problems. Preformation still cannot explain at what point, or how, the transition from inanimate to animate occurs, nor can it offer any account of the size, form, substance or mode of existence of the preformed entity. The notion of an extrinsic vital principle poses not only physical, but metaphysical questions, not least whether the principle is material or spiritual (p.17; Lew. viii.68-69):

Mais qu'est-ce que cet élément? Occupait-il de l'espace, ou n'en occupait-il point? Comment est-il venu ou s'est-il échappé, sans se mouvoir? Que faisait-il là ou ailleurs? A-t-il été créé à l'instant de besoin? Existait-il, attendait-il un domicile? Homogène, il était matériel. Hétérogène on ne conçoit ni son inertie avant le développement, ni son énergie dans l'animal développé.

Both theories, then, are dismissed as absurdly obscurantist and riddled with internal contradictions – unworthy of consideration by the serious philosopher: 'Ecoutez-vous, et vous aurez pitié de vous-même; vous sentirez que [...] vous renoncez au sens commun et vous précipitez dans un abîme de mystères, de contradictions et d'absurdités.'

It has been argued by Got that this theory of an *élément caché* is an alternative formulation of *sensibilité* and thus acceptable to Diderot. He even excuses its vague wording on the grounds that Diderot knew little about the actual process of conception.[45] This reading allows him to maintain his thesis of Diderot's vitalism, 'vitalisme ou, mieux peut-être, animisme, c'est l'inspiration secrète de Diderot',[46] but seems to be based on a misunderstanding. In the first place, Diderot does quite clearly reject both alternatives: whether the *élément* originates within or outside the egg, it is declared to involve 'un abîme de mystères, de contradictions et d'absurdités' (p.17). The preceding questions confirm that his attack is directed at both versions: 'Comment est-il venu?' refers to an external principle, 'ou échappé' to an internal one; similarly with 'Que faisait-il là' and 'ou ailleurs'. Even if the *élément caché* and *sensibilité* could be conflated, Diderot's formulation of the latter in terms of an active and an inert form, that is, as force rather than the substance implied by *élément*, would avoid the vitalistic implications seen by Got.

43. Here again Diderot is referring to the canary's egg.
44. *Rêve de d'Alembert*, p.16-17; Lew. viii.68.
45. 'Le matérialisme de Diderot', p.151.
46. p.163. Cf. above, n.25.

3. Diderot's answer: universal *sensibilité*

Sensibilité alone offers a way out of the 'abîme' identified by Diderot. Only by assuming life to be the result of a form of energy, universal within matter, can an adequately materialist account of conception be formulated. If *sensibilité* (the principle underlying life) is there all the time, the problem of when and how it is introduced does not arise. It is this point which disturbs marxist critics and leads them to conclude that Diderot failed to escape from the traditional thought categories of mechanism/vitalism. Szigeti, in particular, contends that the latency principle prevents Diderot from elaborating a pure form of material-ism, since it makes no provision for the emergence of genuinely new qualitative levels: 'Chez Diderot [...] la qualité nouvelle, celle de la vie, était donnée d'emblée. [...] Son développement n'en est donc pas un dans le vrai sens du mot; il ne s'agit pas là de la naissance de quelque chose de neuf',[47] and again: 'la qualité déjà donnée devient manifeste, grâce à un accroissement quantitatif, mais aucune qualité nouvelle n'est engendrée' (p.76). It needs to be pointed out, firstly, that *sensibilité* is not a quality: it is *life* (active *sensibilité*) which is the quality, or characteristic state, of living matter, and this is not 'déjà donnée', since inanimate matter possesses only potential *sensibilité*, that is, not life. Secondly, life (active *sensibilité*) is not produced by 'un accroissement quantitatif' but by the process of activation, or transition to a completely new qualitative state. Similarly Ehrard sees Diderot's hypothesis of active and latent *sensibilité* as a further example of the same tendency which had given rise to Maupertuis's 'dynamisme psychique'. He claims that, in both systems, perception of a kind precedes the simplest organisation, and blames this 'inadequacy' on the state of chemistry: 'dans l'impossibilité de réduire la vie à un simple processus physico-chimique, on était de plus en plus conduit à admettre l'existence d'un "principe vital" spécifique'.[48] He thus fails to see that Diderot's principle, unlike Maupertuis's, is not of the sort which precludes a 'saut qualitatif' from inert to living matter. As Wartofsky has pointed out, it was only Maupertuis who rejected the possibility of perception and intelligence emerging at a certain qualitative level, by making them essential properties of matter (p.292). Diderot's monism is richer and fuller (p.298).

Szigeti's conclusion, then, does not seem to be borne out by a close examin-ation of what Diderot actually writes, both here and in the works of transition considered in the previous chapter. Firstly, *sensibilité* is primarily a force, a dynamic phenomenon, rather than a qualitative state. Secondly, life is the

47. *Denis Diderot: une grande figure*, p.74.
48. *L'Idée de nature*, i.221-26.

manifestation of this force, its mode of action under certain specific conditions: it simply does not exist in inert matter.[49]

If then the missing element involved in life is not an occult principle, but a purely material force, as *sensibilité* is, it is valid to describe its activation in the same terms as might be applied to any form of energy. And if both bird and man derive from germinal elements already possessing *sensibilité*, the differences between them may indeed be reduced to ones of organisation. Hence the advantages of accepting: 'Une supposition simple qui explique tout, la sensibilité, propriété générale de la matière, ou produit de l'organisation.'[50]

4. Duality of *sensibilité*?

It is important to study the precise significance and implications of Diderot's expression describing *sensibilité* as 'propriété générale de la matière, ou produit de l'organisation': so much depends on a careful interpretation of the single word *ou*. Does Diderot mean that *sensibilité* is to be understood as both 'propriété générale de la matière' and 'produit de l'organisation'? Or that it can be only one of these things? In the first case, does the co-existence of two alternatives imply that it is possible for both to be true simultaneously? Or that sometimes one, sometimes the other offers a more accurate description? In the second case, is Diderot's unwillingness to opt definitively for one version rather than the other to be seen as a strength or a weakness in his thought?

Whilst fully aware of the dangers of 'making Diderot seem more cartesian than he actually is',[51] I believe that this is one occasion when it is valid to reconstruct the underlying logic of Diderot's ideas. Certainly Diderot's expression is ambiguous; nevertheless I suspect that the 'problem' it presents may lie as much in interpreters' preconceptions of the nature of *sensibilité* as in the words themselves.

Diderot has already declared that there are two forms of *sensibilité*, inert (or potential) and active. Further, he has explained that in the male and female seminal elements *sensibilité* is dormant, representing not life itself, but a potential, a capacity for life. Finally, he has suggested that at the moment of conception these seminal elements are subjected to the forces of heat and motion and their inert *sensibilité* released in the form of those activities associated with sentience, the most basic form of life. In other words, even without accepting the energetic nature of *sensibilité*, it is possible to discern the way in which Diderot's elliptical expression may be literally applied to the ideas expressed elsewhere in the *Entretien*. Firstly, all matter, whether animate or inanimate, possesses *sensibilité*

49. Cf. below, Conclusion, p.192-93.
50. *Rêve de d'Alembert*, p.17; Lew. viii.69.
51. Niklaus, during discussion in 1982.

in one of its two forms, inert or active. This is Diderot's 'propriété générale de la matière'. Secondly, organic matter, where activation has taken place, possesses *sensibilité* in its active form, namely sentience as it is conventionally understood, the rudimentary manifestation of life. This is Diderot's 'produit de l'organisation'. Under certain conditions (discussed later in this chapter) universal *sensibilité* is converted to its active form, *via a change in organisation*. 'Propriété générale' and 'produit de l'organisation' are successive forms of the same phenomenon. Once the assumption of simultaneity is set aside, many of the problems of interpretation cease to exist.

For many commentators, Diderot's expression reveals a lack of commitment to the universality of *sensibilité*. Varloot, for instance, remarks that: 'Diderot laisse le choix entre l'hypothèse maximale et la sensibilité restreinte aux êtres organisés.'[52] Lefèbvre, on the other hand, paraphrases the idea in the following terms: 'Et Diderot montre ainsi à d'Alembert [...] que la sensibilité est propriété générale de la matière, ou plutôt *produit de l'organisation*.'[53] He gives no evidence or logical justification for his 'plutôt'; indeed he does not even mention the potential form of *sensibilité*, still less explore its energetic content. Szigeti takes much the same line, conflating general *sensibilité* with life[54] and concluding that, whilst the analogy with motion was Diderot's only hope of avoiding both mechanism and vitalism, he retained the (potentially dialectical) formula of *sensibilité* emerging at a given level of organisation 'car il pensait que l'avenir était susceptible de la doter d'un sens nouveau' (p.75). Only Momdzjan, to our knowledge, amongst the marxist school, accepts Diderot's belief in general *sensibilité* as self-consistent, pointing out that this constitutes 'une position quelque peu divergente' in comparison with contemporaries such as La Mettrie who avoided making a choice between the two conceptual alternatives.[55] He quotes, by way of illustration, the following lines from La Mettrie's *Traité de l'âme*: 'Nous ignorons si la matière a en soi la faculté de sentir ou seulement la puissance de l'acquérir par les modifications ou par les formes dont elle est susceptible; car il est vrai que cette faculté ne se montre que dans les corps organisés.'[56] This, in any case, is a far cry from Diderot's latency concept.

For some, the supposed duality of *sensibilité* represents a serious flaw in Diderot's thesis, for others a commendable eschewing of dogmatism. Varloot, for instance, describes *sensibilité* as a working hypothesis ('Arbeitshypothese')

---

52. *Rêve de d'Alembert*, p.7, n.3. Cf. Varloot, 'Diderots Philosophie', p.713, and Ehrard, 'Matérialisme et naturalisme', p.199-200: 'Nous soulignons ce *ou* qui traduit l'hésitation du philosophe.'
53. *Diderot*, p.158 (Lefèbvre's emphasis).
54. *Denis Diderot: une grande figure*, p.74.
55. 'La dialectique dans la vision du monde de Diderot', p.262-63.
56. p.263. Cf. above, chapter 4, n.91.

adopted only because neither reason nor contemporary experiments rule it out, and claims that intellectual integrity ('intellektuelle Ehrlichkeit') prevents him from choosing between the two alternatives. He does remark that Diderot seems to be using the term *sensibilité* sometimes in a general sense and sometimes with the restricted meaning of active *sensibilité*, but does not explore the possibility that this might provide a key to coherence, rather than contradiction ('Diderots Philosophie', p.713).

Hofmann, another critic in the marxist tradition, sees no tension between the alternatives, and praises Diderot for having opened up not one, but two potentially materialist epistemologies.[57] A similar reaction is evident in Crocker's analysis, which presents the alternatives as equally effective means to resist entropy, both exemplifying 'stability of the power to resist deterioration to a lower level of structuring and degrading of energy'.[58]

Winter devotes almost ten pages to the analysis of what she calls the duality of *sensibilité*. She argues that Diderot's awareness of the provisional, hypothetical quality of his own thought leads him to base his natural philosophy on a dual concept whose alternative formulations each imply a distinct content and a distinct philosophical position (p.229). *Sensibilité* as a general property of matter she sees as an essentially vitalist concept (p.233) on the grounds that it appeals to a concept of matter which is not purely physical: 'Diderots Hypothese der allgemeinen Sensibilität der Materie liegt jedoch schon eine völlig andere als die rein physikalische Konzeption der Materie zugrunde' (p.229-30). *Sensibilité* as the product of organisation, on the other hand, is accepted as a materialist hypothesis on the grounds that it posits the existence of non-sentient matter from which life emerges (as a qualitatively new property) only at a specific level of organisation (p.234). This duality, she concludes, makes it impossible to classify Diderot definitively as either vitalist or materialist (p.235, 277).

In fact, as I have shown, there is no need to 'explain' the duality, since Diderot's words can be acceptably interpreted as a single, uncontradictory formulation of his concept of *sensibilité*. Indeed, if the energetic dimension of this concept is taken into account, further indications of its coherence emerge. Diderot openly invites the conceptualisation of *sensibilité* as a force by means of the analogy he draws with movement, establishing a clear parallel between on the one hand *force morte*, *force vive* and the latter's manifestation in actual movement, and on the other, *sensibilité inerte*, *sensibilité active* and the latter's manifestation in actual sentience.[59] Despite the absence of any explicit statement

57. W. Hofmann, 'Diderots Auffassungen vom allgemeinen Empfindungsvermögen, von der Entstehung und Einheit des Bewußtseins', *Wissenschaftliche Zeitschrift* 13 (1964), p.176.
58. *Diderot's chaotic order*, p.27.
59. Cf. above, A.i.

to the effect that *sensibilité* is a force, it is difficult to see what else Diderot could have in mind.[60]

If this interpretation is correct, the 'duality' of Diderot's statement about *sensibilité* is easily dismissed. Just as motion may be envisaged either as a universal form of energy or as actual movement, so *sensibilité* may be considered to exist either as a universal force ('propriété générale de la matière') or as actual sentience ('produit de l'organisation'). Recasting Diderot's words in the form of a statement about motion will perhaps make this point more clearly. Had he written: 'le mouvement, propriété générale de la matière, ou produit du choc', it seems unlikely that this would have been interpreted as evidence of his uncertainty about the nature of motive force, still less as a regrettable contradiction.

It therefore follows that, far from being contradictory, the two forms of *sensibilité* (inert and active) are mutually indispensable. Ehrard comes close to recognising this, despite his orthodox view that the alternatives represent 'des incertitudes'[61] and that they are basically contradictory. He argues that since contemporary science did not allow Diderot to explain organisation 'sans supposer dans les éléments les propriétés du tout' both hypotheses must be retained: 'il a besoin qu'elles soient vraies en même temps'. In fact Diderot's entire concept of *sensibilité* relies on the assumption that both exist, and could not logically do otherwise. Were this not so, if only one of the alternative formulations were considered to hold the whole truth, the analogy he draws with motion – *force morte* and *force vive* – would be reduced to a meaningless exercise. The problem of accounting for the emergence of life without recourse to vitalism would remain unresolved. Diderot would be in no position to declare that *sensibilité* is 'une supposition simple qui explique tout'[62] were it not for the fact that *sensibilité* is not created, but activated. To recapitulate, *sensibilité* takes on two successive forms. In the seminal elements it is dormant, and represents a potential, a capacity for life. At conception, it is subjected to heat, motion, and released as the activities associated with sentience, the most basic form of life. It is not created, as the conventional accounts suggest, but activated, and thus exists in two, successive forms.

5. Organisation

Organisation plays the vital role in this conversion process. Heat produces

---

60. Nor is the idea as far-fetched as it might appear. Some years later, in the *Eléments de physiologie*, he will actually suggest *sensibilité* as a form of movement: 'Je serais tenté de croire que la sensibilité n'est autre chose que le mouvement de la substance animale' (quoted in Varloot (ed.), *Rêve de d'Alembert*, p.4, n.4). Cf. *Eléments de physiologie*, ed. Mayer, p.21; Lew. xiii.659.

61. *L'Idée de nature*, i.242; cf. 'ce flottement révélateur' (p.243).

62. *Rêve de d'Alembert*, p.17; Lew. viii.69.

motion in the previously inert matter, and thus induces the organisation required for *sensibilité* to be released. Diderot had established in 1761 that the manifestations of an energy resource are determined by the varying physical conditions under which it is deployed; organisation is one such variable. On three occasions in this single portion of dialogue he points out the need for matter to take on an appropriate arrangement before the activation of *sensibilité* can occur:

Comment cette masse passera-t-elle *à une autre organisation*, à la sensibilité, à la vie? [...]

Avec une matière inerte, *disposée d'une certaine manière*, [...] on obtient de la sensibilité, de la vie. [...] [63]

La sensibilité, [...] *produit de l'organisation*.[64]

Modern biology, with its knowledge that male and female germ cells are already highly complex, living entities, has rendered Diderot's account obsolete. Nevertheless it is an ingenious attempt to come to terms with the problem posed by sexual reproduction as it was then understood.

b. Spontaneous generation

To a certain extent this too is a false problem. As on previous occasions, Diderot's belief in spontaneous generation stems from his acceptance of Needham's findings, which were subsequently to be discredited.[65]

The issue of spontaneous generation has two aspects, however. On the one hand is biogenesis, or the current production of living organisms from organic matter by purely physical means. It was this form of spontaneous generation which Needham's work appeared to have proved, but which scientists no longer accept.[66] On the other is abiogenesis, the original emergence of life from inert, inorganic elements, under special conditions no longer prevalent. This process has been replicated in the laboratory and is today widely accepted as the alternative to creationist theories. In certain respects, therefore, Diderot's concern with the issue is not entirely redundant.

As Mendelsohn's lucid and interesting account of the previous history of this concept[67] has pointed out, spontaneous generation was considered 'disproved' three times – by Rédi and Leeuwenhoek in the seventeenth century, Spallanzani

63. *Rêve de d'Alembert*, p.16 (my emphasis); Lew. viii.68.
64. *Rêve de d'Alembert*, p.17 (my emphasis); Lew. viii.69.
65. Cf. above, chapters 1 (*Lettre sur les aveugles*) and 2 (*Apologie de l'abbé de Prades*). Cf. also Chouillet, *Diderot poète de l'énergie*, p.53.
66. Spallanzani had already conducted counter-experiments in 1765, but Diderot failed to be convinced by his findings.
67. 'Philosophical biology versus experimental biology: spontaneous generation in the seventeenth century'. For a detailed, though less felicitous account of the eighteenth-century debate, see Rostand, *Les Origines de la biologie expérimentale*, p.16-46.

in the eighteenth, and Pasteur in the nineteenth. Mendelsohn comments perceptively that the concept 'did not die each time, but rather in descending order of size of organism[68] its usefulness as an explanatory model for the generation of organisms was replaced' and that modern research suggests 'some form of a concept of abiogenetic formation of living "stuff" may well still be a very strong explanatory model' (p.204).

Spontaneous generation is introduced in the *Entretien* to resolve the question of what d'Alembert calls 'la génération première des animaux'.[69] Diderot rejects once again the theory of preformation ('ces germes préexistants') and substitutes a transformist account of the development of present-day forms. If, he speculates, the sun were to be extinguished, these forms would die out; no life would remain on earth. All that would be required, however, to revive the process, to bring about new prototype beings, is the restoration of the sun: 'Rallumez cet astre, – et à l'instant vous rétablissez la cause nécessaire d'une infinité de générations nouvelles' (p.10; Lew. viii.63). This speculative device recalls Descartes's method in his *De mundo*, and incidentally appears to cast doubt on Crocker's claim that Diderot does not share the modern view of a system in entropy having no tendency to change itself.[70] Diderot's words imply that he does hold this to be the case, since an input of extraneous energy is required to bring about new interactions with the 'inert sediment' resulting from the sun's previous extinction. By implication too it is in this way that life arose in the first place: through the action of heat upon inert matter. Although *sensibilité* is not mentioned in these lines, it would appear that essentially the same principle is involved in the hypothetical regeneration of life as in sexual reproduction, namely the transition from an inert to an active (sentient and animate) state, with heat (the sun) and organisation (d'Alembert's reference to 'les mêmes éléments épars, venant à se réunir' under the influence of thermal energy)[71] playing the key roles.

Certainly when d'Alembert returns to this particular theme during his dream, he will make an explicit connection between the microcosmic (spontaneous generation) and macrocosmic (terrestrial regeneration) levels of the process. In the speculative synthesis offered by his vision of nature, the difference between them is one of scale only. Mlle de l'Espinasse reports his speculations on the supposed instances of spontaneous generation observed by Needham:

Le vase où il apercevait tant de générations momentanées, il le comparait à l'univers. Il

68. Insects, infusoria and bacteria respectively.
69. *Rêve de d'Alembert*, p.9; Lew. viii.62.
70. *Diderot's chaotic order*, p.17, n.
71. *Rêve de d'Alembert*, p.11; Lew. viii.63. For Diderot's account of the corresponding process in reproduction, see above, B.i.a.1, 2 and 5.

voyait dans une goutte d'eau l'histoire du monde. [...] Suite indéfinie d'animalcules dans l'atome qui fermente. Même suite indéfinie d'animalcules dans l'autre atome qu'on appelle la terre.[72]

Diderot's hypothetical future world is the subject of further speculation in a later phase of d'Alembert's dream, and on this occasion *sensibilité* does feature in its reanimation. Matter is seen as passing through three successive stages. Starting as 'un grand sédiment inerte et immobile' (that is, where both motion and *sensibilité* are present only in their potential forms) it then becomes 'un amas [...] de points sensibles et vivants' and may ultimately develop into sophisticated animal forms (p.37; Lew. viii.91). The activation of *sensibilité* during this transition is twice attributed to the process of *fermentation*: 'Qui sait si la fermentation et ses produits sont épuisés? [...] L'éléphant, cette masse énorme, organisée, le produit subit de la fermentation? Pourquoi non?' Interestingly, these lines indicate that past, present and hypothetical future are being reintegrated into a single vision. The first reference looks back to the origins of the actual world and Epicurus's view that existing forms had been brought about by fermentation (p.36; Lew. viii.90) and implies that the process may still be going on; the second reference is to the hypothetical future, but is prompted by contemporary beliefs about spontaneous generation. D'Alembert's reasoning, in the dream state where anything seems possible, is that, since it has been proved that a grain of flour can produce a worm (this is what Needham's experiments had claimed to show), an analogous phenomenon at the macrocosmic level – the earth producing an elephant – cannot be ruled out. The spontaneous generation of large or small organisms appears equally feasible, and neither need involve any extra-material principle: 'tous les deux sont également possibles; ils ne supposent que le mouvement et les propriétés diverses de la matière' (p.37; Lew. viii.91).

The 'propriétés diverses de la matière' may be fairly assumed to include *sensibilité*, given Diderot's statement of its universality in the *Entretien*. His use of the word 'propriété', incidentally, might seem to militate against my interpretation of *sensibilité* in energetic terms. In fact, however, Diderot uses the label loosely throughout his philosophical writings, and no particular significance can be attached to it. I shall mention just two examples, widely separated in time. The *Encyclopédie* article 'Asiatiques' refers to movement and 'les autres propriétés de la matière'.[73] Motion, whose energetic status is not in question, is thus classed as a property. In the much later *Eléments de physiologie* Diderot declares that 'la matière en général aura cinq ou six propriétés essentielles, la

72. *Rêve de d'Alembert*, p.34-35. Cf. p.36-37, where the same drop of water is described as 'une image en petit, de ce qui s'était fait en grand à l'origine des temps' (Lew. viii.89).
73. Her., v.521 (quoted above, 2, B.ii.a; cf. also chapter 5, conclusion).

force morte ou vive, la longueur, la largeur, la profondeur, l'impénétrabilité et la sensibilité'.[74] Here aspects we would categorise separately as dimensions, properties and forces all coexist happily under the label of 'propriétés'.

Once the dreaming d'Alembert has accepted Diderot's hypothesis of inert and active *sensibilité*, and hence that there exists a purely material principle to account for the transition from inanimate to animate matter, the phenomenon of spontaneous generation ceases to appear miraculous: 'Le prodige, c'est la vie, c'est la sensibilité; et ce prodige n'en est plus un ... Lorsque j'ai vu la matière inerte passer à l'état sensible, rien ne doit plus m'étonner.'[75] He concludes that, together, spontaneous generation and the process responsible for it, the activation of *sensibilité*, account adequately for vital phenomena, past, present or future: 'Vous avez deux grands phénomènes, le passage de l'état d'inertie à l'état de sensibilité, – et les générations spontanées; qu'ils vous suffisent' (p.38; Lew. viii.92).

For Winter, this declaration exemplifies Diderot's synthesis of philosophical theory (universal *sensibilité*) and scientific experiment (spontaneous generation) (p.40-41). It is unfortunate that the experimental data available to him were ambiguous in the conclusions they suggested:[76] the fanciful instances of biogenesis conjured up by d'Alembert[77] can no doubt be dismissed as the extravagances of a dream, but I think it unlikely that Diderot would have indulged in them, had contemporary biological research offered a more clear-cut answer to the question of whether biogenesis actually occurs.

Abiogenesis is a different matter. The origins of life on earth could obviously be discussed only in speculative terms. Diderot's guess was likely to be as good as anyone else's, and by a happy coincidence his intuitions are strikingly similar to modern scientific opinion on the question. It is not difficult to draw a parallel between Diderot's 'sédiment inerte', 'soleil [...] cause nécessaire d'une infinité de générations nouvelles' and 'points sensibles et vivants' and the twentieth-century account of ultraviolet light energy and heat from the sun catalysing chemical reactions within primitive forms of matter until chance combinations brought about DNA molecules, the basic replicable units of all life forms.[78] Indeed, given that Diderot is thinking of life itself in primarily energetic terms, thanks to his concept of potential and active *sensibilité*, the coincidence may not be so surprising.

74. *Eléments de physiologie*, ed. Mayer, p.24; Lew. xiii.661.

75. *Rêve de d'Alembert*, p.38; Lew. viii.91. Cf. Winter, p.157-58.

76. Cf. above, B.i.a.5.

77. See Mayer, *Diderot homme de science*, p.239.

78. For an early version of this now generally accepted theory, see H. C. Urey, 'On the early chemical history of the earth and the origin of life', *Proceedings of the National Academy of Sciences* 38 (1952), esp. p.356, 362.

ii. *The sentient system: nutritive assimilation*

The activation of *sensibilité* within the organism, which is itself already sentient, presents a rather different problem. Once an organism has come into being, it must grow and develop by the assimilation of extraneous matter. This raises the familiar question of how two heterogeneous portions of matter – one organic, living, the other inorganic and inert – can interact.

Diderot's 1765 letter to Duclos had proposed active and potential categories of *sensibilité* as a source of homogeneity replacing the 'eternal life' of 1759.[79] If *sensibilité*, seen as vital energy, is universal within matter, the process of nutritive assimilation involves merely the activation of a force which already exists. Diderot returns to this principle in the *Entretien*.

D'Alembert disputes the analogy drawn by Diderot between motion and *sensibilité*, on the grounds that, whereas the conversion of potential to kinetic motion is easily accomplished by means of impetus, there appears to be no equivalent procedure where *sensibilité* is concerned: 'Mais il y a un procédé fort simple pour faire passer une force morte à l'état de force vive; c'est une expérience qui se répète sous nos yeux cent fois par jour. Au lieu que je ne vois pas trop comment on fait passer un corps de l'état de sensibilité inerte à l'état de sensibilité active.'[80] Diderot points out in reply that the phenomena of nutrition and digestion perform the same rôle for *sensibilité* as impetus does for motion. In both cases inertia results from an equilibrium of opposing forces, and in both cases this equilibrium can be disturbed. The liberation of motion has already been described: 'Otez l'obstacle qui s'oppose au transport local du corps immobile, et il sera transféré' (p.4; Lew. viii.57). The release of vital energy is accomplished by an equally straightforward method: 'Cela se fait toutes les fois que vous mangez. [...] car en mangeant, que faites-vous? Vous levez les obstacles qui s'opposaient à la sensibilité active de l'aliment; vous l'assimilez avec vous-même; vous en faites de la chair; vous l'animalisez; vous la [*sic*] rendez sensible' (p.5-6; Lew. viii.58).

In 1765 Diderot's attitude towards the participation of plants and minerals in the food chain had been ambiguous.[81] Even now he remains uncertain as to whether plants should be classed as actively sentient or not.[82] Nevertheless he does acknowledge in the *Entretien* that both mineral and plant are potentially capable of life, since their quota of (latent) *sensibilité* can be released as vital

79. Cf. above, chapter 4.
80. *Rêve de d'Alembert*, p.5; Lew. viii.58.
81. Cf. above, chapter 4.
82. He refers earlier to 'certaines actions remarquables dans l'animal et peut-être dans la plante' (p.4) and states that 'l'homme, l'animal, la plante même peut-être sont doués d'une sensibilité active' (p.5; Lew. viii.57bis).

energy at the end of the nutritive chain (p.6-7; Lew. viii.58-60):

Ce que vous exécutez sur un aliment, je l'exécuterai, quand il me plaira, sur le marbre. [...] Lorsque le bloc de marbre est réduit en poudre impalpable, je mêle cette poudre à de l'humus ou terre végétale. [...] J'y sème des pois, des fèves, des choux, d'autres plantes légumineuses. Les plantes se nourrissent de la terre, – et je me nourris des plantes. [...] Je fais donc de la chair, [...] une matière activement sensible.

Guédon claims a chemical source for Diderot's account of nutritive assimilation on the grounds of his declaration that 'il y a un moyen d'union, d'appropriation entre l'humus et moi, – un *latus*, comme vous dirait le chimiste. – Et ce *latus*, c'est la plante' (p.7; Lew. viii.59). For the eighteenth-century chemist, *latus* denoted the particular quality of a composite substance which gave it a certain affinity for another body. Guédon sees this chemical metaphor as a more significant model than d'Alembert's *force vive* and *force morte*,[83] arguing that it enables Diderot to envisage life as a surface phenomenon corresponding to one of matter's many properties and requiring only certain specific circumstances, a certain chemical combination, to emerge (p.200). Whilst Guédon's overall interpretation may be valid, he neglects the central, energetic concept of latency, and fails to acknowledge that the essentials of Diderot's account of nutritive assimilation had been established long before his introduction of *latus* as an illustrative image.

An article by Varloot, on the other hand, offers the interesting hypothesis that Diderot may have been influenced in his choice of a sculptural masterpiece to represent the mineral world (the 'bloc de marbre' is a statue) by the myth of Pygmalion – the subject both of a sculpture by Falconet (quite probably the *chef d'œuvre* to which Diderot refers) and of several contemporary works of fiction. Boureau-Deslandes, for instance, in his novel *Pigmalion* (1741; republished in 1753) speculates that a statue could indeed develop human faculties of sentience and thought: 'Tout dépend peut-être d'un peu plus ou d'un peu moins de mouvement, d'un certain arrangement des parties', and describes its gradual animation in terms which Varloot finds highly significant: 'La machine se développe peu à peu, ses ressorts jouent les uns contre les autres, les fluides et les solides se combattent et résistent tour à tour, c'est *une action et une réaction continuelles.*'[84] This only serves to illustrate the futility of much critical research into 'sources', for what Varloot overlooks is the fact that Diderot's model requires the statue to be broken down into its component parts and assimilated into an existing organism; moreover the mechanistic tenor of Boureau-Des-

83. 'Chimie et matérialisme', p.198-99.
84. 'Le projet "antique" du *Rêve de d'Alembert* de Diderot', *Beiträge zur romanischen Philologie* 2 (1963), p.50-52. Varloot's emphasis.

landes's account is not entirely in keeping with Diderot's concept of *organic* action and reaction.

The distance between Diderot and his 'sources' may be further illustrated by reference to a 1718 extract from Meslier's writings. Meslier's proposition that: 'ce n'est pas précisément la matière qui pense, mais c'est l'homme ou l'animal composé de matière qui pense [...] comme les parties d'une pierre ou d'un morceau de fer [...] peuvent par leurs différentes modifications devenir chair et os'[85] bears only a superficial resemblance to Diderot's thesis; it does not seek to explain the process involved, nor does it describe it in terms of the general properties of matter, still less suggest an energetic dimension. If anything, such a parallel demonstrates the extent of Diderot's originality rather than his borrowings.

Once again, although modern biology would not accept all the details of his account, in his description of nutritive assimilation Diderot has applied the concept of universal *sensibilité* in terms consistent both with the current state of science and with the requirements of materialism. By conceptualising *sensibilité* as a force activated only under certain conditions, he has bridged the gulf between organic and inorganic matter without recourse to a vitalist model.

Szigeti disputes that Diderot's account of nutritive assimilation resolves the issue of inorganic/organic conversion on the grounds that it presupposes 'une substance vivante capable de s'assimiler la substance inorganique' (p.71). This criticism offers a true premise (nutritive assimilation *does* require living matter) but an invalid conclusion. It implies that Diderot has taken the easy way out and failed to address the problem, and thus overlooks the fact that the integration of 'inert' foodstuffs into a living system presents a genuine challenge for the materialist, a challenge to which Diderot has responded imaginatively. More basically, Szigeti omits to mention that this section of the work constitutes only part of Diderot's reflections on the issue; the emergence of life from wholly inert matter is discussed later in the *Entretien* and again in the *Rêve*. Belaval makes a similar slightly unfair observation: 'Le *Rêve* ne paraît pas aller plus loin [que les *Pensées sur l'interprétation de la nature*], puisque les transitions d'un règne à l'autre s'y font toujours en supposant, dans la combinaison, la présence du règne supérieur.'[86] Belaval's 'toujours' is not borne out by Diderot's speculations on the origins of life (abiogenesis). He does, however, make the valuable suggestion that nutritive assimilation should be considered primarily a *chemical* process (and latent *sensibilité* as a chemical force).[87] He agrees with Naigeon in

85. Quoted in Wade, *Clandestine organization*, p.69. The same passage appears as an anticipation of Diderot in Vernière, *Spinoza et la pensée française*, p.368, n.3.
86. 'Sur le matérialisme de Diderot', *Europäische Aufklärung* (München 1967), p.16.
87. See *ibid.*, especially p.17-18, for Belaval's detailed support of this thesis.

seeing Rouelle's influence as decisive in turning Diderot towards chemistry, rather than mechanism, for his answers to the questions posed at the end of the *Pensées sur l'interprétation de la nature*.[88] Such an interpretation would go a long way towards answering Crocker's objection that Diderot does not attempt to relate the laws governing organic function to the laws of the non-organic physical world.[89]

iii. *The outcome of activation: organic unity*

a. The problem

As in sexual reproduction, the activation of *sensibilité* in a sentient system (the food chain) gives rise to two related questions: firstly, what actually happens, and secondly, how this process produces its effect. Nutritive assimilation alone answers only the former question. It gives no account of how combination brings about a unified whole, sentient in all its parts, a problem closely analogous to the issue of corporate consciousness considered by Diderot in the *Pensées sur l'interprétation de la nature* some fifteen years before.[90]

As d'Alembert points out at the start of his dream, it is not clear how the products of digestion are assimilated into the animal body. Even if their vital energy has been activated, this does not necessarily lead to unity with adjacent living matter: 'Tenez, philosophe, – je vois bien un agrégat, un tissu de petits êtres sensibles, – mais un animal? ... un tout? ... un système un, lui, ayant la conscience de son unité? je ne le vois pas ... non, je ne le vois pas.'[91]

The pages which follow attempt to clarify this issue. Diderot has Bordeu approve and complete the dreaming d'Alembert's speculation, so that this particular complex of ideas is worked through twice – dreaming and waking – as if to stress the significance he attaches to it. It is difficult to envisage the grounds on which Crocker states that Diderot does not attempt to explain why or how organic unity develops.[92] Lerel, too, is guilty of oversimplification of this issue. He quotes the passage relating to the fusion of drops of mercury,[93] omits the alternative version and even passing reference to nutritive assimilation, and then declares that Diderot does not investigate the relationship between *sensibilité*

---

88. *Ibid.*, *passim.* Cf. Desné, 'Sur le matérialisme de Diderot', p.101-102, and Belaval, 'Le *philosophe* Diderot', *Critique* 58 (1952), p.244 n.45. Cf. also above, on Guédon.

89. *Diderot the embattled philosopher*, p.317.

90. Cf. above, chapter 3.

91. *Rêve de d'Alembert*, p.26; Lew. viii.80. The reference here is actually to epigenesis, that is, the theory of embryonic growth by addition of matter rather than cellular division, which was unknown in the eighteenth century (cf. *ibid.*, n.1). The principles involved are thus the same as in nutritive assimilation.

92. *Diderot the embattled philosopher*, p.317.

93. See below, b.1.

and continuity (*Diderots Naturphilosophie*, p.52). On the contrary, it is one of the questions which is most fully investigated.

b. Physical continuity

In 1765, Diderot had implied that he believed interactions within organic matter to lead to continuity, rather than mere contiguity between its constituent parts.[94] This concept is at once made explicit in the *Rêve*. It is the first stage of Diderot's response to the problem of unity posed by d'Alembert: 'Mon ami, d'Alembert, prenez-y garde: vous ne supposez que de la contiguïté où il y a continuité' (p.26-27; Lew. viii.80). By attempting to visualise biological unity in terms of contiguity only, d'Alembert has overlooked the fact that organic combination is of a different order from its inorganic counterpart. He reminds himself of this principle twice in the lines which follow (p.27-28; Lew. viii.81):

Il est certain que le contact de deux molécules vivantes est tout autre chose que la contiguïté de deux masses inertes ...
[...]
il doit y avoir de la différence entre le contact de deux molécules sensibles et le contact de deux molécules qui ne la seraient pas.

The key to this distinction is continuity. But how does continuity come about? Diderot elaborates two alternative accounts.

1. Simple model

The first is based on an analogy with the mode of combination observed in fluids. Where two particles of organic matter (both actively sentient) have an identical, simple chemical nature, they merge on contact (p.27; Lew. viii.81):

Comme une goutte de mercure se fond dans une autre goutte de mercure, une molécule sensible et vivante se fond dans une molécule sensible et vivante ... D'abord il y avait deux gouttes; après le contact, il n'y en a plus qu'une ... Avant l'assimilation il y avait deux molécules; après l'assimilation, il n'y en a plus qu'une.

The original identities of the particles are completely submerged in the new whole; the sentience of the molecules – their quota of vital energy – is pooled, becomes corporate sentience: 'La sensibilité devient commune à la masse commune.' The outcome of such a process would be total continuity, perfect organic unity: 'Le contact de deux molécules homogènes, parfaitement homogènes forme la continuité ... et c'est le cas de l'union, de la cohésion, de la combinaison, de l'identité la plus complète qu'on puisse imaginer.'

There are severe limitations to this model, however, as Diderot acknowledges. In the first place it can apply only to the simplest levels of living matter (it is

94. Cf. above, chapter 4.

not, in fact, clear whether Diderot has any concrete instances in mind). It cannot account for the combination of more complex organic entities – such as those actually involved in animal nutrition: 'Oui, philosophe, si ces molécules sont élémentaires et simples; mais si ce sont des agrégats; si ce sont des composés.' Nor has this model any place for the conversion of latent to active *sensibilité*; it assumes that activation has already taken place, and this is at variance to some extent with his declaration that actively sentient matter combines in a wholly different manner from its inert counterpart – such as, presumably, liquid mercury.[95]

Nevertheless, the combination of compound aggregates of organic matter does occur. Here too unity is established in the form of physical continuity, and the resultant, even more complex systems are able to interact in their turn, which implies a common fund of *sensibilité* or vital energy: 'La combinaison ne s'en fera pas moins, et en conséquence l'identité, la continuité … et puis l'action et la réaction habituelles' (p.27; Lew. viii.81). Consequently an alternative model must be sought; having outlined the objections, d'Alembert is unable to leave the subject unresolved: 'Passons, passons … […] Cependant reprenons …'

2. Complex model

A second analogy is introduced: that of a fabric woven from different types of thread. Whether the fibres are of plant, animal or even mineral origin: 'Un fil d'or très pur. Je m'en souviens; c'est une comparaison qu'il m'a faite' (p.27; Lew. viii.81), they intermesh into a continuous whole, despite their diversity. Complex webs of organic matter go to make up the fabric of a living system. The strands considered individually are homogeneous (and possibly, therefore, formed along the lines of the fusion model). Intertwined, they form a heterogeneous yet continuous whole, whose potential complexity knows no bounds: 'Un réseau homogène, entre les molécules duquel d'autres s'interposent et forment peut-être un autre réseau homogène, – un tissu de matière sensible, – un contact qui assimile'.

Unity is ensured by the presence of active vital energy. The original sentient organism communicates its life to the newly assimilated matter in the same way that motion is transferred from one body to another: by activation of the latent energy source: 'un contact qui assimile, de la sensibilité, active ici, inerte là, qui se communique comme le mouvement'.

Thus the matter ingested during the digestive process is qualitatively transformed, its *sensibilité* converted to an active state. It is not therefore true, as Crocker suggests, that Diderot fails to draw the necessary conclusion from his philosophy

95. Cf. Casini, *Diderot 'philosophe'*, p.281.

of organism – that an atom (Crocker's term) may behave differently when part of an organism, being to some extent determined by the whole.[96] It is precisely the nature of matter's activity ('behaviour') which is transformed by its assimilation into a living system. Vital energy bonds the two previously disparate portions of matter, enabling them to participate in a common identity. Organic unity is not the product of a static, crystallised patterning within contiguous systems, but derives from a dynamic flux, an ever-changing pattern of interactions, which amount to a kind of internal finalism akin to Diderot's early principle of optimum organisation. When an external element (energetic or material) is introduced into a balanced system, the resulting modifications tend to restore a state of balance: unity is maintained.[97] Varloot touches on this point, although he does not make it clear (in terms of *sensibilité*) why this should distinguish organic from inorganic matter ('Diderots Philosophie', p.716):

Ihre [of the aggregate] Einheit ist nicht metaphysisch; sie wird durch das Leben des Ganzen herbeigeführt; [...] im Inneren jedes Aggregats gründet sich die Einheit auf die fortwährend stattfindenden Wirkungen und Rückwirkungen: darin besteht die qualitative Besonderheit des organischen Wesens.

Moreover, these are not the interactions associated with the activity of attractive and motive force (as in the inorganic realm) but the special interrelationships for which active *sensibilité*, the uniquely organic energy, is responsible (*Rêve de d'Alembert*, p.27-28; Lew. viii.81):

il doit y avoir de la différence entre le contact de deux molécules sensibles et le contact de deux molécules qui ne le seraient pas; et cette différence? quelle peut-elle être? ... une action, une réaction habituelles ... et cette action et cette réaction avec un caractère particulier ... tout concourt donc à produire une sorte d'unité qui n'existe que dans l'animal.

This model offers a far more detailed and sophisticated account of biological unity than the first. It also accords, incidentally, with a quite modern account of the distinction between organic and inorganic. 'Pour les philosophes', remarked Collin in 1935, 'les êtres vivants sont caractérisés par l'immanence de l'action et s'opposent aux corps bruts qui possèdent seulement l'action transitive' (p.413). Thus the transfer of motion or electricity, together with chemical reactions, may be considered external, whereas such processes as assimilation and self-construction are immanent (p.413-14). In the latter, the original components effectively disappear, yet the organism remains constant, by virtue of a complex kind of self-preserving unity (p.415-16). The network model is still not entirely

---

96. *Diderot the embattled philosopher*, p.317.

97. Cf. R. Collin, 'Mécanisme et animisme en biologie', *Revue de philosophie* 35 (1935), p.393-411, for the role played by this principle in the modern account of nutritive assimilation.

satisfactory to Diderot, however, and he re-examines the issue one more time in an attempt to clarify the form taken by this uniquely organic variety of unity.

c. Animal unity

Diderot has explained how the process of nutritive assimilation leads to the activation of *sensibilité* and the creation of a basic unity within organic matter. He now takes his speculation one step further in an attempt to account for unity on a higher level – not between the individual portions of matter which form the parts of an animal, but between the composite parts themselves.

He considers two different types of animal organisation: those involved in *animaux ordinaires* and *animaux polypeux* (*Rêve de d'Alembert*, p.31; Lew. viii.85). Although modern cellular biology discounts such a distinction,[98] any eighteenth-century attempt to describe the organisation of living forms without reference to the apparently anomalous characteristics of the polyp would have been less than complete.

Diderot's final model of organic unity is based on yet another analogy: between an animal and a swarm of bees. This was a concept which enjoyed a wide currency in the eighteenth century, and Diderot was already acquainted with it from his reading of Maupertuis.[99] Bordeu had also used the image in his writings and is given the rôle of elaborating it here to endorse and extend the dreaming d'Alembert's vision.

1. The swarm of bees: basic version

The swarm of bees represents a developed animal; the individual bees correspond to its organs, themselves complex, composite aggregates of living matter: 'cette grappe est un être, un individu, un animal quelconque. [...] un assemblage d'animaux' (p.28, 30; Lew. viii.82, 83). Within this swarm, unity is maintained by constant interaction between the parts (p.28-29; Lew. viii.82):

Si l'une de ces abeilles s'avise de pincer d'une façon quelconque, l'abeille à laquelle elle s'est accrochée, que croyez-vous qu'il en arrive? [...] il [Diderot] vous dira que celle-ci pincera la suivante; qu'il s'excitera dans toute la grappe autant de sensations qu'il y a de petits animaux.

Thanks to common sentience,[100] the individual identities of the bees are

98. It is realised today that the ability of certain organisms to replicate damaged tissues is not a function of their organisation. Every cell, however specialised, carries the same genetic blueprint and is potentially capable of self-replication. This ability is simply suppressed in the majority of cases.

99. Cf. above, chapter 3. Cf. also Dieckmann, 'Bordeu und Diderots *Rêve de d'Alembert*', p.109, n.125.

100. Cf. Chouillet, *Diderot poète de l'énergie*, p.231: 'Il y a déjà, au-delà de la juxtaposition des individus, un début d'agglutination et de vie commune; qui plus est, une sensibilité commune.'

transcended, merged into a corporate identity, which allows the swarm to behave as if it were a single organism (p.29; Lew. viii.82):

le tout s'agitera, se remuera, changera de situation et de forme; [...] celui qui n'aurait jamais vu une pareille grappe s'arranger, serait tenté de la prendre pour un animal à cinq ou six cents têtes, et à mille ou douze cents ailes.

As the last sentence implies, however ('serait tenté'), the analogy is not complete. For the individual bees are linked only in a contiguous, not continuous fashion: 'une longue grappe de petits êtres ailés, tous *accrochés* les uns aux autres par les ailes' (p.28; Lew. viii.82; my emphasis). Consequently the swarm, as it occurs in nature, does not provide a full model for animal organisation: 'L'homme qui prendrait cette grappe pour un animal se tromperait' (p.29; Lew. viii.83).

2. First reformulation: the continuous swarm

This can only be achieved by substituting continuity for contiguity, by fusing the insects' feet where the contact occurs: 'voulez-vous transformer la grappe d'abeilles en un seul et unique animal? Amollissez les pattes par lesquelles elles se tiennent; de contigües qu'elles étaient, rendez-les continues.' By means of this device, genuine unity is achieved: 'Entre ce nouvel état de la grappe et le précédent, il y a certainement une différence marquée; et quelle peut être cette différence, sinon qu'à présent c'est un tout, un animal, un, et qu'auparavant, ce n'était qu'un assemblage d'animaux' (p.29-30; Lew. viii.83). The continuous swarm, as Bordeu explains, represents the way in which individual organs are related in the animal body, and not, therefore, as Varloot and Wartofsky assume, molecules and aggregates of matter. Even if this were the case, Varloot's analysis of the point would be inadequate, since he omits any reference to the process of nutritive assimilation in this part of his account. He dismisses Diderot's analogy as 'reine Phantasie' on the grounds that it is applicable only to the erroneous theory of epigenesis in foetal development. Certainly the concept of cellular division does not occur to Diderot, but this does not diminish the need for a model to account for the nutritive assimilation of matter, equally an additive process. In the same way, Varloot's suggestion that modern science has limited fusion to the case of sexual fertilisation[101] overlooks its wider relevance.

Whether the continuous swarm model represents, as Rostand has claimed, an intuition of cellular structure[102] is debatable. I feel that on logical grounds

---

101. 'Diderots Philosophie im *Rêve de d'Alembert*', p.715. Cf. Wartofsky, p.315.

102. 'La molécule et le philosophe', p.7. Cf. his *Biologie et humanisme* (Paris 1964), p.221. A similar conclusion is implicit in Niklaus's 'The mind of Diderot', p.932, and Winter appears to accept Rostand's view, which she quotes, p.48, 161. It is shared even by Vartanian, *La Mettrie's L'Homme machine*, p.118. Canguilhem's account of the philosophical implications of cellular biology,

it cannot do so. If, as Diderot states, the beehive corresponds to the world[103] and the (continuous) swarm to an animal (p.29, 30; Lew. viii.83, 85), the individual bees (because they are themselves complex and organised) would logically stand for individual organs. Cells would seem to require a further stage of subdivision. This reading is consistent with Diderot's remarks in the later *Eléments de physiologie*[104] and is the one I shall adopt. Nevertheless, the cellular interpretation cannot be ruled out on this occasion; Bordeu's words are, admittedly, ambiguous: 'Tous nos organes [...] ne sont que des animaux distincts que la loi de continuité tient dans une sympathie, une unité, une identité générale.'[105] Does this mean that the organs *are* interrelated 'animals', or that they *are composed of* interrelated 'animals'? Either is literally possible, and the latter would certainly validate the cellular thesis. The subsequent development of the passage, however, suggests that here at least it is the former, more obvious meaning which is intended. In this version, each organ would have its own identity – its internal configuration and its function differ from those of its neighbour – and yet all work together. As in the original swarm it is shared sentience (implied by the etymology of Diderot's term *sympathie*) which enables this dynamic unity to come about.

The association of bees/organs is, however, reversible, even in the continuous swarm. An individual bee may be separated from the swarm and yet live. Whilst it may be damaged, its portion of life (that is, in Diderot's terms, participation in the energetic phenomenon of *sensibilité*), its own organic identity, will be retained: 'Prenez vos ciseaux [...] et séparez-moi ces abeilles, [...] – vous les blesserez un peu, – mais vous ne les tuerez pas [...]. Voyez-vous comme elles s'envolent, chacune de son côté?' (p.30; Lew. viii.84). In the same way, an organ can survive even apart from its original body.[106]

In such instances, the retention of life and sentience is only temporary. The

'Le tout et la partie dans la pensée biologique', although not discussing this particular model, demonstrates that any attempt to conceptualise organic composition in analogical terms necessarily falls seriously short of the reality represented by the interrelationship of cells, *passim*.

103. *Rêve de d'Alembert*, p.28; Lew. viii.82.

104. See the following two notes.

105. *Rêve de d'Alembert*, p.30; Lew. viii.84. F. Piselli has labelled this conception perceptively as 'une théorie coloniale de l'organisme', 'La philosophie et les sciences dans la pensée de Diderot', p.189. Cf. also *Eléments de physiologie*: 'Voilà donc des organes sensibles et vivants, accouplés, sympathisant et concourant à un même but sans la participation de l'animal entier. L'homme peut donc être regardé comme un assemblage d'animaux où chacun garde sa fonction particulière et sympathise [...] avec les autres' (p.286-87; Lew. xiii.809). The idea that individual organs are distinct 'animals' recurs frequently throughout the *Eléments de physiologie*, for example, p.56, 106, 113, 284-89; Lew. xiii.679, 706, 710, 808, 809-11 *passim*.

106. Cf. *Rêve de d'Alembert*, p.30, n.3, and *Eléments de physiologie*, p.284-89; Lew. xiii.808, where Diderot takes up this idea in similar terms: 'Point d'organe qui séparé de l'animal ne conserve quelque temps la sensibilité, la vie. L'abeille a les pattes coupées, et vole.' The cellular interpretation seems unlikely here.

organ's *sensibilité* soon reverts to the inactive state. Not so, however, in the case of the polyp, whose life it is impossible to destroy by division.

3. Second reformulation: the polypous swarm

A third version of the swarm analogy is therefore proposed: it is the original, contiguous swarm, but rendered microscopic in scale. In this way the individual bees are so small that they escape damage by the hypothetical scissors (p.31; Lew. viii.85):

Supposez ces abeilles si petites, si petites que leur organisation échappât toujours au tranchant grossier de votre ciseau; vous pousserez la division si loin qu'il vous plaira, sans en faire mourir aucune; et ce tout formé d'abeilles imperceptibles sera un véritable polype que vous ne détruirez qu'en l'écrasant.

The polypous version of the swarm, with its 'abeilles imperceptibles', does lend itself more readily to the cellular interpretation, but even then, since this model applies only to 'animaux polypeux' and not to 'animaux ordinaires', cellular structure would not appear to be a particularly widespread phenomenon in Diderot's view. For the polyp's unity is of a different nature from that of ordinary animals; if it were based on continuity, its unique divisibility would be impossible.[107] Along with certain other organisms which were believed at the time to display similar characteristics, it must therefore be placed in a separate category: 'La différence de la grappe d'abeilles continues et de la grappe d'abeilles contigües est précisement cellc des animaux ordinaires, tels que nous, les poissons, et des vers, des serpents, et des animaux polypeux' (p.31; Lew. viii.85).

4. Reintegration of polypous and normal animals

The boundaries of this category are not fixed, however. Diderot entertains the hypothesis that the polypous form of organisation could occur even within normal animals: 'Eh bien, philosophe, vous concevez donc des polypes de toute espèce, même des polypes humains? ... Mais la nature ne nous en offre point' (p.32; Lew. viii.86). Diderot counters this objection by quoting a case of Siamese twins documented by Buffon. Here the two forms of unity coexist: the twins' individual physiology represents normal, continuous organisation (since separately they are, one assumes, 'animaux ordinaires'), but they are joined only contiguously, 'accolées' (p.32; Lew. viii.87).

107. Cf. Winter, p.40. It should be noted that this introduces an element of inconsistency into Diderot's account of organic unity, since he had previously declared continuity essential if unity is to be achieved through nutritive assimilation. Niklaus feels that Diderot's concept of the oneness of nature (discussed below, B.iii.d) indicates the possibility of reconciling contiguous and continuous organisation within a single whole. This is certainly true at the macrocosmic level, but does not resolve the problem where nutritive assimilation is concerned.

Furthermore, he argues, the absence of 'polypes humains' does not rule out the possibility of such forms. In another time and place, they may well exist: 'Cela est passé ou cela viendra; et puis qui sait l'état des choses dans les autres planètes?' (p.32-33; Lew. viii.87). The details which follow are little more than flights of fancy, reminiscent of Cyrano de Bergerac's speculations in the previous century.[108] Nevertheless, Bordeu interrupts d'Alembert's vision to point out that it is not entirely extravagant. Man may not be a polyp, but he is composed of organic matter. Disintegration of the human body does not extinguish the *sensibilité* of its parts. The energy remains, awaiting reactivation in a new combination, a new form: 'Si l'homme ne se résout pas en une infinité d'hommes, – il se résout du moins en une infinité d'animalcules dont il est impossible de prévoir les métamorphoses et l'organisation future et dernière.'[109] Ultimately the matter concerned may even, like that of the polyp, return to its original form: 'Qui sait si ce n'est pas la pépinière d'une seconde génération d'êtres séparée de celle-ci par un intervalle incompréhensible de siècles et de développements successifs?' The principle of the circulation of matter does not abolish the distinction between polypous and normal organisation, but does reduce it to one of timescale.

d. Universalisation of unity

For *sensibilité* renders all matter equal. In the final analysis there are no categories, no boundaries; biological unity gives way to total unity. By associating life with a particular mode of energetic *sensibilité*, Diderot blurs the conventional distinctions between kingdoms: 'tout animal est plus ou moins homme; tout minéral est plus ou moins plante; toute plante est plus ou moins animal ... Il n'y a rien de précis en nature' (p.43; Lew. viii.97). Gradation is universal and no longer operates according to a single, simple, linear model. Diderot's image of nature is not that of a scale, or ladder, but of an organic entity whose parts are in constant flux through a succession of forms: 'Naître, vivre et passer, c'est changer de formes' (p.45; Lew. viii.98). These forms stand in the same relationship to each other as two particles of organic matter in an aggregate, as organs in an animal body, as bees in a swarm: one of dynamic unity. The whole of nature, thanks to the vital energy intrinsic to all matter, is but a single entity: 'Que voulez-vous donc dire avec vos individus? ... il n'y en a point. Non, il n'y

108. Cf. *L'Autre monde*'s conceit of 'dancing men' (ed. H. Weber, Paris 1968, p.220-21) and Cyrano's contention that 'notre chair, notre sang, nos esprits, ne sont autre chose qu'une tissure de petits animaux qui [...] produisent tous ensemble cette action que nous appelons la vie' (p.127).
109. *Rêve de d'Alembert*, p.33; Lew. viii.87-88. It is not entirely clear how the notion of 'animalcules' (implying the permanence of life in organic matter, once established) is to be reconciled with the concept of active and potential *sensibilité*. The problem of molecular life is discussed more fully below, C.iii.a, D.iii.a and conclusion.

en a point ... Il n'y a qu'un seul grand individu; c'est le tout.'[110]

In this way, even the most ambitious conclusions of Diderot's philosophy of nature, expressed at the climax of d'Alembert's dream, can be traced back to the deceptively modest proposal with which the *Entretien* opened: universal *sensibilité*.

No part of the *Rêve de d'Alembert* illustrates more clearly the distance which Diderot has travelled since his early philosophical works. The unity of nature as expressed in the *Essai sur le mérite et la vertu* and even the *Pensées sur l'interprétation de la nature* was an instinctive, but nebulous principle, eclectic in its inspiration and expression and lacking a coherent conceptual foundation. It is still possible to claim a variety of sources for Diderot's belief. Crocker invokes Toland's 'all things are but one'[111] and Fabre lists this form of unity amongst the intuitions Diderot may have encountered in his study of the theosophists for the *Encyclopédie*.[112] Another scholar argues at some length that what he calls Diderot's 'cosmic mysticism' ('the notion of the underlying and ultimate oneness of all things') stems from the vestiges of mystical thought.[113] Both Spinoza and Leibniz have been attributed key rôles in the elaboration of the form of unity finally expressed in the *Rêve de d'Alembert*.[114] Hazard claims that the principle of continuity constitutes Diderot's main debt to Leibniz. Certainly this principle corresponds to many of Diderot's central concerns: as Tonelli points out, it took several forms, notably in the areas of biology and psychology.[115] An uninterrupted scale from pure spirit to brute matter, constant flux of the individual form, birth and death as simple changes of state, continuity between the different forms of perception and knowledge are among its many implications which find an echo in Diderot's account of unity. Diderot himself endorses this link by remarking in his article 'Leibnizianisme', 'Le voilà tout voisin [...] de la sensibilité, propriété générale de la matière, et de beaucoup d'autres idées qui nous occupent à présent' (Her., vii.683). Whatever Diderot's debt to Leibniz in this respect, however, the overall philosophical context (of materialism) in which unity is set is very much his own.

Diderot had claimed that his hypothesis of universal *sensibilité* could account for all those vital phenomena which would otherwise have had to be referred

---

110. p.44; Lew. viii.97-98. Cf. below, Conclusion, p.186-87, for further comment on this issue.

111. 'John Toland et le matérialisme de Diderot', p.292-93.

112. 'Diderot et les théosophes', p.221.

113. Forno, 'The cosmic mysticism of Diderot', p.128.

114. Forno, p.130, 135-36; Perkins, 'Diderot et La Mettrie', p.58, 59; Hazard, 'Les origines philosophiques de l'homme de sentiment', p.152.

115. G. Tonelli, 'The law of continuity in the eighteenth century', *Studies on Voltaire* 27 (1963), p.1621-23.

to an extrinsic cause. The conversion of inert to living substance (whether in abiogenesis, sexual reproduction or nutritive assimilation) was one such phenomenon. Organic unity was another. A third broad area requires clarification before Diderot can justify *sensibilité*'s label, 'une supposition simple qui explique tout': the exact function of sentience, or active *sensibilité*, within the organism.

C. Active *sensibilité* within the organism

i. *The problem*

Of the various stages linking inert *sensibilité* with sophisticated intellectual activity within the most highly developed organisms, only the earliest are elucidated by Diderot's account of the activation of *sensibilité* and its contribution to organic unity. That a direct relationship exists is made clear by Diderot in the *Entretien* on more than one occasion. From the inert matter involved in sexual reproduction, he claims: 'on obtient de la sensibilité, de la vie, de la mémoire, de la conscience, des passions, de la pensée'.[116] That it takes the form of a linear, sequential development is also made clear, not only by implication in the statement just referred to, but explicitly: 'celui qui exposerait à l'Académie le progrès de la formation d'un homme ou d'un animal n'employerait que des agents matériels dont *les effets successifs* seraient un être inerte, un être sentant, un être pensant' (p.8-9; Lew. viii.61; my emphasis). Finally, that it presents a problem is underlined twice by d'Alembert. He acknowledges that Diderot has accounted for the conversion of a marble block into a sentient being, and that this may well be a more challenging task than explaining the next stage. Nevertheless, he insists: 'Avec tout cela, l'être sensible n'est pas encore l'être pensant' (p.7; Lew. viii.60). A little later he reminds Diderot that this issue is still outstanding: 'rappelez-vous que c'est au passage d'être sentant à l'Etre pensant que vous m'avez laissé. [...] Franchement, vous m'obligeriez beaucoup de me tirer de là. Je suis un peu pressé de penser' (p.11; Lew. viii.63).

Surprisingly, few studies have been devoted to the details of the relationship between *sensibilité* and higher organic functions such as thought. The terms in which memory, consciousness, etc. are presented have received a great deal of critical attention, but not the specific character these take on as a result of

116. *Rêve de d'Alembert*, p.16; Lew. viii.68. Cf. his detailed account of a bird's development a few lines earlier, and of human development, p.8. Cf. also p.12, 51, 88; Lew. viii.61, 65, 104, 145.

Diderot's own particular concept of *sensibilité*.[117] In fact Diderot's solution to these issues proves to be complex and detailed, and its elements are dispersed throughout the *Entretien* and the *Rêve*. His examination takes account of two separate phases in the development of animal sentience: firstly the origin of animal tissue and its diversification in the higher animals, and secondly its role in the emergence of intellectual faculties.

ii. *Development of sentience within the organism*

Diderot has already given an account of the beginning of life at the moment of conception. In the *Rêve* he has Bordeu take up this account and trace the subsequent stages of embryonic development.

The newly conceived animal exists at first as nothing more than 'un point imperceptible' (p.50; Lew. viii.104). This point is transformed, by degrees, into a filiform structure which then multiplies to form animal tissue: 'ce point devint un fil délié; puis un faisceau de fils'. Diderot's terminology is imprecise, and the possibility that the 'faisceau de fils' may refer to the rudimentary nervous system cannot be ruled out.[118] It seems more likely, however, that he is thinking in terms of the concept of *fibre*, which many eighteenth-century physiologists, including Haller, held to be the basic unit of animal tissue.

It is interesting to note that the *Eléments de physiologie* discuss *fibre* in the terms used here for *fils*. Diderot quotes Marat's 1775-1776 *De l'homme*: 'La fibre simple est un *faisceau* de fibrilles mille fois plus déliées que le cheveu le plus fin' and adds his own comment: 'J'estime que la fibre est plus vraisemblablement de la chair ajoutée à de la chair, formant un tout continu, à peu pres homogène, vivant.'[119] This is strikingly similar to the *Rêve*'s explanation of how unity results from nutritive assimilation and epigenesis by means of 'un réseau homogène' and thus tends to confirm that Diderot is thinking of animal tissue in general.

Certainly it is quite evident that these threads develop from the conjoined germinal elements and thus that these lines do not constitute, as Grava has

117. Even Hofmann's article devoted to general *sensibilité* and the emergence of consciousness ('Diderots Auffassungen vom allgemeinen Empfindungsvermögen, von der Entstehung und Einheit des Bewußtseins') is dominated by marxist preconceptions and fails to live up to the promise of its title. Diderot's actual ideas are presented only in the sketchiest of paraphrases, and Hofmann pays greater attention to the reappearance of kindred notions in later materialist thought in support of his thesis of Diderot's contribution to the 'ideologischen Kampf gegen die feudale Ordnung' (p.179).

118. This is Varloot's view; he comments that in this passage 'Diderot [...] construit avec raison et génie l'embryogenèse à partir du système nerveux' (p.50-51, n.4); cf. p.lxxx. Mayer reaches the same conclusion (*Eléments de physiologie*, p.62 n.1).

119. *Eléments de physiologie*, p.64 (my emphasis) and 65. Cf. also p.66: 'La fibre est la matière du faisceau qu'on appelle organe' and p.67's reference to muscular tissue as 'un faisceau de fibres sensibles et vivantes' (Her., xiii.685-86).

claimed, an intuition 'of what we would call today the genes and chromosomes'.[120]

Like the original living point from which it develops, this tissue is sentient: 'le faisceau est un système purement sensible' (*Rêve de d'Alembert*, p.50; Lew. viii.104). It is therefore capable of reaction to the most basic physical stimuli – tactile qualities such as temperature and texture: 'S'il persistait sous cette forme, il serait susceptible de toutes les impressions relatives à la sensibilité pure, comme le froid, le chaud, le doux, le rude' (p.51; Lew. viii.104). The rudimentary form is not retained, however. Through the nutritive assimilation of new matter, each thread follows a distinct developmental path, giving rise to specialised organs: 'Chacun des brins du faisceau de fils se transforma par la seule nutrition et par sa conformation, en un organe particulier' (p.50; Lew. viii.104). Since there is diversity within the organisation ('conformation') of the individual threads,[121] their *sensibilité* is manifested in a variety of forms. Each organ possesses its own characteristic and unique mode of sentience: 'cette sensibilité pure et simple, ce toucher se diversifie par les organes émanés de chacun des brins' (p.51; Lew. viii.104-105).

This process accounts for the emergence of the other four named senses, each of which is but a variant of basic tactile sentience (p.51; Lew. viii.105):

un brin formant une oreille donne naissance à une espèce de toucher que nous appelons bruit, ou son; un autre formant le palais donne naissance à une seconde espèce de toucher que nous appelons saveur; un troisième formant le nez et le tapissant donne naissance à une troisième espèce de toucher que nous appelons odeur; un quatrième formant un œil donne naissance à une quatrième espèce de toucher que nous appelons couleur.

It also accounts for the involvement of all parts of the animal body in a network of sentience. For the remaining threads or strands of tissue also continue to grow and metamorphose as the foetus develops: 'Le reste des brins va former autant d'espèces de toucher qu'il y a de diversité entre les organes et les parties du corps' (p.52; Lew. viii.106). Not only sense organs, but limbs, bones, indeed all identifiable physiological elements, are 'les développements grossiers d'un réseau qui se forme, s'accroît, s'étend, jette une multitude de fils imperceptibles' (p.46; Lew. viii.100). Every element has its own portion of *sensibilité*, resulting in an 'infinie diversité de toucher' (p.53; Lew. viii.107), a 'multiplicité de

120. A. Grava, 'Diderot and recent philosophical trends', *Diderot studies* 4 (1963), p.82. Cf. Niklaus's (admittedly more cautious) use of these terms in 'The mind of Diderot', p.932. The assumption recurs in Wilson, *Diderot: the testing years*, p.567, Crocker, *Diderot the embattled philosopher*, p.567, and Wartofsky, 'Diderot and the development of materialist monism', p.314, 324.

121. Diderot does not explain how this diversity arises from the homogeneous product of conception.

sensations' (p.52; Lew.viii.106) impossible to discriminate by means of physiological labels.

This specific concept, the differentiation of *sensibilité* (together with the notion of organic autonomy evoked earlier) is almost certainly taken straight from Bordeu.[122] As Dieckmann points out, Diderot and Bordeu shared a twofold aim – to stress the unity of nature, abolishing divisions by means of a single principle underlying all vital phenomena, and yet at the same time to account for spontaneity and diversity (p.113-17). The first aim was achieved by *sensibilité* itself, the second by theories of autonomy and diversification.

This particular model allows Diderot to explain the occurrence of aberrant forms without recourse to Maupertuis's psychism. Absence, deformity or excess of bodily parts is simply attributed to destruction, damage, accidental adhesion or duplication of the relevant 'threads' at the foetal stage: 'Les variétés du faisceau d'une espèce font toutes les variétés monstrueuses de cette espèce' (*Rêve de d'Alembert*, p.57; Lew. viii.111). The development, through epigenesis, of animal tissue – or just possibly the nervous system – is thus responsible for the transition from the speck of sentient organic matter produced by conception to the diversity of forms and sensory capacities which constitute the developed animal. Roger points out that there is nothing particularly original in this account: it is Stahlian embryology, with *sensibilité* assuming the function Stahl had attributed to soul, a substitution already made by Fouquet in his *Encyclopédie* article 'Sensibilité'.[123] Nevertheless, the implications are Diderot's own. For it is as a result of this development that active *sensibilité*, or vital energy, is provided with the channels through which it may be released in the forms associated with animal life – the 'actions remarquables' to which Diderot had earlier referred.[124]

iii. *Function of sentience within the organism*

a. Sensibilité *and life distinguished*

Diderot's initial presentation of *sensibilité* implied that living matter is matter whose *sensibilité* is active.[125] He suggests, furthermore, that life and sentience are present together in the most rudimentary forms of organic matter. Thus d'Alembert evokes, at the climax of his dream: 'la molécule sensible et vivante' (p.45; Lew. viii.98), and Mlle de l'Espinasse's speculations on the effect of depriving animal substance of its organisation arrive at: 'une masse informe qui n'a retenu que la vie et la sensibilité (p.88; Lew. viii.145). Since her account

122. See Dieckmann, 'Bordeu und Diderots *Rêve de d'Alembert*', p.80, 85-87, 89, 104-105.
123. Roger, *Les Sciences de la vie*, p.660-61.
124. Cf. above, section A.
125. Cf. above, A.ii.

refers explicitly only to removing the 'brins [...] de l'écheveau' responsible for the functioning (not the development) of the sense organs and brain of the adult (not embryonic) individual, the nervous system (rather than tissue fibres in general) may be intended by the image here. But Diderot is not dealing in physiological realities in this particular instance anyway; a more important point to extract is that, even when organic specialisation is absent, sentience and life remain.

There is not, however, complete identity between life and sentience. Bordeu interrupts Mlle de l'Espinasse's account to point out that they are: 'Deux qualités presque identiques; la vie est de l'agrégat, – et la sensibilité est de l'élément' (p.88; Lew. viii.145). Life then is the sum of the *sensibilité* present in an organism's constituent parts, just as the organism's substance is the sum of the matter composing it. Actively sentient elements must *combine* to produce the phenomenon which may properly be called life. This is consistent with Diderot's concern to develop an acceptable model of organic unity, for without unity there would be only sentience, not life: the matter involved in a food chain must not only have its *sensibilité* activated, it must also be fully assimilated into the organism. The distinction is, however, almost certainly an artificial one: Diderot offers no example of a case where sentience exists and life does not, precisely because incorporation into an already living system (or at least combination of inert components under special energetic circumstances, as in generation, spontaneous and sexual) is normally required for *sensibilité* to be activated in the first place.[126] It is significant, however, as an indication of Diderot's concern to establish distinct qualitative levels in the organisation of matter, a concern which will be evident throughout his examination of *sensibilité*'s various functions and manifestations in the organism.[127]

A further indication of the same concern is given by d'Alembert's remarks (in the same phase of his dream) on the difference between the dead and living states. Implicitly acknowledging the essentially energetic character of life, he distinguishes molecular or elemental activity from its corporate counterpart: 'Vivant, j'agis et je réagis en masse ... mort, j'agis et je réagis en molécules' (p.45; Lew. viii.98). The aggregate's activity is thus of a qualitatively different type from that displayed by the element: the former constitutes life, the latter

126. D'Alembert's 'molécule sensible et vivante', since it is described as 'l'origine de tout', seems to refer back to the 'points sensibles et vivants' involved in the origin of life on earth (p.37; Lew. viii.91), that is, elements which have undergone activation and combination; the phrase does not imply that all matter is living.

127. In particular it will enable him to avoid equating universal *sensibilité* with universal thought. Cf. below, C.iii.c.5.

does not.[128] Whether the 'molécule' is considered equivalent to Bordeu's 'élément' (that is, possessing sentience but not life) or to d'Alembert's 'molécule sensible et vivante' (that is, remaining organised, actively sentient and alive after the organism's death),[129] or whether it reverts to the inert state and interacts only chemically with other matter, is not clear. What is clear is that the qualitative distinction between life and death is based on activity, that is, on the complex of forces which includes *sensibilité*, and the way they are actually deployed in any given form of organisation.

It is this perspective which Diderot brings to his survey of the forms *sensibilité* may take in organisms of varying complexity.

b. Basic function of sensibilité

The possession of basic, active *sensibilité* equips an organism to react with its environment. Sentience (now equivalent to life) is characterised by a twofold, dynamic interchange: reception of and reaction to external or internal physical stimuli. This is the action and reaction to which Diderot repeatedly refers and which, at the organic level, characterises life: 'La vie? une suite d'actions et de réactions'.[130]

Sensibilité may thus in this respect be equated with the modern physiologist's view of irritability (the debated principle on which it was loosely based) as 'the specific response to stimuli manifested by practically all organic systems, from bacteria and protozoa, through plants, to such complex animal structures as the brain itself'.[131] Vartanian suggests an analogy between La Mettrie's version of irritability and Diderot's *sensibilité*, although, as Callot has pointed out, La Mettrie's view of perception as a passive process dependent on the movement of cartesian animal spirits reveals how far removed in other ways his concept is from Diderot's.[132]

Of more immediate relevance in 1769 is the work of Bordeu, which, despite its vitalistic tendencies,[133] is close in both inspiration and documentation to Diderot's own. Bordeu's definition of life reveals their kinship clearly: 'on voit

---

128. *Sensibilité* and life were related in a similar way in the *Encyclopédie* articles 'Naître' and 'Reptiles' (above, chapter 4, B.i), though in less explicitly energetic terms.

129. Cf. above, B.iii.c 4, n.109.

130. *Rêve de d'Alembert*, p.45; Lew. viii.98. Cf. 'une action, une réaction habituelles' (p.28; Lew. viii.81); 'l'action et la réaction habituelles' (p.27; Lew. viii.81). Cf. Hofmann, p.175, and Alexander, 'Philosophy of organism', p.8, which argues that Diderot's concept of sensory perception as an active process distinguishes him from such contemporaries as Helvétius, for whom perception was a mere receptive capacity. Perkins draws the same contrast with La Mettrie, 'Diderot et La Mettrie', p.77. Cf. also above, p.169 and section A.

131. Vartanian, *La Mettrie's L'Homme machine*, p.21.

132. *Six philosophes français*, p.113.

133. Dieckmann, 'Bordeu und Diderots *Rêve de d'Alembert*', p.67, 76ff.

qu'elle consiste dans la faculté qu'a la fibre animale de sentir et de se mouvoir elle-même. C'est là une faculté innée dans les premiers éléments du corps vivant, qui n'est pas plus étrange que la gravité ou l'attraction',[134] as does his declaration that 'la sensibilité [...] peut très bien servir de base à l'explication de tous les phénomènes de la vie'.[135] Bordeu's ideas were reinforced by contributions to the *Encyclopédie* from his pupils Ménuret and Fouquet. The latter's article 'Sensibilité' (despite some uncertainty as to whether *sensibilité* should be considered a property or a substance) reiterates the duality crucial to Diderot's account: for Fouquet it involves both sentiment (reception of impressions) and movement (reaction to them).[136]

These ideas no doubt complemented the conclusion of La Mettrie's work, so that 'irritability at long last replaced the soul or the vital principle as a concept essential to biology and [...] became [...] the basis for investigating the psychic aspects of the life process' (Vartanian, p.89). Diderot and La Mettrie's aims are essentially similar: to derive all the higher organic functions from the basic units of living matter, to bridge the gap between mechanism and vitalism. Accordingly, 'By *sensibilité* Diderot actually means the autonomous mode of reactivity that is peculiar to living systems, and he consistently proposes to explain its emergence quite mechanistically in terms of physicochemical factors' (Vartanian, p.119). Hence his emphasis upon the rôle of *sensibilité* in establishing, at all levels, an interactive process.

c. Memory: an exclusively organic faculty

1. Memory and psychological unity

Psychological unity is not achieved by sentience alone. There is no continuity between the interactions of an organism possessing only *sensibilité*. D'Alembert points out clearly in the *Entretien* that the faculty of memory is indispensable to an organism's identity: 'Sans cette mémoire il n'aurait point de lui, puisque ne sentant son existence que dans le moment de l'impression, il n'aurait aucune histoire de sa vie. Sa vie serait une suite interrompue de sensations que rien ne lierait' (p.12; Lew. viii.64). It is just possible, concedes Diderot, that such a faculty could exist in the embryo. For the bundle of threads (as yet undifferentiated into organs) is 'un système purement sensible' (p.50; Lew. viii.104) capable of registering external impressions: 'Ces impressions successives [...] y produiraient peut-être la mémoire, la conscience de soi, une raison très bornée' (p.51; Lew. viii.104). Such memory would, however, be of the most rudimentary kind,

---

134. Quoted in Hoffmann, 'L'idée de liberté dans la philosophie médicale de Bordeu', p.773, n.12.

135. Quoted in Dieckmann, 'Bordeu und Diderots *Rêve de d'Alembert*', p.80.

136. Roger, *Les Sciences de la vie*, p.632-35.

since only the most basic, exclusively tactile stimuli would be received ('le froid, le chaud, le doux, le rude' are Diderot's examples). For the completely developed faculty, access to the full range of sensory stimuli is necessary, and this can be attained only by the higher animal forms in which the sentient network has diversified into a number of specialised sense organs: 'un être qui sent et qui a cette organisation propre à la mémoire, lie les impressions qu'il reçoit, forme par cette liaison une histoire qui est celle de sa vie'.[137]

2. Memory and sentience

To explain the operation of memory, Diderot draws upon his concept of a filiform, sentient nervous system. The nerves of sense organs react to physical stimulus in much the same way as would the strings of a musical instrument; this reaction may be prolonged after the initial stimulus has ceased. The problem of memory, he explains: 'm'a fait quelquefois comparer les fibres de nos organes à des cordes vibrantes sensibles. La corde vibrante, sensible, oscille, résonne longtemps encore après qu'on l'a pincée.'[138] As Proust has pointed out, the image itself dated back to classical thought. Only recently, however, had it been treated in a literal, rather than metaphorical manner, the strings being identified with the fibres of human tissue and in particular with the threads of the nervous system.[139] The 'vibratory' model was a common alternative to the more strictly cartesian 'hydraulic' models of nerve function.[140] Both were dynamic concepts to the extent that they represented an attempt to introduce the language of physics into physiology, argues Jackson: 'Forces [...] were transmitted in nerves, sometimes in terms of a fluid which was caused to flow by a force and which exerted a force in turn, and sometimes in terms of undulations caused by an impact and causing an impact in turn' (p.548). As Jackson acknowledges, however, this transposition was frequently little more than an effort 'to increase the prestige of explanations by borrowing from other successful and respected endeavours', doomed to failure at the scientific level on account of the difficulty of identifying measurable variables and thus quantifying the processes involved (p.550-51).

On the more philosophical plane with which Diderot is concerned, no such problems arise; he is able to pursue his speculations in terms of *sensibilité*, of

---

137. p.12; Lew. viii.65. Cf. Mayer, *Diderot homme de science*, p.241-42, for a brief account of the relationship between memory and unity.

138. p.13. Cf. 'il y a une impression qui a sa cause au dedans ou au dehors de l'instrument, une sensation qui naît de cette impression, une sensation qui dure' (p.15; Lew. viii.65).

139. Notably by Bonnet and Haller. Proust, 'Variations sur un thème de *l'Entretien avec d'Alembert*', *Revue des sciences humaines* 28 (1963), p.112.

140. S. W. Jackson, 'Force and kindred notions in eighteenth-century neurophysiology', *Bulletin of the history of medicine* 44 (1970), p.404.

vital energy, rather than of the physicist's mechanical forces. The vibrations – or sense impressions – may be communicated from one part of the instrument – or nervous system – to another, thanks to their energetic quality. Indeed the process is facilitated by the continuity of the organic 'instrument': 'Si le phénomène s'observe entre des cordes sonores, inertes, et séparées, – comment n'aurait-il pas lieu entre des points vivants et liés, – entre des fibres continues et sensibles?' (*Rêve de d'Alembert*, p.13; Lew.viii.66). By this means, a present sensation may recall a past impression. For all impressions are stored, and may be reactivated by stimulation of the appropriate nerve (or other) fibre, from either within or without. The basic physiological theory may well be drawn from Bonnet, as Mayer suggests,[141] but it is integrated into a quite distinct conceptual context (p.324).

3. A specialised memory organ

Diderot clarifies this process later, in the *Rêve*, where the musical analogy is reformulated. Mlle de l'Espinasse vizualises the nervous system as a spider's web, and assigns to it a co-ordinating spider, an image which Bordeu takes up and elucidates. The probable source of the image is Brucker's account of Persian Sufism, which Diderot used for his article 'Asiatiques'. It also occurs in the 1767 *Salon*.[142]

Imaginez une araignée au centre de sa toile. Ebranlez un fil, – et vous verrez l'animal alerte accourir. [...] – Vous imaginez en vous, quelque part, dans un recoin de votre tête, [...] un ou plusieurs points où se rapportent toutes les sensations excitées sur la longueur des fils. [...] Les fils sont partout. Il n'y a pas un point à la surface de votre corps auquel ils n'aboutissent; et l'araignée est nichée dans une partie de votre tête [...][143]

This analogy incorporates both the 'network of threads' responsible for nervous development and functioning and the 'swarm of bees' adopted as an explanatory concept for organic unity.[144] For the spider and its web are one, distinct only in their organisation. Memory, and its active counterpart, recall, are nothing more than the particular form taken by sentience in the specialised organic matter which constitutes the brain (p.78; Lew. viii.134):

Et qu'est-ce donc que la mémoire?
– La propriété du centre. Le sens spécifique de l'origine du réseau.

This organ is capable of overcoming the limitations of the individual senses. It co-ordinates isolated sense impressions, maintaining and comparing them with

141. *Diderot homme de science*, p.320, 322.
142. L. Schwartz, 'L'image de l'araignée dans le *Rêve de d'Alembert*', *Romance notes* 15 (1973), p.264. Cf. Vernière, *OPhil*, p.250.
143. *Rêve de d'Alembert*, p.46-47; Lew. viii.99-100.
144. Cf. Chouillet, *Diderot poète de l'énergie*, p.267, 275.

previous experience. In this way psychological unity is achieved (p.77-78; Lew. viii.134):

Chaque brin n'est susceptible que d'un certain nombre déterminé d'impressions, de sensations successives, isolées, sans mémoire. L'origine est susceptible de toutes, elle en est le registre; elle en garde la mémoire ou une sensation continue, et l'animal est entraîné dès sa formation première à s'y rapporter soi, à s'y fixer tout entier, à y exister.

4. Memory and consciousness

Memory, then, is the key not only to unity but to awareness of unity – consciousness in the animal. For these are not identical. D'Alembert draws the distinction between unity and consciousness at the outset of his dream, by referring to the organism as: 'un système un, lui, ayant la conscience de son unité' (p.26; Lew. viii.80). Similarly Bordeu points out that whilst the swarm analogy may have accounted for the emergence of a corporate identity within the organism, consciousness has not been explained: 'Chaque molécule sensible avait son moi avant l'application; mais comment l'a-t-elle perdu, et comment de toutes ces pertes en est-il résulté la conscience d'un tout?'[145] The problem is exacerbated by Diderot's belief, adopted from Bordeu's work, of the continuing autonomy of organs within the body, bees within the swarm:[146] 'S'il n'y a qu'une conscience dans l'animal, il y a une infinité de volontés; chaque organe a la sienne. [...] Les abeilles perdent leurs consciences et retiennent leurs appétits, ou volontés' (p.69; Lew. viii.125).

Corporate consciousness makes sense only in terms of a specialised memory organ. Elsewhere in the body, impressions can be only temporarily prolonged; this limited survival is insufficient to lead to full consciousness.[147] If consciousness is dependent (as Diderot has implied) upon the indefinite survival and recall of past sensations, it is clear that it can exist only where the faculty of memory exists, in the co-ordinating centre: 'elle ne peut être que dans un endroit, au centre commun de toutes les sensations, là où est la mémoire, là où se font les comparaisons' (p.77; Lew. viii.134). The brain alone, as already noted,[148] possesses memory, that, is the particular form of sentience which permits continuity to be established between individual sense impressions. Just as continuity of substance is a prerequisite of animal life (as opposed to simply sentience) so continuity of sentience is a prerequisite of memory (again as

145. p.40; Lew. viii.94. Varloot sees Diderot's use of the term *moi* as a return to the psychism of Maupertuis (n.1). Both this quotation (which implies that self and consciousness of self are distinct) and the ideas I am about to examine in this section indicate, however, that the molecular *moi* is not a conscious faculty.
146. Cf. above, B.iii.c.
147. Cf. above, C.iii.c.1.
148. Cf. above, C.iii.c.3.

opposed to simply sentience). The sentient organism would possess unity by virtue of the sharing and communication of *sensibilité* between its parts (that is, spatially); only memory, however, by giving this continuity a temporal dimension, can produce consciousness.[149]

Diderot's account implies that the quality of consciousness, and hence the intellectual faculties dependent on it, are determined by the degree of complexity and development of both the nervous system and the brain. For it follows that the more sensitive and discriminating the sense organs, the more detailed and extensive the data which they are able to transmit to an organism's 'memory banks'. The more highly sophisticated the brain, the greater the range of data which can be stored and the efficiency with which they can be recalled.[150]

This implies in turn that it is organisation which brings about the transition from sentience to memory/consciousness – a qualitative change. Alexander seems to capture the essence of this process when he argues that consciousness for Diderot involves a new form of sentience, a qualitatively distinct stage of organic existence, dependent on, but not caused by, physical sentience. He suggests that Diderot sees the individual as an 'active entity' (thanks to the energetic nature of *sensibilité*) which absorbs objective data (that is, sense impressions) into itself and actively processes them.[151] As Diderot himself points out, contemporary knowledge of the brain did not equip him to be more specific about the nature of memory or its exact relationship with consciousness. Accused by Mlle de l'Espinasse of avoiding the question, Bordeu protests: 'Je n'élude rien. Je vous dis ce que je sais; et j'en saurais davantage, si l'organisation de l'origine du réseau m'était aussi connue que celle des brins; si j'avais eu la même facilité de l'observer' (*Rêve de d'Alembert*, p.78; Lew. viii.134). Memory and consciousness must therefore be considered jointly, as complementary expressions of *sensibilité* at a certain level of organisation.

5. Memory and thought

Thought, consequently, is but another aspect of the same dynamic continuum, so that memory and consciousness form the conceptual bridge between sentience and thought. Diderot stresses this link in his opening conversation with d'Alembert: 'Si donc un être qui sent et qui a cette organisation propre à la mémoire, lie les impressions qu'il reçoit, forme par cette liaison une histoire qui est celle de sa vie, et acquiert la conscience de lui, il nie, il affirme, il conclut, il

149. The crucial role played by continuity certainly suggests that Diderot's account of consciousness is based on the 'continuous swarm' model of organic unity and not, as Winter suggests (p.48), on the simple juxtaposition of sentient molecules.

150. Cf. Alexander, 'Philosophy of organism', p.8.

151. pp.7 and 9: 'Unless we assume such a predisposed activity, capable of selecting, unifying and absorbing external data, the growth and development of the specific entity are inexplicable.'

pense' (p.12; Lew. viii.65). *Sensibilité*, plus appropriate organisation (that is, the existence of specialised brain tissues) leads to memory and hence consciousness and the capacity for thought. The relationship is reiterated by Mlle de l'Espinasse and Bordeu. Memory enables sense impressions to be retained and compared one with another. Comparison involves a constant process of internal action and reaction, which by its very ceaselessness unites the organism. To sentience, memory and thought, as cognate developments of the same energy resource, correspond physiological, historical and intellectual[152] unity respectively. Mlle de l'Espinasse and Bordeu's joint declaration of this threefold relationship (a trilogy within the trilogy) is almost poetic in its symmetry:

– Que c'est le rapport constant, invariable de toutes les impressions à cette origine commune qui constitue l'unité de l'animal.
– Que c'est la mémoire de toutes ces impressions successives qui fait pour chaque animal l'histoire de sa vie et de son soi.
– Et que c'est la mémoire et la comparaison qui s'ensuivent nécessairement de toutes ces impressions qui font la pensée et le raisonnement.[153]

The need for a heterogeneous, possibly non-material, thinking substance is thus abolished. Thought (intellectual activity) is simply the physiological behaviour peculiar to the organ of memory – another of the animal's 'actions remarquables' (p.4; Lew. viii.57).

Varloot sees Diderot's characterisation of thought in terms of property rather than substance as perhaps the most original part of his philosophy. He goes on, however, to dismiss Diderot's actual account of thought as 'far less significant' and devotes only two lines to the relationship between thought and sentience. Memory is not even mentioned.[154] Winter's treatment is rather more thorough, despite an initial confusion between memory and thought.[155]

When Diderot originally proposed the analogy of 'cordes vibrantes sensibles' to explain the communication of sense impressions within the organism[156] d'Alembert had objected that this required an idealistic distinction to be made between body and mind: 'Vous faites de l'entendement du philosophe un être distinct de l'instrument, une espèce de musicien qui prête l'oreille aux cordes

152. I use this term (for want of a better) to indicate a mental counterpart to the physical unity engendered by *sensibilité*.
153. *Rêve de d'Alembert*, p.59; Lew. viii.113-14. This significant declaration comes almost exactly at the mid-point of the *Rêve*.
154. 'Diderots Philosophie im *Rêve de d'Alembert*', p.719.
155. She summarises Diderot's conclusion as follows: 'Das Denken ist nicht das Attribut einer unerklärlichen Substanz, sondern die Tätigkeit eines bestimmten Organs, das seine Funktionen ebenso ausübt wie das Auge und jedes andere Organ', but supports this statement with Bordeu's definition of memory (quoted above, C.iii.c.3), p.49.
156. Cf. above, C.iii.c.1.

vibrantes' (*Rêve de d'Alembert*, p.14; Lew. viii.66). Diderot's concept of unity based on sentience allows him to counter this objection by explaining that 'musicien' and 'instrument' are combined in an organic whole: 'L'instrument philosophe est sensible; il est en même temps le musicien et l'instrument. Comme sensible, il a la conscience momentanée du son qu'il rend; comme animal, il en a la mémoire; cette faculté organique, en liant les sons en lui-même, y produit et conserve la mémoire.'[157] Since memory is merely a specialised mode of sentience exclusive to the brain, the reception, retention and interpretation of sense impressions are inseparable facets of the same reality.

We are able to carry out all three operations, explains Diderot, precisely because 'Nous sommes des instruments doués de sensibilité et de mémoire', and, as he had remarked earlier: 'un être qui sent et qui a cette organisation propre à la mémoire [...] pense'.[158] Thought, like consciousness, exists only where memory exists, and memory exists only where organisation is appropriate to its development. Bordeu stresses in his conversation with Mlle de l'Espinasse that any organic aggregate is potentially capable of intellectual activity, *if* its form allows memory to arise: 'et si mon doigt pouvait avoir de la mémoire ... – Votre doigt penserait' (p.78; Lew. viii.134). The finger does not, however, possess such a form. Sentience develops into memory only in the brain, just as sight develops only in the eye; memory is exclusively 'La propriété du centre. Le sens spécifique de l'origine du réseau, – comme la vue est la propriété de l'œil; et il n'est pas plus étonnant que la mémoire ne soit pas dans l'œil, – qu'il ne l'est que la vue ne soit pas dans l'oreille.' Consequently, intellectual activity of any kind cannot exist outside the brain.

By his insistence upon organisation, the specialisation and diversification of actively sentient animal tissue during the course of foetal development, Diderot avoids equating universal *sensibilité* with universal thought, and finally lays to rest the paradox of 1759.

d. Sensibilité's wider role in man

By establishing a concept of memory which explains the transition from sentience to thought in terms of organisation, Diderot has laid the foundations for an examination of all intellectual faculties in similar terms. Thought derives ulti-

---

157. p.14; Lew. viii.67. For Chouillet, this image is one of Diderot's most striking intuitions. He points out that, although La Mettrie's work contained the idea of man as a self-winding clock and the idea of vibrating cords to explain language, no-one had previously thought to combine the two. He concludes: 'C'est pourquoi il est permis de considérer le texte de 1769 comme un événement. L'idée que nous puissions être à la fois le clavecin et le philosophe, l'instrument dont on joue et l'instrumentiste qui en joue est, à notre connaissance, nouvelle et productrice d'idées nouvelles' (*Diderot poète de l'énergie*, p.263).

158. p.12; Lew. viii.65. Cf. above, C.iii.c.4.

mately from *sensibilité*, which is an energetic phenomenon. It is the expression of *sensibilité* under given physical circumstances. Consequently, other forms of intellectual activity may be viewed as variants of thought, each occurring under slightly different physical circumstances. Diderot has Bordeu offer a catalogue of the various psychological phenomena elucidated by his concept of sentience and memory: 'La raison, le jugement, l'imagination, la folie, l'imbécillité, la férocité, l'instinct' (p.78; Lew. viii.135). It is an ambitious catalogue, ranging widely over intellectual, psychological and even moral phenomena, but as Diderot will explain, all its items derive from the existence of rudimentary thought processes and thus ultimately from *sensibilité* and the dynamic interrelationships within an organism for which this characteristic is responsible. Just as *sensibilité* allows an organism to interact with its environment,[159] so its specialised form, memory, allows internal relationships to be established, and it is the precise nature of these which determines the type of intellectual or psychological activity which will occur: 'Toutes ces qualités [Bordeu's catalogue] ne sont que des conséquences du rapport originel ou contracté par l'habitude de l'origine du faisceau à ses ramifications' (p.78; Lew. viii.135).

Diderot's ensuing speculations on the relationships between brain ('l'origine du faisceau') and other parts of the organism, particularly where its sentient tissue is organised into individual sense organs and the nervous system ('ses ramifications') are complex and intriguing. It is for that very reason, however, that I am obliged to leave them unexplored. Despite the admirable start made by Chouillet,[160] no critical study has yet analysed the intellectual, emotional and even moral facets of Diderot's theory of *sensibilité* in the detail which they deserve; to remedy this omission, however, would exceed the brief of my study.

'Rappelez-vous que c'est au passage d'être sentant à l'Etre pensant que vous m'avez laissé', remarks d'Alembert at one point in his conversation with Diderot. 'Franchement, vous m'obligeriez beaucoup de me tirer de là' (p.11; Lew. viii.63). His appeal has been answered. By opening the way to an integrated account of human activity, Diderot has offered a solution to the last of the major issues raised by his examination of matter and life at the physical level. It remains only for me to assess the extent to which his concept of universal energetic *sensibilité* proves satisfactory at the metaphysical level; whether it is adequate to the requirements of Diderot's adoption, in 1749, of an atheist perspective on nature. Does energy effectively replace God?

159. Thus echoing Diderot's early 1750s intuition of *sensibilité*'s role, above, 2, D.iii. Cf. also C.iii.b.
160. *Diderot poète de l'énergie*.

D. *Sensibilité* and metaphysics

i. *Logical advantage of* sensibilité *over spiritual substance*

Diderot labels *sensibilité* 'une supposition simple qui explique tout' (p.17; Lew. viii.69). He makes it clear from the very outset that his thesis has been formulated explicitly for the purpose of abolishing the concept of a spiritual substance: d'Alembert introduces it as 'cette sensibilité que vous lui substituez' (p.3; Lew. viii.55). He enumerates the logical difficulties associated with dualism. Spiritual substance must be presumed to exist, but to occupy no point in space; to be compatible but not identical with extended matter. It must be indivisible, yet animate what is divided; both active and passive, causing change whilst remaining unchanged itself. Finally, despite these apparently contradictory requirements, it must remain acceptable to human reason. Such a concept, contends d'Alembert, is indeed difficult to grasp:

> J'avoue qu'un être qui existe quelque part et qui ne correspond à aucun point de l'espace; un être qui est inétendu et qui occupe de l'étendue; qui est tout entier sous chaque partie de cette étendue; qui diffère essentiellement de la matière et qui lui est uni; qui la suit et qui la meut, sans se mouvoir; qui agit sur elle et qui en subit toutes les vicissitudes; un être dont je n'ai pas la moindre idée; un être d'une nature aussi contradictoire est difficile à admettre.

It seems clear that spiritual substance in general is intended here, rather than either God or even simply human soul, as Fellows contends.[161]

Unlike spiritual substance, *sensibilité*, considered as a force, is capable of reconciling these otherwise mutually exclusive features. For energy exists without being extended, is integral to matter yet can undergo modification within that matter (by passage from the inert to the active state, or by transformation into a kindred force or simply by variation of its effects under different physical circumstances).

D'Alembert later questions the compatibility of *sensibilité* with matter, on the grounds that matter is divisible and *sensibilité* not: 'si c'était une qualité essentiellement incompatible avec la matière? [...] je vois que la sensibilité est une qualité simple, une, indivisible, et incompatible avec un sujet ou suppôt divisible' (p.17-18; Lew. viii.69). Diderot dismisses this objection as 'galimatias métaphysico-théologique'. More importantly, however, his reply twice appeals to the analogy with motive force, thus stressing the energetic character of *sensibilité*. In the first place, he claims, d'Alembert cannot pretend to know the

---

161. Fellows, 'Metaphysics and the *Bijoux indiscrets*', p.535. If the 'être' were God, or human soul, it would hardly be appropriate for it to exist in an inert form in some parts of matter; universal *sensibilité* would not make sense as a substitute.

essential nature of anything; since this does not prevent him from accepting the reality of motion, it should pose no greater obstacle to *sensibilité*:

Et d'où savez-vous que la sensibilité est essentiellement incompatible avec la matière, vous qui ne connaissez l'essence de quoi que ce soit, ni de la matière, ni de la sensibilité? Entendez-vous mieux la nature du mouvement, son existence dans un corps et sa communication d'un corps à un autre?

Furthermore, several attributes of matter are, like *sensibilité*, indivisible in themselves, despite the divisibility of the substance in which they inhere. Motion is one such attribute: 'Il y a plus ou moins de mouvement; mais il n'y a ni plus ni moins mouvement' (p.18; Lew. viii.69).

Consequently it is valid to consider *sensibilité* superior to spiritual substance on rational grounds: 'Soyez logicien, – et ne substituez pas à une cause qui est, et qui explique tout, une autre cause qui ne se conçoit pas, dont la liaison avec l'effet se conçoit encore moins, qui engendre une multitude infinie de difficultés et qui n'en résout aucune' (p.18-19; Lew. viii.70).

ii. *Elimination of the spiritual by* sensibilité

For *sensibilité* appears to provide an adequate substitute for both God and soul. The materialist principles of eternal matter in motion left only two essential issues unresolved: the emergence of life (and its corollaries, the relationship between organic and inorganic, animate and inanimate) and the origin of intelligence. Both these functions have been assumed by *sensibilité*.

In conjunction, the two modes of *sensibilité* – latent and active – offer for Diderot a fully monist and materialist account of phenomena otherwise attributable only to a supra-material entity of some kind.[162] Latent *sensibilité* explains the potential participation of all matter in life processes, be it through spontaneous generation, sexual reproduction or nutritive assimilation. Activated *sensibilité* explains the development of increasingly complex organic systems, memory, and ultimately thought.

Diderot is particularly adamant in his denial of the spiritual where thought is concerned. In order to effect the transition from sentient to intelligent being, it is quite unacceptable, he declares, to have recourse to a non-material principle:

Et pour aller plus loin, nous serait-il permis d'inventer un agent contradictoire dans ses attributs, un mot vide de sens, inintelligible?
– Non.[163]

162. Cf. Casini, *Diderot 'philosophe'*, p.277.
163. *Rêve de d'Alembert*, p.11; Lew. viii.64. Despite Varloot's gloss: 'D'Alembert accepte de nier le déisme', n.2, it is not clear on this occasion whether Diderot's 'agent' refers to God or soul.

The notion of a spiritual soul instilled during the course of foetal development is denounced in equally emphatic terms, as 'un abîme de mystères, de contradictions et d'absurdités' (p.17; Lew. viii.69). As far as Diderot is concerned, there is no longer any need for a spiritual soul, any more than for a creating, ordering deity.

iii. *Avoidance of vitalism and spinozism*

Nor, on this occasion, does Diderot's attempted monism take on a vitalistic or pantheistic tenor, contrary to the views of such critics as Janet, who writes of 'une sorte de panthéisme vitaliste et hylozoïste', and Lerel.[164] Vitalism is avoided thanks to the distinction not only between latent and active *sensibilité*, but also between basic vital energy and its actual effects, and spinozism by his handling of the issue of contiguity versus continuity. There are two points at which such implications seem to arise, but on both occasions the threat is averted.

a. *Vitalism*

The dreaming d'Alembert's vision of universal *sensibilité* appears to attribute emotional faculties to basic organic matter: 'Depuis l'éléphant jusqu'au puceron, ... depuis le puceron, jusqu'à la molécule sensible et vivante, l'origine de tout ... pas un point dans la nature entière qui ne souffre ou qui ne jouisse' (p.45; Lew. viii.98). Rostand quotes these lines in support of his view that Diderot's materialism is 'une sorte d'*hylozoïsme*'.[165] Such a supposition would, however, negate the concept of latent *sensibilité* and make a mockery of Diderot's careful account of the hierarchy pertaining between sentience, memory, thought and the more sophisticated psychological phenomena. In fact d'Alembert had initially qualified this statement in terms which make it clear that even in the delirium of his dream he is not reverting to molecular psychism. For each form of matter experiences only that degree of emotion appropriate to its organisation: 'Chaque forme a le bonheur et le malheur qui lui est propre' (p.45; Lew. viii.98). At the molecular level, therefore, where organic diversity and specialisation are by definition absent, such faculties can be nothing more than the most fundamental forms of action and reaction. 'Bonheur' may be nothing more than a vestige of Diderot's concept of optimum organisation: sentience dictating the most appropriate position or configuration for each particle or aggregate of matter. In the case of inorganic matter, *sensibilité* would be inert anyway, as in the 'feeling stone' discussed earlier.[166]

164. Janet, 'La philosophie de Diderot', p.698; Lerel, *Diderots Naturphilosophie*, p.14, 50, 146, 152.
165. Rostand, 'Diderot et la biologie', p.13. Rostand's emphasis.
166. Cf. above, section A.

For Winter, as has already been pointed out,[167] Diderot's hypothesis of universal *sensibilité* constitutes a vitalist position, co-existing with the materialism of *sensibilité* as a product of organisation. Matter, in the first formulation, does not produce life, she argues, since it already contains it in a potential form, and such a concept cannot be considered as an expression of materialism (p.233). Similar arguments are used by Szigeti.[168] This interpretation appears to be based on two misconceptions. In the first place, Winter, like Szigeti, overlooks the essential distinction between *sensibilité* and life. Secondly, despite her claims to treat each of Diderot's works as a 'provisional stopping place', she assumes that his position on this issue remains constant from 1753 to 1769. Thus the genuinely vitalistic conclusions of the *Pensées sur l'interprétation de la nature*, the letter to Sophie and the article 'Naître' are quoted in support of the supposed vitalism of 1769. Her remark that: 'Diderot bezeichnet in mehreren Texten die Entstehung von Leben aus der Kombination anorganischer Moleküle als *absurd*, und verwirft die Möglichkeit einer Ableitung der Lebensphänomene aus dem Bereich des Unbelebten' (p.230), may be true in itself, but proves nothing about his views in 1769. Such an argument denies both the evolution which has taken place within Diderot's thought and the actual rôle played by organisation in the *Rêve de d'Alembert's* account of the activation of *sensibilité*.

Nor is it valid to associate *sensibilité* with vitalism on account of its connection with Bordeu and hence with Renaissance neo-platonism. Like Diderot, Bordeu had followed Rouelle's lessons and often invoked Van Helmont and Paracelsus;[169] Rouelle's belief in a mysterious vital principle cannot, however, be equated with Diderot's adoption of the term *sensibilité*. As Varloot points out, Diderot's *sensibilité* has little to do with occultism. Ehrard, on the other hand, does interpret *sensibilité* as an occult property to which Diderot had recourse in place of a physico-chemical explanation of life, since the contemporary state of chemistry did not permit the conception of a passage from quantity to quality. He concludes, 'L'outillage mental dont dispose Diderot n'est pas au niveau de ses ambitions. [...] c'est pourquoi, en dernière analyse, le matérialisme de Diderot avorte en naturalisme'.[170] I do not feel that this conclusion stands up to scrutiny. Despite certain interesting parallels, Diderot's ideas have little in common with alchemical doctrine beyond a common opposition to 'life-denying mechanism',[171] and this, in itself, does not amount to vitalism.

167. Cf. above, B.i.a.4.
168. Cf. above, n.47. Cf. also M. D. Tsebenko, *La Lutte des matérialistes français du XVIIIe siècle contre l'idéalisme* (Paris 1955), p.40, and Roger, 'Science et Lumières', p.165.
169. Ehrard, 'Matérialisme et naturalisme', p.198.
170. p.201. Cf. also his *L'Idée de nature*, p.225, 243.
171. Varloot, 'Diderots Philosophie im *Rêve de d'Alembert*', p.715 and n.19. His argument is echoed in more general terms by both Winter, p.115-16, and Briggs, 'The Enlightenment's

It has been argued that concepts of 'vital force' (such as Stahl's *anima*, Barthez's *forces sensitives* and Bordeu's *sensibilité*) draw less on strictly scientific developments than on an older tradition of *immaterial* forces.[172] It is such principles which may properly be termed vitalism.[173] Collin offers a useful distinction between vitalism and mechanism (in its general, rather than narrowly cartesian sense) in terms which clarify Diderot's position. The true vitalist, he argues, holds that 'le principe vital, immatériel, inétendu et intemporel est capable de capter les énergies physico-chimiques, de mouvoir les atomes et les électrons, d'imprimer à la matière un cachet nouveau et, en somme, de la vitaliser',[174] whereas the mechanist 'se propose toujours comme but la réduction des phénomènes vitaux les plus compliqués à des composantes physicochimiques' (p.388). From this it would seem that vitalism and Diderot's principle of a strictly physical *energy* underlying vital phenomena cannot be conflated. *Sensibilité* is not an entity over and above what Collin calls 'les énergies physico-chimiques', but a constituent part of that energy complex.

b. Spinozism

Spinozism, or pantheism, is raised by Mlle de l'Espinasse's analogy of the spider's web. In an echo of his debate with Maupertuis on cosmic unity, Diderot speculates that, since nature is a whole, the web of sentience may be universal. In this case there would be identity between an individual thinker and the reality around him. Universal perception would give rise to universal memory: 'Par votre identité avec tous les êtres de la nature, vous sauriez tout ce qui se fait. Par votre mémoire, vous sauriez tout ce qui s'y est fait' (p.48; Lew. viii.101). A mind of such infinite proportions, omnipresent and omniscient, albeit material, would to all intents and purposes be divine: 'vous seriez Dieu', a point which Schwarz's gloss on this passage recognises: 'il semble rejoindre le Soufisme mahométan en le [l'analogie] douant d'un caractère spinoziste'.[175] Schwarz fails to point out, however, why this resemblance *is* only apparent.

Winter concludes from these lines that Diderot does not exclude the possibility of pantheism.[176] She dismisses Bordeu's counter-argument: 'puisqu'il serait matière dans l'univers, sujet à vicissitudes, il vieillirait, il mourrait' (p.48; Lew. viii.102) on the grounds that matter, for Diderot is eternal (Winter, p.237, n.4),

reception of the Italian Renaissance', p.22-23.

172. Jackson, 'Force and kindred notions', p.546-48.

173. See, for example, the definition offered by the *Oxford concise dictionary* (1964): 'Doctrine that life originates in a vital principle *distinct from* chemical and other physical forces' (my emphasis).

174. 'Mécanisme et animisme en biologie', p.385. Cf. Delaunay, 'L'évolution philosophique et médicale du biomécanisme', p.1338.

175. Schwarz, 'L'image de l'araignée dans le *Rêve de d'Alembert* de Diderot', p.266.

176. p.237. Cf. Forno, 'The cosmic mysticism of Diderot', p.137.

overlooking the fact that its forms, on the other hand, are not.

In fact, however, the pantheist implication is valid only if the universe is considered to be a *continuous* whole, a principle that Diderot rejects: 'C'est qu'entre Saturne et vous, il n'y a que des corps contigus, au lieu qu'il y faudrait de la continuité' (p.47; Lew. viii.101). Memory and thought can only occur within a context of continuous, organic unity. The universe is discontinuous; it is therefore neither an organism nor a god.[177]

iv. *Closing the circle: atheism*

Thus, through *sensibilité*, Diderot has elaborated a philosophy of nature which validates his boldly declared materialist atheism of two decades earlier. The *Lettre sur les aveugles* had given him a metaphysical position which could not, at the time, have been adequately defended. The intervening years have seen an inexorable, if uneven, progress towards a scientific defence of that atheism.

In the *Rêve*, Diderot has Bordeu ask Mlle de l'Espinasse: 'Croyez-vous qu'on puisse prendre parti sur l'intelligence suprême, sans savoir à quoi s'en tenir sur l'éternité de la matière et ses propriétés, la distinction des deux substances, la nature de l'homme et la production des animaux? (p.39; Lew. viii.93). Diderot's answer, like that of Mlle de l'Espinasse, had been categorically negative. By following a speculative programme broadly identical with the one outlined here, Diderot has elaborated a scientific framework which allows him to confirm the decision provisionally taken in 1749, the rejection of any reality beyond material nature: 'Il n'y a plus qu'une substance dans l'univers' (p.19; Lew. viii.70).

Even now, however, his atheism is of primarily methodological, rather than anti-religious concern. He is no more interested in actively disproving the existence of God than he had been in the *Apologie de l'abbé de Prades*.[178] What matters, above all, is that the challenge of explaining the universe and its phenomena in terms of energy rather than spirit appears to have been met.

As Vernière remarks, Diderot has been concerned less with the destination than with the journey in this particular quest: 'Diderot fait dépendre la religion d'une métaphysique qui elle-même dépend des résultats contestés d'une science inachevée; mais la recherche lui plaît plus que la découverte, et comme l'homme de Pascal, la chasse plus que la prise' (*OPhil.*, p.306, n.1).

---

177. Cf. Varloot, 'Diderots Philosophie im *Rêve de d'Alembert*', p.720-71, and Crocker, *Diderot's chaotic order*, p.21: 'His universe is holistic, but not organicist.' It is only now that Crocker's rejection of the label 'organic' to describe Diderot's view of unity (cf. above, 3, A.i.d.) is justified.

178. Cf. Winter, p.176, 179.

Conclusion

In fact, despite Diderot's declaration at the very outset of his philosophical career: 'On doit exiger de moi que je cherche la vérité, mais non que je la trouve',[179] his search has yielded a striking amount, if not precisely of truth (for that is less easy to assess than Diderot himself would perhaps have admitted), at least of rich and resonant intuition about the nature of Nature.

By 1769, energy, in one form or another, has been made responsible for every mode of existence and every mode of action in the universe, from the decomposition of the earth's crust to the most highly refined human intellectual faculties. Everything which exists is an effect of energy, a moment of equilibrium in the cosmic flux: 'mais le tout change sans cesse ... L'homme n'est qu'un effet commun, – le monstre qu'un effet rare; tous les deux [...] également dans l'ordre universel et général' (*Rêve de d'Alembert*, p.43; Lew. viii.97). Individual and species are purely dynamic phenomena: 'Qu'est-ce qu'un être? ... la somme d'un certain nombre de tendances. [...] Et les espèces? ... Les espèces ne sont que des tendances à un terme commun qui leur est propre' (p.45; Lew. viii.98). This conception, like the principle of optimum organisation which preceded it, may be interpreted in terms of resistance to entropy. Crocker suggests that the organism's purpose is 'to preserve its being, that is to protect its complex ordering from the invasion of disorder'.[180]

The potential forms of this matter/energy continuum are infinite, for the circumstances governing their development are infinitely variable.[181] Diderot is well aware of the significance of time and space: 'Si une distance de quelques mille lieues change mon espèce,,, que ne fera point l'intervalle de quelques milliers de diamètres terrestres? [...] que ne produiront point ici et ailleurs la durée et les vicissitudes de quelques millions de siècles?' (p.41-42; Lew. viii.95). It has been suggested, rather ambitiously, that such remarks in the *Rêve de d'Alembert* amount to an intuition of time as a fourth dimension, on the strength of an observation in d'Alembert's *Encyclopédie* article 'Dimension': 'Un homme d'esprit de ma connaissance croit qu'on pourrait [...] regarder la durée comme une quatrième dimension.'[182] The same scholar also points out that Diderot considers movement in similar terms in his *Principes sur la matière et le mouvement*: 'le mouvement est une qualité aussi réelle que la longueur, la largeur et la profondeur' (p.130; Lew. ix.611). Varloot makes the more restrained comment that Diderot's greatest originality is to have analysed old problems in terms of

179. p.27 (*Pensées philosophiques* no. XXIX); Her., ii.34.
180. *Diderot's chaotic order*, p.32.
181. Cf. Laidlaw, 'Diderot's teratology', p.113.
182. R. Debever, 'Du dialogue d'Alembert-Diderot?', *Etudes sur le XVIIIe siècle* 2 (1975), p.129.

a very new concept of time – as an irreversible, forward-moving *durée*, quite unlike the mechanists' mathematical model.[183]

Since nature is in flux, no effect can be exactly repeated, for the same combination of time and place, matter and energy, will never recur. Absolute unity leads, paradoxically, to absolute heterogeneity: 'Y a-t-il un atome en nature rigoureusement semblable à un autre atome? ... Non.'[184] Through energy, unity and diversity are at last reconciled.

183. 'Diderots Philosophie im *Rêve de Alembert*', p.727. Cf. also Mayer, *Diderot homme de science*, p.205, although he discusses the issue only in relation to the *Eléments de physiologie*.

184. *Rêve de d'Alembert*, p.44; Lew. viii.97. Cf. Varloot, p.709. For Forno ('The cosmic mysticism of Diderot', p.130) this is yet another leibnizian debt.

Conclusion

CHOUILLET'S *Diderot poète de l'énergie* concludes with a survey of Diderot's major contributions to the philosophy of energy. On the one hand, he declares, Diderot plays a key rôle in ridding the concept of energy of its 'résidus occultistes' (p.300) and simultaneously challenging the cartesian view of extended, passive matter, offering in its place a radically redefined concept of substance. On the other, and for Chouillet more importantly, Diderot was able to intuit the relevance of energy to the unity of nature: 'Enfin et surtout son intelligence surplombante lui a fait deviner le pouvoir d'unification que recélait le concept d'énergie. [...] l'énergie, telle qu'il l'a définie, dépasse et en même temps réunit les différents secteurs de la connaissance' (p.301). It may be that Diderot's concept of energy offers a key not only to the unity of nature, but to the unity of his own thought. I have attempted to give an impression of this double unity, by stressing the evolutionary, organic quality of his ideas on physical energy alongside their constantly underlying aim of explaining nature in terms of 'un seul acte'.

This study is, however, only the start of the beginning, and several paths are open for future exploration. It may be necessary – or at the very least useful – to reappraise whole areas of Diderot's thought (I am thinking particularly of his moral and aesthetic ideas) in the light of his philosophy of energy and *sensibilité*, as indeed Chouillet's suggestive study has begun to do. More specifically, questions need to be asked about the fortunes of the concepts dealt with here, in the years following the *Rêve de d'Alembert*. Diderot's notion of universal *sensibilité* is a case in point. Received wisdom has it that Diderot subsequently recoiled from his original bold conjectures about the universality of *sensibilité*: the truth of the matter can be established only via a systematic and comparative close study of later works, notably the *Réfutation d'Helvétius*, *Commentaire sur Hemsterhuis* and the chronologically problematic *Eléments de physiologie*, all of which contain crucial – and at first sight conflicting – material.

The text on which most critics have based their assumption that Diderot later rejects the thesis of universal *sensibilité* is his statement in the *Réfutation d'Helvétius* (*OPhil.*, p.566):

Il faut en convenir: l'organisation ou la co-ordination de parties inertes ne mène point du tout à la sensibilité, et la sensibilité générale des molécules de la matière n'est qu'une supposition, qui tire toute sa force des difficultés dont elle débarrasse, ce qui ne suffit pas en bonne philosophie.

Is this, as Vernière claims, '[un] recul manifeste depuis les thèses du *Rêve de d'Alembert*'?[1] I do not think it is as simple as that. As far as the first part of the statement is concerned, Diderot had said as much himself in the *Rêve de d'Alembert* and on several previous occasions. The inadequacy of organisation alone to bring about sentience is a recurrent theme in his writings: indeed it was precisely to resolve this difficulty that universal *sensibilité* was proposed (which may of course be implied by his use here of 'et').

What then of Diderot's contention that universal *sensibilité* is no more than a 'supposition'? In citing this term as evidence of Diderot's denial of his earlier position – 'Le mot même de "supposition" n'a pas la noblesse d'une "hypothèse"' (p.566) – Vernière forgets that the fictional Diderot of the *Rêve de d'Alembert* had called the notion '*une supposition* simple qui explique tout'.[2] Even in 1769 then, he had been fully aware of its purely speculative status and the fact that its strength lay primarily in its potential as an explanatory concept.

Compare the grounds on which the *Rêve de d'Alembert* rejects the theory of preformed germs: 'cela est contre l'expérience et la raison' (p.9; Lew. viii.61). Diderot's thesis of universal *sensibilité* is compatible with both, and therein lies its superiority (p.18; Lew. viii.70). Moreover, Diderot uses the term 'supposition' elsewhere in the *Réfutation d'Helvétius* to denote the inspired hypothesis which frequently has to precede practical experimentation (*OPhil.*, p.598; my emphasis):

[Helvétius] Il faut s'avancer à la suite de l'expérience et ne la jamais précéder. [Diderot] cela est vrai, mais fait-on des expériences au hasard? L'expérience n'est-elle pas souvent précédée d'*une supposition*, d'une analogie, d'une idée systématique que l'expérience confirmera ou détruira?

Far from contradicting his 1769 position, this is not so far removed from Bordeu's comment on d'Alembert's visionary dream: 'Voilà de la philosophie bien haute; systématique dans ce moment, je crois que plus les connaissances de l'homme feront de progrès, plus elle se vérifiera.'[3] In both cases, Diderot is calling for experimental verification, and rather than rejecting the hypothesis – which he seems to find as attractive in 1773 as he had four years earlier – simply appealing for the empirical support Helvétius has failed to provide. Diderot's main grievance, perhaps, in this instance, is that Helvétius, unlike Diderot himself, has attempted to make a prematurely definitive, *published* statement of the idea. His 1773 remark continues: 'Je pardonne à Descartes

1. This is despite Vernière's belief that it would be wrong to interpret the *Réfutation* as 'une sorte d'abjuration des audaces d'autrefois' (p.559).
2. *Rêve de d'Alembert*, p.17 (my emphasis); Lew. viii.69.
3. *Rêve de d'Alembert*, p.45; Lew. viii.98. Note the similarity of terms: 'systématique' / 'une idée systématique'.

d'avoir imaginé ses règles du mouvement, mais ce que je ne lui pardonne point, c'est de ne s'être pas assuré par l'expérience si elles étaient ou n'étaient pas, dans la nature, telles qu'il les avait imaginées' (*OPhil.*, p.598). It seems likely that the extensive documentation accumulated in the *Eléments de physiologie* represents, in part, Diderot's attempt to establish an empirical basis for his theory of universal *sensibilité* and thus to avert (albeit by means of others' researches) the accusation levelled at Descartes. His explicit and urgent appeal for research in this area: 'J'invite tous les physiciens et tous les chimistes à rechercher ce que c'est que la substance animale, sensible et vivante' (p.565), while destined to remain unheard (since he did not publish the *Réfutation*), is nevertheless indicative of the importance Diderot attaches to the question.

In the event, Diderot's speculations on energy, matter, life and the unity of nature are rarely supported by detailed experimental data, and this is how it had to be. As Mayer has pointed out, contemporary science simply did not offer the necessary documentation for an intuitive philosophy ahead of its time. The *Rêve de d'Alembert* is not an exposé of eighteenth-century science, but 'un pari sur la science de l'avenir'.[4] As Chouillet has indicated, although it is futile to present Diderot as a prophet in the literal sense, we can acknowledge the qualities which enable him, in so many respects, to win that wager:

Notre objectif n'est pas de légaliser la science passée au nom d'un futur de la science dont les hommes du dix-huitième siècle n'avaient pas la moindre idée. Qu'il nous suffise de constater que Diderot est allé plus loin que ses contemporains dans le sens de l'audace et de l'imagination.[5]

For Diderot's monist materialism comes strikingly closer to modern than to classical models of nature.

The eighteenth century in general saw a transition from emphasis on the passivity of material entities to the concept of active principles (often divinely imparted rather than inherent, and thus contingent rather than essential). Chouillet sees Diderot's philosophy of energy in terms of a common eighteenth-century tendency to extrapolate from the particular to the general, which meant, in the case of materialist thinkers, a tendency to generalise energy: 'Puisque l'énergie, comme définition première de l'homme, leur paraissait une vérité expérimentale, ils ont pensé qu'il ne pouvait en être autrement à l'échelle cosmique' (p.45). Ultimately, this was to lead to the quite distinct concept of active substance[6] rather than active principles, and it is within the context of

---

4. Mayer, *Diderot homme de science*, p.272. On the other hand, Mayer has also warned against the pointlessness of presenting Diderot as a prophet (p.450, 457).

5. *Diderot poète de l'énergie*, p.66. Cf. also previous note, and Introduction.

6. P. M. Heimann and J. E. Mcguire, 'Newtonian forces and Lockean powers', *Historical studies in the physical sciences* 3 (1971), p.235-36.

this evolution that Diderot's modernity appears most striking, given that clear expressions of the third concept do not emerge until the 1780s and 90s (Heimann and Mcguire, p.273, 286).

Diderot's philosophy of energy is far closer in spirit to John Playfair's declaration in 1822 of matter/energy equivalence: 'Thus it appears that power is the essence of matter, and that none of our perceptions warrant us in considering even body as involving anything more than force, subjected to various laws and combinations' (p.294) than to the naturalistic or vitalistic thought forms with which his speculations are traditionally associated.[7]

Three concepts in particular, each of which represents an aspect of unity, were to find an echo in the theories of later centuries: the interconvertibility of energy forms (unity of energy); the emergence of qualitative from quantitative change (unity of inorganic and organic, of sentience and intelligence, through energy); the identification of elementary particles with the forces they deploy (unity of matter and energy).

Diderot's works up to 1769 contain no explicit declaration of energy transformation. Nevertheless it is not unreasonable to interpret the activation of *sensibilité* in such terms. Heat releases (or activates) motion, which in turn releases (or activates) sentience. These are not, however, discrete qualities of matter, but may well be envisaged as three alternative modes of a single energetic entity.

Heat is defined in the *Encyclopédie* as a form of motion: 'la chaleur dans le corps qui la donne, n'est autre chose que le mouvement' (*Enc.*, iii.23). In point of fact, considerable confusion reigned amongst both physicists and chemists as to the nature of heat. Locke had considered it to represent the 'motions of parts'[8] and Bacon had declared 'Heat itself, its essence and quiddity, is Motion and nothing else.'[9] By the time of the *Encyclopédie* it was interpreted variously as a fluid composed of special particles (a form of matter) or as a phenomenon which could be produced in any body by mechanical means (a form of movement).[10]

Varloot is impressed by the fact that Diderot sees a causal connection between heat and molecular change long before the principles of combustion were fully elucidated[11] but does not comment on its energetic aspect. Kiernan, on the other hand, suggests that the association of heat and motion was a characteristic

---

7. Cf. Perkins, 'Diderot and La Mettrie', p.70-72.
8. Gillispie, *The Edge of objectivity*, p.372.
9. Quoted in Boas, 'The establishment of the mechanical philosophy', p.440, n.3.
10. Vassails, '*L'Encyclopédie* et la physique', p.308-309. Cf. the similar confusion over electricity (above, chapter 3).
11. 'Diderots Philosophie im *Rêve de d'Alembert*', p.709. Cf. Wartofsky, p.314.

view of the 'ferment theorists' (of which Rouelle was the foremost),[12] whose anti-mechanist tendencies predominated in the *Encyclopédie* (p.137, 139): 'they rejected the mechanisation of phlogiston theory. [...] Combustion was explained as a sort of fermentation in matter, as a chemical reaction induced by the air, with heat as an additional catalyst rather than a cause' (p.118). This may be so, but has little relevance to Diderot's use of an energetic concept of heat in the entirely different context of generation.

Sensibilité too appears to be an energy form, having latent and active modes, and being presented as a dynamic phenomenon of action and reaction or, in one of Diderot's analogies, as vibration, yet another specialised type of motion. This interpretation was put forward in 1904 by Païtre, who saw both the relationship between *sensibilité* and motion: 'il en est de la sensibilité comme du mouvement, ou même la sensibilité n'est qu'une forme du mouvement',[13] and the energetic character of the entire sequence (though he erroneously reverses the relationship between heat and motion): 'Mais comment s'explique la vie? Par la génération spontanée favorisée elle-même par la chaleur qui est une manifestation du mouvement – car Diderot avant Carnot a émis le principe de la transformation des forces.'[14]

Mayer, too, though his analysis of this point is necessarily brief, does stress the modernity of Diderot's concept of energy, particularly in relation to vital phenomena: 'pour Diderot, la vie est une forme de l'énergie: c'est là sa définition et le vingtième siècle n'en possède pas de meilleure'.[15]

As Wartofsky points out, Diderot posits a process of qualitative change, based on energy and changing levels of organisation, a process which unites organic and inorganic, physical and mental, continuity and discontinuity, part and whole, quantity and quality (p.310, 312-14, 321).

To claim, therefore, as marxist criticism has invariably done, that Diderot fails to reach an intuition of the dialectical principle of the emergence of qualitative from quantitative change, is to misrepresent his philosophy. For new qualities – in the form of new energy modes – do arise precisely from a change in the complexity of matter. Life belongs only to an aggregate of matter, not to

12. 'Additional reflections', p.119.

13. *Diderot biologiste* (Genève 1971 [reprint]), p.42.

14. p.44. This seems to be a chance intuition on Païtre's part, however, as his study generally lacks academic rigour. For an account of the actual nineteenth-century development of this theory, see Gillispie, *The Edge of objectivity*, chapter 10, especially p.370-71.

15. *Diderot homme de science*, p.196, 237. For a discussion of the scientific counterpart of Diderot's philosophical intuition, see Canguilhem, *Etudes d'histoire* III/1/II, 'Bioénergetique', which traces the development of this concept in nineteenth-century physiology (for example, p.260: the experimental verification by Liebig (1842) and Mayer (1845) 'que la cause de chaque phénomène vital réside dans l'énergie fournie par l'alimentation').

its elements; intelligence belongs only to the sophisticated organism which possesses the specialised configuration appropriate to memory.

Varloot gives Diderot credit for this distinction between the various levels of matter, but claims that his desire to avoid both cosmic unity (total continuity) and rigid classification, held him back from achieving the truly pre-dialectical insight into the transition from one qualitative state to another which Wartofsky had claimed for him.[16]

Lefèbvre too denies him this insight, on the grounds that his desire for unity and continuity in nature prevents him from grasping the significance of discontinuity: 'il ne pourra ni comprendre, ni même pressentir les *bonds* dans la nature, [ce qui] va donc lui interdire d'approfondir les rapports de la qualité et de la quantité, rapports qui impliquent la notion du bond dialectique'.[17] This judgement appears to be based on Lefèbvre's imprecise reading of Diderot's philosophy of energy in general.[18] For, as Mayer has indicated, Diderot's concept of stages of development is based on distinctions of nature, rather than degree, that is to say a principle of discontinuity quite modern in spirit.[19]

Crocker, too, whilst pointing out that dialectic in the sense of 'unity of contraries producing a new synthesis' has no place in Diderot's views,[20] nevertheless acknowledges that 'Beyond a certain level of complexity, a structuration comes about that creates a new type of interrelationships, an enhancement of organised energy to the point of a new way of existing'[21] and writes of 'the leap to a new level of emergence'.[22]

Moreover, the relationship between energy and organisation is twofold. On the one hand, organisation determines the form in which energy is deployed. On the other, however, it is energy which determines the form in which matter is organised. Ehrard's contention that Diderot chooses to explain organisation by *sensibilité* rather than vice versa[23] acknowledges only one side of this relationship. It is energy, just as much as matter, which constitutes the essence of nature. Or rather, as Diderot was to write just a year after the *Rêve de d'Alembert*, matter itself is essentially energy: 'La molécule, douée d'une qualité propre à

16. Varloot, 'Diderots Philosophie im *Rêve de d'Alembert*', p.727-28.

17. *Diderot*, p.143. Cf. Szigeti's similar arguments, *Denis Diderot, une grande figure*, p.35-36, 73-74, 76, and the more moderate judgement of Momdzjan, 'La dialectique dans la vision du monde de Diderot', p.259, 260.

18. Cf. above, 5, B.i.a.4.

19. *Diderot homme de science*, p.16.

20. *Diderot's chaotic order*, p.46.

21. p.30. Cf. Winter, p.234, although she applies this interpretation only to part of Diderot's concept of *sensibilité*. Cf. also above, chapter 5, p.147.

22. p.27. Cf. his *Diderot the embattled philosopher*, p.313, and above chapter 5, p.144-45.

23. 'Matérialisme et naturalisme', p.200.

sa nature, par elle-même est une force active.'[24] It should be noted that the *qualité* referred to is in turn energetic. Diderot posits, a few lines later: 'une action, une force, [...] ou extérieure à la molécule ou inhérente, essentielle, intime à la molécule, et constituant sa nature de molécule ignée, aqueuse, nitreuse, alcaline, sulfureuse'.

Wartofsky's analysis of the *Principes philosophiques sur la matière et le mouvement* clarifies the relationship between energy and qualitative transformation. He points out that Diderot effectively equates force and motion, thus making energy not a conditional state of matter (as in mechanist thought) but an essential property, the mode in which matter exists (p.299, 302). Energy (in this case motion) is thus responsible for the qualitative differentiation – heterogeneity – of matter (p.301). It has both quantitative and qualitative aspects (p.302); ultimately all force is inherent, and all effects follow from it.[25]

Although Wartofsky's conclusions are based on a work of 1770, they coincide with the implications I have drawn in an earlier chapter from *Modification* and *Sur la cohésion des corps*.[26] Contrary to Lefèbvre's assertion, the concept of matter/ energy equivalence is not explicitly present in the *Rêve de d'Alembert* itself (*Diderot*, p.157). It is never, however, very far from the surface.

Gillispie remarks of Mayer and Helmholtz, the nineteenth-century founders of energetics, that they 'raised force to a status equivalent to that of matter – equivalent ontologically, but more interesting physically'.[27] This had already been achieved, at the speculative if not the experimental level, by Diderot in the previous century. Almost 100 years after Diderot's own *Pensées* on the subject, Helmholtz, the German physicist who formulated in 1847 the law of energy conservation which remains a foundation block of modern physics (Gillispie, p.386), laid down an objective for the 'interpreter of nature':

The mission of theoretical science will have been accomplished when it has defined all phenomena in terms of elementary forces, and demonstrated that this definition alone is compatible with the facts. Such a definition should be considered as the necessary form in which to conceive nature.[28]

Diderot would certainly have concurred.

24. Lew. ix.611 (*Principes philosophiques sur la matière et le mouvement*).
25. p.304. Cf. Chouillet's remark that the *Principes*, 'texte souvent et injustement négligé' (*Diderot poète de l'énergie*, p.61), offer a valuable attempt to clarify the broad energetic issues raised in the *Rêve de d'Alembert*: 'Non pas que les *Principes* traitent directement du problème de la sensibilité, mais ils appliquent au problème du mouvement et du repos une méthode de réflexion qui pourrait sans trop d'inconvénient être transposée en termes de biologie' (p.54).
26. Cf. above, chapter 4, n.88.
27. *The Edge of objectivity*, p.385.
28. Gillispie, p.386. The quotation is from *On the conservation of force*.

Bibliography

Alexander, I. W., 'Philosophy of organism and philosophy of consciousness in Diderot's speculative thought', *Studies in romance philology and French literature presented to John Orr*, Manchester 1953, p.1-21

Bachelard, G., *La Formation de l'esprit scientifique*, Paris 1947

Barber, W. H., *Leibniz in France from Arnauld to Voltaire: a study in French reactions to Leibnizianism 1670-1760*, Oxford 1955

Belaval, Y., 'La crise de la géométrisation de l'univers dans la philosophie des Lumières', *Revue internationale de philosophie* 21 (1952), p.337-55

– 'Note sur Diderot et Leibniz', *Revue des sciences humaines* 112 (1963), p.435-51

– 'Le *philosophe* Diderot', *Critique* 58 (1952), p.230-53

– 'Les protagonistes du *Rêve de d'Alembert*', *Diderot studies* 3 (1961), p.27-53

– 'Sur le matérialisme de Diderot', *Europäische Aufklärung: Herbert Dieckmann zum 60. Geburtstag*, ed. Friedrich and Schalk, Munich 1967, p.9-21

Benot, Y., 'Diderot épistolier: de ses lettres à ses livres', *Pensée* 99 (1961), p.98-105

Boas, M., 'The establishment of mechanical philosophy', *Osiris* 12 (1952), p.412-541

Briggs, E. R., 'The Enlightenment's reception of the legacy of the Italian Renaissance', *British Society for Eighteenth-Century Studies newsletter* 11 (1977), p.19-23

– 'L'incrédulité et la pensée anglaise en France au début du XVIIIe siècle', *Revue d'histoire littéraire de la France* 41 (1934), p.497-538

Callot, E., *Six philosophes français du XVIIIe siècle: la vie, l'œuvre et la doctrine de Diderot, Fontenelle, Maupertuis, La Mettrie, d'Holbach, Rivarol* Annecy 1963

– *La Philosophie de la vie au XVIIIe siècle* (chapter 6: Diderot), Paris 1965

Canguilhem, G., *Etudes d'histoire et de philosophie des sciences*, Paris 1970

– 'Le tout et la partie dans la pensée biologique', *Les études philosophiques* 31 (1966), p.3-16

Casini, P., *Diderot 'philosophe'*, Bari 1962

Charpentier, J., 'Diderot et la science de son temps', *Revue du mois* 16 (1913), p.537-52

Chouillet, J., *La Formation des idées esthétiques de Diderot*, Paris 1973

– 'Le personnage du Sceptique dans les premières œuvres de Diderot', *Dix-huitième siècle* 1 (1969), p.195-211

– *Diderot poète de l'énergie*, Paris 1984

Cohen, I. B., 'A note concerning Diderot and Franklin', *Isis* 46 (1955), p.268-72

Collin, R., 'Mécanisme et animisme en biologie', *Revue de philosophie* 35 (1935), p.385-418

Crocker, L. G., *Diderot's chaotic order: approach to synthesis*, Princeton 1974

– *Diderot the embattled philosopher*, New York 1966

– 'John Toland et le matérialisme de Diderot', *Revue d'histoire littéraire de France* 53 (1953), p.289-95

– 'Pensée XIX de Diderot', *Modern language notes* 67 (November 1952), p.433-39, and ensuing correspondence, 68 (April 1953), p.282-288

Crosland, M., 'The development of chemistry in the eighteenth century', *Studies on Voltaire* 24 (1963), p.369-441

Cyrano de Bergerac, *L'Autre monde (les états et empires de la lune; les états et empires du soleil)*, ed. H. Weber, Paris 1968

Daumas, M., 'La chimie dans l'Encyclopé-

die', *Revue d'histoire des sciences* 4 (1951), p.334-43

Debever, R., 'Du dialogue d'Alembert-Diderot? Un trait d'esprit à propos de la quatrième dimension', *Etudes sur le XVIIIe siècle* 2 (1975), p.129-33

Delaunay, P., 'L'évolution philosophique et médicale du biomécanisme de Descartes à Boerhaave, de Leibniz à Cabanis', *Le Progrès médical* (20.8.1927), p.1289-93; (27.8.1927), p.1331-34; (3.9.1927), p.1369-84

Desné, R., 'Sur le matérialisme de Diderot', *Pensée* 108 (1963), p.98-108

Diderot, D., *Correspondance*, ed. G. Roth and J. Varloot, Paris 1955-1970

– *De l'interprétation de la nature* (with *Articles de l'Encyclopédie*), ed. J. Varloot, Paris 1953

– *Eléments de physiologie*, ed. J. Mayer, Paris 1964

– *Lettre sur les aveugles*, ed. R. Niklaus, Lille Genève 1951

– *Pensées philosophiques*, ed. R. Niklaus, Genève 1965

– *Œuvres complètes*, ed. J. Assézat and M. Tourneux, Paris 1875-1877

– *Œuvres complètes*, ed. R. Lewinter, Paris 1972

– *Œuvres complètes*, ed. Wilson, Hanna, Desné and others, Paris, Hermann, 1975-

– *Œuvres esthétiques*, ed. P. Vernière, Paris 1968

– *Œuvres philosophiques*, ed. P. Vernière, Paris 1964

– *Œuvres romanesques*, ed. H. Bénac, Paris 1962

– *Le Rêve de d'Alembert*, ed. J. Varloot, Paris 1962

Dieckmann, H., 'Diderots Naturempfinden und Lebensgefühl', *Travaux du séminaire de philologie romane*, Istanbul, 1 (1937), p.57-83

– 'Diderot's *Promenade du sceptique*: a study in the relationship of thought and form', *Studies on Voltaire* 55 (1967), p.417-38

– 'The first edition of Diderot's *Pensées*

sur l'interprétation de la nature', *Isis* 46 (1955), p.251-67

– 'The influence of Francis Bacon on Diderot's *Interprétation de la nature*', *Romanic review* 34 (1944), p.303-80 (reprinted *Studien zur europäische Aufklärung*, München 1974, p.34-57)

– 'Théophile Bordeu und Diderots *Rêve de d'Alembert*', *Romanische Forschungen* 52 (1938), p.55-112

– 'Zur Interpretation Diderots', *Romanische Forschungen* 53 (1939), p.47-82

Doolittle, J., 'Robert James, Diderot, and the *Encyclopédie*', *Modern language notes* 71 (1956), p.431-34

Ehrard, J., *L'Idée de la nature en France dans la première moitié du dix-huitième siècle*, Chambéry, Paris 1963

– 'Matérialisme et naturalisme: les sources occultistes de la pensée de Diderot', *Cahiers de l'Association internationale des études françaises* 13 (1961), p.189-201

El Nouty, H., 'Le panthéisme dans les lettres françaises au dix-huitième siècle: aperçus sur la fortune du mot et de la notion', *Revue des sciences humaines* 100 (1960), p.435-57

Encyclopédie, ou Dictionnaire raisonné des sciences, des arts et des métiers, Paris 1751-1780

Etiemble, R., 'Structure et sens des *Pensées philosophiques*', *Romanische Forschungen* 74 (1962), p.1-10

Fabre, J., 'Actualité de Diderot', *Diderot studies* 4, 1963, p.17-40

– 'Le chemin de Diderot', *Europe* 405-406 (1963), p.3-16

– 'Diderot et les théosophes', *Cahiers de l'Association internationale des études françaises* 13 (1961), p.203-22

Fellows, O. E., 'Metaphysics and the *Bijoux indiscrets*: Diderot's debt to Prior', *Studies on Voltaire* 56 (1967), p.509-40

Forno, L. J., 'The cosmic mysticism of Diderot', *Studies on Voltaire* 153 (1975), pp.113-40

Fusil, C.-A., 'Lucrèce et les philosophes

du XVIIIe siècle', *Revue d'histoire littéraire de la France* 35 (1928), p.194-210

Gay, P., *The Enlightenment: an interpretation*, London 1967

Gillispie, C. C., *The Edge of objectivity: an essay in the history of scientific ideas*, Princeton 1960

Got, M., 'Sur le matérialisme de Diderot', *Revue de synthèse* 3/26-28 (1962), p.135-64

Grava, A., 'Diderot and recent philosophical trends', *Diderot studies* 4 (1963), p.73-103

Greenwood, T., 'The philosophy of nature of Denis Diderot', *Revue de l'Université d'Ottawa* (1947), p.169-86

Gregory, A., 'Denis Diderot', *Horizon* 9 (1944), p.32-47

Groethuysen, B., 'La pensée de Diderot', *Grande revue* 22 (25.11.1913), p.322-41

Guédon, J.-C., 'Chimie et matérialisme: la stratégie anti-newtonienne de Diderot', *Dix-huitième siècle* 11 (1979), p.185-200

Gusdorf, G., *Dieu, la nature, l'homme au siècle des Lumières*, Paris 1972

Hazard, P., *La Pensée européenne au XVIIIe siècle de Montesquieu à Lessing*, Paris 1946
– 'Les origines philosophiques de l'homme de sentiment', *Quatre études*, New York 1940

Heimann, P. M. and McGuire, J. E., 'Newtonian forces and Lockean powers: concepts of matter in eighteenth-century thought', *Historical studies in the physical sciences* 3 (1971), p.233-306

Heisenberg, W., *Physics and philosophy* (translated from the German), London 1959

Helvétius, *De L'Esprit*, ed. G. Besse, Paris 1959

Hill, E. B., 'Materialism and monsters in *Le Rêve de d'Alembert*', *Diderot studies* 10 (1968), p.67-93
– 'The rôle of *le monstre* in Diderot's thought', *Studies on Voltaire* 97 (1972), p.147-261

Hofmann, W., 'Diderots Auffassungen vom allgemeinen Empfindungsvermögen, von der Entstehung und Einheit des Bewußtseins', *Wissenschaftliche Zeitschrift*, Humboldt Universität, Berlin, 13 (1964), p.175-80

Hoffmann, P., 'L'idée de liberté dans la philosophie médicale de Bordeu', *Studies on Voltaire* 88 (1972), p.769-87

Iltis, C., 'Leibniz' concept of force: physics and metaphysics', *Akten der internationalen Leibniz Kongress* 2 (*Studia Leibnitiana supplementa* 13) Wiesbaden 1974, p.143-49

Jackson, S. W., 'Force and kindred notions in 18th-century neurophysiology and medical psychology', *Bulletin of the history of medicine* 44 (1970), p.397-410, 539-54

Janet, P., 'La philosophie de Diderot: le dernier mot d'un matérialiste', *Nineteenth century* 9 (1881), p.695-708

Jasinski, R., *Histoire de la littérature française* (vol.ii), Paris 1966

Jugnet, L., 'Essai sur les rapports entre la philosophie suarézienne de la matière et la pensée de Leibniz', *Revue des sciences humaines* 3 (1935), p.126-36

Kiernan, C., 'Additional reflections on Diderot and science', *Diderot studies* 14 (1971), p.113-42
– *Enlightenment and science*, 2nd edition, Studies on Voltaire 59A (1973)

Krauss, W., 'Diderot in dieser Zeit', *Wissenschaftliche Zeitschrift*, Humboldt Universität, Berlin, 13 (1964), p.115-18

Lach, D. F., 'Leibniz and China', *Journal of the history of ideas* 6 (1945), p.436-55

Laidlaw, G. N., 'Diderot's teratology', *Diderot studies* 4 (1963), p.105-29

Landucci, S. C., 'Diderot philosophe', *Belfagor* 18 (1963), p.323-35

Laplassotte, F., 'Quelques étapes de la physiologie du cerveau du XVIIe au XIXe siècle', *Annales: économies, sociétés, civilisations* 25 (1970) p.599-613

Lefèbvre, H., *Diderot*, Paris 1949

Lemay, P., 'Les cours de Guillaume-François Rouelle', *Revue d'histoire de la pharmacie* 13 (1949), p.434-42

– 'Du nouveau sur le *Rêve de d'Alembert*', *Le Progrès médical* 15-16 (10-24.8.1951), p.423a-424b

Lerel, A. C., *Diderots Naturphilosophie*, Wien 1950

Leroy, J.-F., 'La notion de vie dans la botanique du XVIIIe siècle', *Histoire et biologie* 2 (1969), p.1-9

Lough, J., *The Encyclopedie in eighteenth-century England and other studies*, Newcastle-upon-Tyne 1970

Luppol, I. K., *Denis Diderot, ses idées philosophiques*, Paris 1936

Luxembourg, L. K., *Francis Bacon and Denis Diderot: philosophers of science*, Copenhagen 1967

Maupertuis, P. L. Moreau de, *Œuvres*, Lyon 1756 (vol.ii: *Système de la nature* and *Réponse aux objections de M. Diderot*)

Mayer, J., *Diderot homme de science*, Rennes 1959

Mendelsohn, E. I., 'Philosophical biology vs. experimental biology: spontaneous generation in the 17th century', *Actes: 12e Congrès international d'histoire des sciences*, 1b (1971), p.201-26

Metzger, H., *Les Doctrines chimiques en France du début du XVIIe siècle à la fin du XVIIIe siècle. Première partie*. Reprint, Paris 1969

Momdzjan, H. N., 'La dialectique dans la vision du monde de Diderot', *Au siècle des Lumières*, ed. M. Duchet and M. Launay, Paris, Moscow 1970, p.249-67

Moravia, S., 'Dall' Homme machine all' Homme sensible: meccanismo, animismo e vitalismo nel secolo XVIII', *Belfagor* 29 (1974), p.633-48

Mornet, D., *Diderot, l'homme et l'œuvre*, Paris 1941

Mousnier, R., *Progrès scientifique et technique au XVIIIe siècle*, Paris 1958

Naigeon, J. A., *Mémoires historiques sur la vie et les ouvrages de D. Diderot*, Genève 1971 [reprint]

Niklaus, R., 'The Mind of Diderot', *Filosofia* 14 (1963), p.926-38

– 'Les *Pensées philosophiques* de Diderot',

Bulletin of the John Rylands Library 26 (1941), p.121-29

– 'Présence de Diderot', *Diderot studies* 6 (1964), p.13-28

Paître, F., *Diderot biologiste*, Genève 1971 [reprint]

Paty, M., 'Matière, espace et temps selon Newton', *Scientia* 107 (1972), p.995-1026

Perkins, J. A., 'Diderot et La Mettrie', *Studies on Voltaire* 10 (1959), p.49-100

Piselli, F., 'La philosophie et les sciences dans la pensée de Diderot', *Studia leibnitiana supplementa* 15 (1975), p.187-92

Polonoff, I. I., *Forces, cosmos, monads and other themes of Kant's early thought*, Bonn 1973 (*Kantstudien* 107)

Pommier, J., *Diderot avant Vincennes*, Paris 1939

Proust, J., *Diderot et l'Encyclopédie*, Paris 1962

– '*L'Encyclopédie* dans la pensée et dans la vie de Diderot', *Europe* 405-406 (1963), p.110-17

– 'Variations sur un thème de l'*Entretien avec d'Alembert*', *Revue des sciences humaines* 28 (1963), p.454-70

Raghuveer, S., 'Herakleitos and the law of nature', *Journal of the history of ideas* 24 (1963), p.457-72

Rappaport, R., 'G.-F. Rouelle: an eighteenth-century chemist and teacher', *Chymia* 6 (1960), p.68-101

Ritterbush, C., *Overtures to biology*, New Haven 1964

Roger, J., 'Le déisme du jeune Diderot', *Europäische Aufklärung: Herbert Dieckmann zum 60 Geburtstag*, ed. Friedrich and Schalk, München 1967, p.237-45

– 'Diderot et Buffon en 1749', *Diderot studies* 4 (1963), p.221-36

– *Les Sciences de la vie dans la pensée française du dix-huitième siècle*, Paris 1963

– 'Science et lumières', *Revue de l'Université de Bruxelles* (1972), p.157-65

Rostand, J., 'Diderot et la biologie', *Revue d'histoire des sciences* 5 (1952), p.5-17

- 'Diderot, philosophe de la biologie', *Biologie et humanisme*, Paris 1964
- 'La molécule et le philosophe', *Nouvelles littéraires* (19.12.1963), p.7
- *Les Origines de la biologie expérimentale et l'abbé Spallanzani*, Paris 1951

Russell, B., *History of western philosophy*, 2nd ed., London 1979

Schmidt, O., 'Die Anschauungen der Encyclopädisten über die organische Natur', *Deutsche Rundschau* 7 (1876), p.82-96

Schwartz, L., 'L'image de l'araignée dans le *Rêve de d'Alembert*', *Romance notes* 15 (1973), p.264-67

Sheldon, W. H., 'Leibniz's message to us', *Journal of the history of ideas* 7 (1946), p.385-96

Singh, C. M., 'The *Lettre sur les aveugles*: its debt to Lucretius', *Studies in 18th-century French literature presented to R. Niklaus*, ed. Fox and others, Exeter 1975, p.233-42

Smith, C. I., 'Heraclitus and fire', *Journal of the history of ideas* 27 (1966), p.125-27

Smith, I. H., 'Le *Rêve de d'Alembert* and *De rerum natura*', *Australasian Universities Modern Languages Association publications* 10 (1959), p.128-34

Spink, J. S., *French free-thought from Gassendi to Voltaire*, London 1960

Spinoza, B. de., *Œuvres*, ed. Appuhn, Paris 1964

Szigeti, J., *Denis Diderot: une grande figure du matérialisme militant du XVIIIe siècle*, Budapest 1962

Thielemann, L. J., 'Diderot and Hobbes', *Diderot studies* 2 (1952), p.221-78

Tocanne, B., *L'Idée de nature en France dans la seconde moitié du XVIIe siècle*, Paris 1978

Tonelli, G., 'The law of continuity in the eighteenth century', *Studies on Voltaire* 27 (1963), p.1619-38
- 'La nécessité des lois de la nature au XVIIIe siècle et chez Kant en 1762', *Revue d'histoire des sciences* 12 (1959), p.225-41

Torrey, N. L., 'Voltaire's reaction to Diderot', *Publications of the Modern Language Association of America* 50 (1935), p.1107-43

Trahard, P., *Les Maîtres de la sensibilité française au XVIIIe siècle, 1715-1789*, Paris 1932

Tsebenko, M. D., *La Lutte des matérialistes français du XVIIIe siècle contre l'idéalisme*, Paris 1955

Urey, H. C., 'On the early chemical history of the earth and the origin of life', *Proceedings of the National Academy of Sciences* 38 (1952), p.351-63

Varloot, J., 'Sur Diderot et *l'Encyclopédie*', *Pensée* 3 (1963), p.87-97
- 'Diderots Philosophie im *Rêve de d'Alembert*: Materialismus in Aktion', *Sinn und Form* 14 (1962), p.704-28
- introduction to Diderot, *Textes choisis*, Paris 1953
- 'Le projet 'antique' du *Rêve de d'Alembert* de Diderot', *Beiträge zur romanischen Philologie* 2 (1963), p.49-61

Vartanian, A., *Diderot and Descartes: a study of scientific naturalism in the Enlightenment*, Princeton 1953
- 'From deist to atheist: Diderot's philosophical orientation 1746-1749', *Diderot studies* (1949), p.46-63
- introduction to La Mettrie's *L'Homme machine: a study in the origins of an idea*, Princeton 1960
- 'The problem of generation and the French Enlightenment', *Diderot studies* 6 (1964), p.339-52
- 'Trembley's polyp, La Mettrie, and eighteenth-century French materialism', *Journal of the history of ideas* 11 (1950), p.259-86

Vassails, G., '*L'Encyclopédie* et la physique', *Revue d'histoire des sciences* 4 (1951), p.294-323

Venturi, F., *La Jeunesse de Diderot (1713-1753)*, Paris 1939

Vernière, P., *Spinoza et la pensée française avant la Révolution*, Paris 1954

Villey, P., 'A propos de la *Lettre sur les aveugles*', *Revue du XVIIIe siècle* (1913), p.410-33

Wade, I. O., *The Clandestine organization and diffusion of philosophic ideas in France from 1700-1750*, Princeton 1938

– 'Organic unity in Diderot', *L'Esprit créateur* 8 (1968), p.3-14

Wartofsky, M. W., 'Diderot and the development of materialist monism', *Diderot studies* 2 (1952), p.279-329

Weinert, H. K., 'Die Bedeutung des Abnormen in Diderots Wissenschaftslehre', *Festgabe Ernst Gamillscheg*, Tübingen 1952, p.228-44

Wilson, A. M., *Diderot: the testing years 1713-1759*, New York 1957

Winter, U., *Der Materialismus bei Diderot*, Geneva, Paris 1972

Zempliner, A., 'Leibniz und die chinesische Philosophie', *Akten der internationalen Leibniz Kongress* 5, Wiesbaden 1971 (*Studia leibnitiana supplementa* 5), p.15-30

Index